Success
International
English skills for IGCSE

Marian Barry

Jealousy

GEORGIAN PRESS

Vivian 9G

Georgian Press (Jersey) Limited
8 Duhamel Place
St Helier
Jersey JE1 3WF
Channel Islands

First published by Georgian Press (Jersey) Limited 1998
Reprinted 1999

ISBN 1-873630-18-2

Produced by AMR Limited

Printed in Egypt by International Printing House

Acknowledgements

The author and publishers are grateful to the following for permission to reproduce copyright material:

Camp Beaumont for their publicity material (pages 98/9).

Egypt Today for the article originally entitled 'Faces – Signs of concern' by Manal el-Jesri (page 183).

Explore Worldwide for extracts from their publicity brochure (page 115).

Friends of the Earth for 'Bike to the future' (page 68) from *Earth Matters* Spring 1995, © Friends of the Earth.

Guardian News Service Ltd for the abridged articles 'How safe is air travel?' (page 63) and 'A bar is born' (pages 174/5), both by John Crace, © The Guardian.

Robert Harding for the abridged article 'Insomnia – In search of the big sleep' from *BBC Vegetarian* (page 58).

Hobsons Publishing for 'An interview with Nick Park' by Philip Gray (pages 84/5), from *Springboard* magazine, volume 4:4.

IPC Magazines Ltd for the adapted article 'Happy not to be a high flyer' from *Options* magazine (page 8).

The Lady magazine for the abridged article 'Fear of swimming' by Beverly Davies (page 57).

Lancashire Evening Post for the film descriptions from *Seven Days* (pages 82/3).

Ewan MacNaughton Associates for 'Facing the fear', an adaptation of 'A mother makes up for lost years' by Angela Neustatter (page 14), © Telegraph Group London 1996.

The National Magazine Company Ltd for the adapted/abridged articles from *Good Housekeeping*: 'Exam tension: What can you do?' (pages 122/3), 'Offshore Italy' (page 107), 'Who dares, wins' (page 29), © Good Housekeeping/The National Magazine Company, and 'To test or not to test' (page 158), from *Zest,* © Zest Magazine/The National Magazine Company.

Rosemary Conley's Diet & Fitness Magazine for the adapted article 'I went down four dress sizes!' by Hilary Talbot (page 55).

Solo Syndication for the adapted article 'Back from the dead' by Luke Harding (page 142), © Daily Mail/Solo Syndication 1995.

The Times Educational Supplement for the abridged articles 'Games for a laugh' by Sally Smith (page 41) and 'Boxing shapes up for a come-back' by Michael Prestage (page 51), © Times Supplements Limited 1997.

Times Newspapers Ltd for 'Kwik way for cricket to catch them young' by John Goodbody (page 49), © Times Newspapers Limited 1996, and 'Hometown: Diane Modahl' by Candida Crewe (page 23), © Times Newspapers Limited 1995.

Judy Wall for the adapted quiz 'Are you living the life you want?' (page 5).

Illustrations by Josephine Blake

Photographs by permission of:

Camp Beaumont (pages 98, 99, 101 bottom left and right); Judith Brown (pages 25, 97, 105, 109, 115, 122, 133 left); Rachel Brown (pages 101 top, 142, 154, 168, 169 top); Colorsport (pages 23, 46, 48); Greg Evans (pages 39, 60, 72 bottom, 107, 185 right); Mary Evans Picture Library (page 10 left); Friends of the Earth (page 68 top); Sally and Richard Greenhill (page 29); Robert Harvey (pages 68 centre and bottom, 72 top, 73, 133 right, 134, 149, 153, 165, 169 centre and bottom, 170); The Image Bank (page 123 top); Images Colour Library (pages 5 left, 8, 163, 177, 185 left); Rex Features (pages 10 right, 12, 84, 85, 92, 140, 141, 187); Liz & Chris Rodgers (page 123 bottom); Royal Fleet Auxiliary (page 146); The Stock Market (pages 5 right, 15, 77, 88, 112, 120, 157, 173, 179, 180); The Telegraph Colour Library (pages 51, 55); Thomson Holidays (page 113)

Cover photograph by permission of Visual Hellas

Cover design by George Mansolas

Contents

Happiness and Success

What is happiness?

1 Quiz

Do this quiz in pairs to find out how happy you are. Don't worry about individual words – just try to understand the main ideas.

Are you living the life you want?

1 Which statement best summarises your feelings about your education?
  A My talent is unrecognised.
  B I'm very clear about what way of working suits me.
  C Other people's approval is very important.

2 How do you feel about relationships?
  A I think people should accept me for who I am.
  B I know what I have to give, but sometimes I fail.
  C I try hard to be an ideal son/daughter/friend.

3 Which statement best describes your relationship with your closest friend?
  A Our relationship is so good we never argue.
  B We do argue, but we make up afterwards.
  C We like to get every niggle off our chests.

4 Which statement best describes your feelings about your home?
  A It's a place to rest my head.
  B My heart lifts when I come home.
  C I feel proud when I tell someone my address.

5 You've got a chance to redecorate your bedroom. Do you
  A let your parents choose the colour scheme and carpet, etc?
  B go for something outrageous or soothing – whatever makes you feel good?

  C select something stylish you saw in a magazine?

6 What are your feelings about other people?
  A I believe there is usually an ulterior motive in people's behaviour.
  B I give individuals the benefit of the doubt.
  C I trust people and then feel let down.

7 You've been invited to a big party. All your friends will be there. You hate parties. Do you
  A tell everyone you're going but don't turn up?
  B explain your feelings in a light-hearted way?
  C go anyway and feel miserable?

8 You're feeling proud of a new outfit. A 'friend' makes a hurtful remark. Do you
  A give a sharp reply/say something nasty back?
  B ignore it?
  C vow never to be seen in it again?

9 How do you choose your clothes?
  A I go for classics.
  B For comfort and personal taste – favourite colours, cuts and fabrics.
  C I like to be fashionable.

10 What are your feelings about family and personal relationships?
  A I believe that I have a duty to others.
  B I'll make sacrifices, but I know my limits.
  C I believe I must be happy in whatever I do.

11 What is the most important part of your home?
  A Main reception room.
  B Bathroom, kitchen, bedroom or 'den'.
  C Front entrance.

12 How do you deal with difficult situations?
  A I avoid situations that might hurt me.
  B I remove myself from any situation that keeps causing me pain.
  C I persevere in situations that are hurting me.

13 How would you describe your life?
  A I've no time to pursue personal goals.
  B I've a clear sense of meaning and purpose.
  C I'm over-committed and I feel all over the place.

14 Which best describes your friendships?
  A I'd like to have more.
  B I choose my friends.
  C My friends choose me – I'm liked and accepted.

15 You're relaxing in the bath after a hard day when a friend phones. Do you
  A get someone to tell her you're out?
  B get someone to tell her you'll call back?
  C take the call?

See page 191 for quiz scores.

2 Discussion

A   The quiz suggests the happiest people are those who live life in their own way. They know what they want and don't feel the need to do things just because others want them to. How far do you agree with this interpretation?

Do you think living like this can make people selfish? Does everyone have a right to happiness? Try to explain your ideas to your group.

B   What makes you happy? Read some comments made by students.

"Finding a £1 coin in the pocket of my jeans when I thought I was broke."

"Going to a football match and seeing my side win."

"A surprise long-distance call from a really close friend."

Now add your own ideas. Be specific!

....

....

C   Share your ideas around your group.

D   What can you do when you feel unhappy?

Study these comments.

"I ride my horse down to the river and just sit and think. It's my real place to escape."

"I talk to my dad and he tells me how he coped in a similar situation."

Discuss your ideas with your partner or keep them private.

3 Formal and informal styles

Here is some informal or colloquial language from the quiz. Match it to the more formal equivalents.

B **1**   I feel all over the place.
E **2**   We like to get every niggle off our chests.
A⊘ **3**   I go for classics.
E C **4**   You're waiting for life to come and dish out the happiness.
D⊅ **5**   You've hardly got off the launch pad.

A   I prefer clothes that will not go out of fashion.
B   I lack a clear sense of my goals in life.
C   You aren't taking responsibility for making yourself happy.
D   You haven't started moving.
E   We always tell each other our bad feelings even if they are about something unimportant.

4 Spelling patterns and speech sounds

You've just completed a quiz. In English spelling, **q** is always followed by **u**. **Qu** is a spelling pattern. The speech sound is /kw/.

Can you guess the following words, each containing the pattern **qu**? Use your dictionary to check that your spelling is correct.

1   The king is married to her. queen
2   He started the essay with words from his favourite poem. quotation
3   This is the sound a duck makes. quack
4   A celebration meal which a very large number of people attend. banquet

Ph is another spelling pattern, and sounds like /f/. It's in **ph**one, **ph**otogra**ph** and **ph**rase.

What other sounds and spelling patterns do you know?

....

....

5 Approaches to spelling

Tick the strategies you use to help you spell.

☐ I remember how the word looks on the page (visual recall).

☐ I use spelling rules.

☐ I link spelling patterns with speech sounds (e.g. **q+u** is a pattern and sounds like /kw/).

Everyone makes spelling mistakes! To improve your spelling you need to use a combination of all these approaches. One method which is particularly useful and quick to learn is called the 'look, say, cover, write, check' method, described below.

6 Look, say, cover, write, check

This method concentrates attention on each letter group in a word so you won't miss any letters out. It also stops you putting letters into a word which don't belong there – even if they sound as if they do! It can be used with other strategies such as spelling rules and linking speech sounds to spelling patterns.

Break into syllables
To help you remember how a word looks, break it into syllables. For example, *quality* has three syllables: qua/li/ty.
Qualification has five syllables: qua/li/fi/ca/tion.

Break these words into syllables: *quota, question, automatic, quarrel.*

Take a mental photograph

Cover the word with a piece of paper. Then move the paper so that you can see the first syllable only. Study the syllable carefully, 'photographing' it in your mind and saying the syllable to yourself. Then move the paper along so that you can see the next syllable. Repeat the process, until you have mentally 'photographed' the complete word.

Testing yourself

Cover up the whole word. Write it from memory. Then check your spelling with the original. If your spelling was correct, write out the word three times from memory to reinforce the visual recall. If you didn't get it right, repeat the whole process until you are sure you can spell the word accurately.

7 Tricky words

Here are some words IGCSE students find hard to spell correctly. Make sure you understand the meaning of each one. Can you pronounce it properly? Say it aloud to your partner to check.

cupboard	committee
truthful	honour
activities	curable
responsible	embarrassment
calm	wrist

How well can you spell these tricky words? Use the 'look, say, cover, write, check' method. Remember to break each word into syllables first. When you have mastered the spelling of each word, move on to the next. Finally, use each word in a sentence to show its meaning.

8 Why are words misspelled?

A Try this exercise in a pair or group of three. Study each tricky word in exercise 7 again. Do you notice anything about the word which makes it extra hard to spell? Think about these questions.

Is the problem the fact that we do not pronounce some of the letters in the word? These are called **silent letters**.

Is the problem the **ending** of the word? Do we make mistakes because the sound of the ending is different from the correct spelling?

Is the problem the fact that the word is a **plural**? What happens to the word when it changes from singular to plural?

Is the problem the fact that there are **double letters** in the word? Do we make mistakes because we are not sure whether to use a double or single letter?

B When you have decided why each word is tricky, make a note.

Examples:
Cupboard is tricky because you can't hear the *p*, so you might forget to put it in.

Activities is a tricky word because the singular is *activity*. You might forget to change the ending to *ies* when you write the plural form.

C Write down examples of other words which have silent letters and *ies* plurals.

Examples:
p is not only silent in *cupboard*. You can't hear it in *receipt*, *raspberry*, *psychology*.

Dictionary, *story* and *memory* are other words which have an *ies* plural. But words like *boy* and *railway* just add *s* to make the plural.

D When you have written as much as you feel you can, discuss your results with other groups.

9 How helpful is your dictionary?

Dictionaries give you the meaning of words and help you to spell. Does your dictionary also

* tell you how to pronounce the word?
* tell you the grammatical class (verb, noun, adverb, etc)?
* tell you if the word belongs to more than one grammatical class (nouns which can be used as verbs etc)?
* tell you if a noun is countable or uncountable?
* give you example sentences?
* give you any idiomatic expressions with the word(s)?

If the answer to most of these questions is no, you need a new dictionary! Choosing a good dictionary is complex. Before you spend a lot of money, ask your teacher or your classmates for their ideas.

10 Getting organised

Have you got a spelling and vocabulary book? If not, start one now. Plan the layout carefully. Use columns, notes on pronunciation, space for translations and example sentences. Keep it nicely organised and you'll find it a great aid to memory. It will be a enormous help in understanding the patterns of English.

Happy not to be a high flyer

A Compare this description with the photograph.

Tina's black hair is drawn back from her smooth, dark-skinned face. She has a beaming smile and looks alert, confident and ready for anything.

Do you agree with the description? Would you change anything?

B You are going to read about Tina's way of being happy. Before you read, try to answer these questions.

Where do you think the text comes from?
What do you think the style is going to be – chatty and informal, or formal and serious?
Who do you think the article is written for?

VOCABULARY CHECK
Make sure you know the meaning of these words from the text.

- priority
- insignificant
- trivial

12 Comprehension check

Now read the article. Then answer the questions which follow.

Tina Lanzi, 32, acquisitions assistant of a TV company, is happy standing still on her career ladder.

'My mum always wanted me to do well at school and to have a high status job, but that sort of thing isn't a big priority for me. I did have the potential to do well and go to university, but I was just too busy having a good time. My relationships have always been far more important to me than academic or career success.

'My present job basically involves working as an assistant, and friends still insist I could have achieved more in my working life. When I was younger, I did feel I had to set myself goals and attain them within a certain period. I successfully ran my own business for a while, but having kids put life back into perspective.

'There have been times when I could have taken on a lot more responsibility at work, but I imagine that if I had a more senior role at work, another part of my life would have to give, and I'm not prepared to risk that. I'm just not the sort of person who can trample on others to get to the top. I find it satisfying to do a productive job because I like to feel I'm doing something useful, but I'm not into climbing the career ladder now.

'The biggest priorities in my life are my husband David, our son Rory, who's nine, and daughter Rachel, who's four. If I'm ever fed up after a day at work, I just spend some time with the children, and the enjoyment I get from them makes me realise how insignificant and trivial my worries at work can be.

'Occasionally, I'm reminded of how tied down I am – if a friend goes off travelling, for example. But I suppose an important part of contentment is to accept life's limitations, and to learn to enjoy the things that you *can* do.'

---

1 Why do Tina's friends think her job isn't good enough for her?

2 What does Tina think is the most important part of her life?

3 Why is Tina not ambitious?

4 Describe Tina's attitude to life.

13 Principles of a happy life

Psychologists, analysing the ingredients for a happy life, have come up with the following do's and don'ts. Unfortunately, the words *do* and *don't* are missing.

Working with a partner, write *Do* or *Don't* next to each point.

.... regret decisions you made in the past.

.... hold resentment against your parents.

.... value status and material possessions more than people.

.... spend a lot of time envying other people.

.... be realistic about how much you can achieve.

.... choose a job which gives you real satisfaction.

Now discuss your opinions in groups.

14 Finding examples

Working in groups of two or three, look back at Tina's comments about her life. Try to find specific examples in what she says which illustrate the principles about happiness in the list above.

Example:
She says she had the potential to go to university but it wasn't a priority. She was too busy having a good time. This shows she doesn't regret decisions made in the past.

....

....

....

15 Sharing ideas

A   When your group has finished, check your examples with those of another group. Are there any differences? Make any corrections you need to. Include new, interesting ideas on your own list.

B   Suggest some 'happiness principles' to share with your group. Try to base them on your own experience.

Examples:
Do try to be tolerant of other people.
Don't be too self-critical.

16 Discussion

Tina says she's happy not to be a high-flyer. On the other hand, people say they get great fulfilment from being promoted to highly demanding jobs. Would you be prepared to make any sacrifices in your personal life in order to have a high-flying career? Why/Why not?

17 Goal setting

A   Tina says that, when she was younger, she set herself goals. Is goal-setting a good idea? Does it help you achieve things, or should you take each day as it comes? Should you ever change your goals?

B   Have you any goals of your own? Take a few minutes to think and then write them down. Divide them into daily, medium-term and long-term goals. Share them with others or keep them private if you prefer.

Examples:
A goal for today is to tidy my bedroom.
A medium-term goal is to improve my fitness by swimming twice a week.
A long-term goal is to travel the world.

Daily goal..

Medium-term goal..

Long-term goal ....

18 Figurative meanings

Tina says, *'I'm just not the sort of person who can trample on others to get to the top.'*

The literal meaning of *'trample'* is to tread heavily on something in a way which damages it.

Example: *They trampled over the garden, ruining the new plants.*

Tina uses *'trample'* figuratively, meaning that she would not behave in a way which would hurt the feelings of others.

In each of the following sentences, one word is used figuratively. Underline the word, and then discuss its meaning with your partner. Finally, write sentences of your own to illustrate the meanings. Don't forget to use a dictionary when you need to.

1   I spent the day <u>wrestling</u> with our financial problems.
2   My heart <u>lifts</u> when I come home.
3   She was unhappy because her older sister always <u>squashed</u> her ideas.
4   We're <u>fighting</u> the authorities who want to close our village school.
5   His face <u>broke into a smile</u> when he heard the news.
6   I'm tired of <u>battling with staff</u> who refuse to accept different working conditions.
7   After his wife's death, <u>he buried himself</u> in his work.
8   He's <u>crippled by shyness</u>.

The English language is full of figurative uses of words. Reading and listening to authentic English will develop your awareness. Work towards including examples in your own vocabulary.

19 Homophones

Tina says that she doesn't want a more senior role at work. *Role* here means job.

Role has the same sound as *roll*, but each word has a different spelling and meaning. *Roll* can refer to a bread roll, or be used as a verb meaning movement, e.g. *roll the ball along the ground*. Words of the same sound but different spellings are called homophones.

The following sentences are based on IGCSE students' writing. Choose the correct homophone in each case. Can you explain the meaning of the incorrect one?

1 There's no plaice/place like home.
2 I was in terrible pane/pain when I broke my arm.
3 You need peace/piece and quiet for your work.
4 I read the hole/whole book in one evening.
5 We're not aloud/allowed to stay out late.
6 We have a pear/pair tree in the garden.
7 The wind farms will be a horrible site/sight.
8 Their/There are six people in my family.
9 I answered four/for questions.
10 He's got a saw/sore throat.

20 More homophones

Work in small groups to try to find a homophone for each of these words.

1 steal _steel_
2 male
3 your
4 week _weak_
5 hour
6 bear
7 tail _tale_
8 sale _sail_
9 poor
10 wail

Now put each word into a sentence to show its meaning.

The price of greatness

21 Before you listen

Name someone who you think deserves to go down in history for their work or achievements. Why do you think this person should be admired? Try to be specific.

Example: *Alexander Fleming – because his discovery of penicillin means that many illnesses which used to kill people are now curable.*

Make a few notes.

What do you know of this person's background and personal life? If you don't know very much, what picture do you have in your mind of it? Do you imagine a happy home life or one dominated by struggle and conflict? Why/Why not? Write down your ideas.

Share your ideas with the rest of the group.

22 Vocabulary check

Match the words which you are going to hear with their definitions.

1	genius	A	something which makes it difficult for you to do what you want
2	inner drive	B	inherited through your parents
3	genetic	C	reach an extremely high standard
4	setback	D	unhappy feelings, anxiety, depression
5	excel	E	average, not particularly good
6	psychological unease	F	a strong determination to achieve
7	mediocre	G	(a person of) exceptional ability

23 Listening: Radio interview

Listen to this radio interview and choose the best answer for each question.

1 According to Steve, the disadvantages suffered by great achievers when they were children
  a made it more difficult for them to reach their potential.
  b drove them to excel. ✓
  c made the public more sympathetic to their achievements.
  d embittered them for life.

2 The interviewer's attitude to the information that suffering is a significant factor in great achievement is
  a doubtful. ✓
  b amused.
  c horrified.
  d intrigued.

3 What, according to Steve, did great achievers need when they were children?
  a understanding
  b companionship
  c solitude ✓
  d training

4 Steve's message to ordinary children who are hoping to fulfil their potential is
  a discouraging – you'll probably never make it as a real superstar.
  b supportive – everyone should develop his/her abilities. ✓
  c cautious – try to achieve but take care not to get depressed.
  d excited – there's a wonderful future ahead of you.

24 Post-listening discussion

A According to the speaker, the greatest thinkers had unhappy lives.
Does this surprise you at all? Why/Why not?

B Do you agree that being very successful is '5% talent and the rest hard work'?
Explain your views.

25 Apostrophes (1)

These sentences come from the script of the radio interview. Why are the apostrophes used, do you think? Discuss your ideas with your partner.

1 Steve's been reading an absolutely wonderful book.
2 You can't just pick out one or two factors.
3 It's a very complex web.
4 They've probably suffered from depression.
5 I wouldn't say you ought to stop trying to achieve your potential.
6 You mightn't be the next superstar.

PRONUNCIATION
Practise saying the contracted forms to your partner. Try to make the contraction smooth and natural-sounding.

26 Apostrophes (2)

With a partner, study the exact position of the apostrophes in these sentences.

1 Someone's stolen the doctor's bag.
2 He got a parents' guide to zoos.
3 All the passengers' luggage goes in the hold.
4 There are no men's toilets on this floor.
5 Give me Brendan's shoes.
6 I spoke to the children's favourite teacher.
7 Can I introduce Maria's husband?

What conclusions can you come to about using apostrophes? Write down your ideas.

....

....

27 Correcting sentences

Now correct the following sentences by adding apostrophes where they are necessary.

1   The teachers listened to Carols views.
2   Theyve bought a new car.
3   I went to my mothers office.
4   Please dont touch the babies clothes.
5   Its hard to explain the programmes success.
6   She works in the womens ward of the hospital.
7   Hes training to be a ladies hairdresser.
8   Youll find her in the teachers workroom – all the staff go there.
9   He mightve become the next Einstein.
10   She couldnt understand why her cat had lost its appetite.

Practise saying the sentences aloud to your partner.

28 Speculating about a photograph

Study this photograph with a partner. Read how three students have described the person in it. Which comments do you most agree with? Try to explain why.

A   *"He's a burly, bearded man with a thick mop of grey hair. He's rather severe-looking. He could be a doctor or a teacher."*

B   *"He looks big and heavy set. He's got a warm, humorous expression and a rugged, outdoor appearance. He could be a farmer or a sailor."*

C   *"He's fair-skinned with bushy eyebrows and swept-back grey hair. He's rather sensitive-looking. He could be an artist or a ballet dancer."*

The photograph is of David Bellamy, a famous naturalist and environmental campaigner. He has improved people's understanding of the ways we can protect our planet.

29 Describing personal qualities

Here are some comments people have made about David's life. Study them with a a partner. Make sure you understand each one.

When he's carrying out an environmental campaign, he gets letters from children who say, 'It's not worth it, David, the world is dying.' But he doesn't think it is. He thinks nature can adapt and we never need lose hope.

He campaigned to save the rainforests and ended up in prison. But he says that it was worth it because now, all over the world, people are starting to understand about the forests.

He thinks the earth is in a mess. And the seas are in trouble too. But he reminds us that we've got a global agreement from governments about protecting the environment, so things will gradually improve.

When he starts on a project he's filled with enthusiasm. He relies on friends saying 'Wait a minute David, you've got to do this or do that to avoid disaster.'

He believes the countryside has to be managed and that sometimes means killing things. Even if it annoys people, he just has to do what he thinks is right.

His work is exhausting and sometimes dangerous, but what has kept him going is having friends who believe in him.

After reading people's comments about David's life, do you think it is right to draw the following conclusions about him? Answer yes or no.

He has:

1   the courage to take risks.
2   benefited from positive criticism.
3   bad memories he cannot forget.
4   accepted stress as part of his life.
5   encouragement and support from friends.
6   trouble trusting others.
7   self-belief.
8   a positive, optimistic outlook.
9   determination.
10   difficulty adjusting to change.

30 Discussion

1 David might be successful, but is he happy? What are your views?

2 Is there anything about David's approach to life you would choose for yourself? Try to explain why.

3 Do you think David is a good example to younger people? Could he be a role model (a person who inspires others to copy them)? Why/Why not?

4 Does David share any qualities with your own personal heroes or heroines?

31 Drafting a paragraph

Write a paragraph of about 75 words describing the kind of person you think David is. Try to give reasons for your opinions.

When you've finished writing, show your paragraph to a partner. Does he/she think you should change anything? Do you agree? Make a second draft, putting in the changes you both agreed on.

Obstacles and challenges

32 Expressing fears and giving reassurance

In pairs, read the following dialogue.

A: I've got to recite a poem in front of the whole school.

B: How do you feel about it?

A: To tell you the truth, I'm a bit worried about it.

B: Don't worry. You'll be fine. Everyone thinks you're great!

When people want to express fears, they use these expressions. Tick the one(s) which sound most fearful.

I feel sick every time I think about it.

To tell you the truth, I'm a bit scared about it.

I'm not really sure I can cope.

To be honest, I'm not sure I'll be able to do it.

The thought of it bothers me.

I'm terrified!

Here are some expressions you can use to calm someone's fears. Which do you prefer?

There's nothing to worry about. You'll do a wonderful job.

You'll be fine. Nothing can go wrong.

Things will be all right. We're all supporting you.

Don't get too upset. It'll all go well.

PRACTICE

Practise expressing fears and giving reassurance in pairs. A should explain what he/she has to do. B should give reassurance. Then swap over. Base your dialogues on these situations.

- a fear of taking an exam
- a fear of competing in a race
- a fear of giving a talk in front of the school
- a fear of going to the dentist

33 Pre-reading discussion

You are going to read about Monica, a woman who didn't learn to read until she was grown-up. Discuss the following questions.

1 What everyday problems do you think not being able to read would present?

2 Why might someone who was unable to read not try to get help to learn?

3 What effect do you think not being able to read might have on him/her?

34 Vocabulary check

Make sure you know the meaning of these words from the text. Use a dictionary if necessary.

- taunted
- illiterate
- volunteer

35 Reading: Textual organisation

Read the text carefully and match each paragraph with one of these headings.

A Effects on Sally's education

B Hiding the problem

C Unhappy school days

D Qualifying as parent-educator

E Sally's birth

F Monica's work today

G Learning to read

Facing the fears

1 Monica Hegarty's childhood memories are of crippling stomach aches each morning before school, of missing lessons through illness and falling so far behind that she understood little but did not dare to ask for help, of silent misery as other children taunted her as 'stupid'. She says, "I spent all those years feeling I had failed at school, but now I think school failed me, and when I had Sally, 17 years ago, I was determined it would not be the same for her." She is sitting in her immaculately tidy flat in south London. Sally, a rangy, striking teenager joins us – at first shy, then exchanging memories with her mother.

2 Monica is describing how it feels to be unable to read and write, to be illiterate in a world where just about everything we do, how we are judged, depends on our literacy skills. Few people, she says, realise what it means to be unable to read a road sign, safety instructions or the contents of a food packet, when every form you have to fill in, every note you need to write, is an impossible task. Monica remembers it very clearly: "I felt so conscious of not being able to join in the life other people were living." Nor do many people realise the elaborate charades people put on to disguise this inadequacy. Monica explains, "I would have the names of places I wanted to go to written down, and then I'd show this and ask someone to help, explaining that I'd left my glasses at home or some such story. I'd carry a book or paper around and pretend to read it. You get good at fooling other people, but you can't fool yourself. It makes the world a scary place."

3 Her husband Derek, who died earlier this year, was unaware of her secret. She says, "I'd just ask him to do the things I couldn't cope with and he accepted that. But it really came home to me when Sally was born. I felt very insecure as a mother, and as she grew up everyone around me was saying, 'You must read to her.' I felt so stupid because I couldn't." Even then she did not tell Derek, although she smiles now and says, "I think he must have known in his heart of hearts, but he was such a sweet man he never let on. I made sure he did the reading with Sally – I'd say I had to cook tea and that it was a good way for them to be close." Sally remembers, "Sometimes Mum would sit with us and seem to join in. I never realised she wasn't actually reading."

4 Things changed when Sally went to primary school and Monica became a volunteer, helping with the children. One morning the head said they wanted to offer her a paid job as a helper. "I just froze. I knew that would involve reading and writing – the things I'd avoided so far. But the head had recognised my problem. She took me under her wing and did reading with me every day so that I could take the job. As I learned, she put me in with older children and I realised I could read and write. It was like a miracle."

5 That was the beginning. When the present head took over he set up a parents' group and Monica was part of it. He asked them to write a book for parents teaching their children. Monica says, "My first reaction was, 'Ooh, I can't do that,' but then I realised I could contribute. And I wanted to because I realised there were other parents 'in the closet', as I had been, and that I could help them. By now she was doing a training course to become a parent educator. "The day I got my certificate – the first in my life – Sally and I went out for a really nice meal to celebrate."

6 These struggles are in the past. Monica now works in several different schools and has just returned from a conference in Cyprus where she gave a presentation on involving parents in reading. Her delight is obvious. "Learning to read has made the world a different place. Suddenly I feel there are so many things I can do. But the most important thing is that Sally hasn't been held back."

7 Sally pulls a face. "Mum was very pushy about studying and homework. She'd find fault with everything because she was so keen I should do well." But Monica is unapologetic. "Perhaps I pushed harder than other parents because I knew what failing feels like, and I suppose I was living my life through her. But we were both bursting with pride the day she did really well in her GCSEs. I was in tears in front of everyone at school because I was so proud." Sally is no less proud. She sits on the arm of the sofa near her mother, listening, her smile overflowing with affection. She says, "I think it was brave of Mum. She's also shown me how important it is to take opportunities when they come. If she hadn't done that, she wouldn't have become the person she is now, with a great future."

36 Comprehension check

1 Why did Monica dislike school? Give two reasons.
2 How did she hide from other people the fact that she couldn't read? Give two examples.
3 Explain how Monica felt when she was offered paid work by the headteacher.
4 What has Sally learned from her mother's experiences?

37 Vocabulary: Odd one out

The following groups of adjectives each contain a word which doesn't describe Monica. Cross it out.

1 Monica as a child:
anxious   robust   delicate   tense
shy   sensitive

2 Monica as a young mother:
secretive   insecure   abrasive
gentle   worried

3 Monica now:
fulfilled   timid   cheerful
understanding   frank

38 'Bird' idioms

Monica explains that the headteacher *'took me under her wing'* (paragraph 4) when she was learning to read. This image comes from birds. What does it mean, do you think?

Now try to complete the sentences, choosing a suitable expression from the box to fill each space.

> a bird in the hand is worth two in the bush.
> a bird's eye view
> took me under her wing
> kill two birds with one stone
> a hen party
> an ugly duckling

1 He's seven years old and has just lost his front teeth. He's going through _____ phase.
2 We climbed to the top of the tower to get _____ of the town.
3 She had _____ on the night before she got married.
4 I decided to take the job I was offered rather than wait for the results of my next interview. After all, _____.
5 Eleni was nervous when she joined her new school but one of the older girls _____.
6 I went home to visit my mother. She told me my old friend Ahmed had moved into the area, so I decided to _____ and go and see him as well.

39 Post-reading discussion

A Monica accepted the challenge of learning to read as an adult. Why are challenges important? What challenges do you have in your own life?

B Monica says *'I suppose I was living my life through her'* (paragraph 7). What bad effects might living your life through another person have?

C Some people feel they will be happy if they have success, achievement, material things. Other people claim happiness comes from inside you. Where does Monica's happiness come from? Try to explain your views.

INTERNATIONAL OVERVIEW

> Nearly a quarter of the world's population is illiterate.
>
> Of the world's nearly 900 million illiterate adults, nearly two-thirds are women.
>
> In 1995 UNICEF decided to double its funding for basic education and give special attention to girls' schooling. This money will be spent on education in developing countries.

How far do you think literacy is important to the progress of a country?

Do you have any idea of the literacy rates in your own country? If you don't know, try to find out.

40 Describing people

Sally is described as a *'rangy, striking teenager'* (paragraph 1). *Rangy* means tall and very slim with long, slender limbs. What does the adjective *striking* tell us about her appearance?

The writer uses only two adjectives before the noun. Do you think this is enough? How well do you think he/she manages to convey the impression Sally makes?

The writer tells us that Sally listens to her mother with a *'smile overflowing with affection'* (paragraph 7). What kind of person does Sally seem to be? What is her relationship with her mother like? How does the language used emphasise warmth and closeness?

41 Using a wide range of adjectives

When you are trying to describe the impression a person makes, you can refer to their appearance and their character. Try to use adjectives which are fresh and individual.

You can use:

- specific single adjectives.   *striking, sensitive, charming.*

- adjective compounds (adjective + noun + *-ed*):
  broad-shouldered, fair-skinned, good-natured.

- compounds with *-looking:*   *stern-looking* (instead of saying 'He looked as if he were a stern person').

Compounds with *-looking* usually refer to a person's inner qualities: *capable-looking, studious-looking, miserable-looking.* *Good-looking* is an exception.

42 Adjective collocations

Study the adjectives in the box. Divide them into four groups, under the four headings. Work with a partner and use a dictionary to help you. Find translations if you need to.

APPEARANCE   HAIR   VOICE   CHARACTER

> deep   wavy   tight-fisted   grating   straight   genial   husky
> shy   placid   ambitious   melodious   slim   tolerant   wispy
> absent-minded   tender-hearted   well-proportioned   quiet
> self-centred   dreamy   plump   ill-mannered   altruistic   balding
> high-pitched   burly   rugged   generous   well-dressed
> considerate   outgoing   luxuriant   gentle   rangy   elegant
> scruffy   argumentative   overweight   curly-haired   skinny
> bad-tempered   close-cropped   domineering   frank   bushy
> humorous

43 Positive and negative

You might not mind being called *slim,* but you probably wouldn't like to be called *skinny*! *Slim* has a positive connotation, whereas *skinny* is negative.

Study your word groups in exercise 4 again. Tick (✓) the words you think are definitely positive, and mark with a cross (✗) the ones you think are definitely negative.

44 Negative prefixes

Make the character traits below into their opposites by adding a prefix from the box.

> dis-   im-   in-   ir-   un-

responsible   mature
secure   trustworthy
reliable   efficient
happy   loyal
contented   honest

Now put the words into sentences to show their meanings.

45 Colour

Colour is a big part of people's appearance. You could write *'He had black hair and blue eyes'*. However, your writing will get a better response if you say what shade of blue and what kind of black you mean.

Using an image from the natural world helps identify an exact shade of colour and produces more vivid writing.

Examples:
Her eyes were sapphire-blue.
His hair was coal-black.
He was wearing olive-green trousers.

Write sentences about people's appearance using these colour images.

chestnut-brown	emerald-green
chocolate-brown	lime-green
cherry-red	jet-black
rose-pink	sky-blue
strawberry-blonde	lemon-yellow

BEING CREATIVE

Make up some other associations of your own by linking colours to natural objects. Think about the people and colours around you.

Examples:
He's wearing a leaf-green jacket.
She was carrying a banana-yellow shopping bag.

46 Developing a more mature style

Try to avoid stringing lots of adjectives together. Using clauses beginning with *which/that ...* and phrases beginning with *with ...* makes your descriptive style more mature. Underline the examples in these descriptions.

'He had straight, dark-yellow hair and milky blue eyes that made him seem dreamy and peaceful.' (Anne Tyler, *The Ladder of Years*)

'She was a tall, fragile-looking woman in a pretty blue hat that matched her eyes.' (Barbara Pym, *An Unsuitable Attachment*)

'He was a tall, melancholy man with curly hair, rather romantic-looking in his long, sewer-man's boots.' (George Orwell, *Down and Out in Paris and London*)

Conjunctions such as *but* introduce a contrast:

'He had grown to be a large-boned man, but his face was still childishly rounded, with the wide eyes, the downy cheeks, the delicate lips of a schoolboy.' (Anne Tyler, *Dinner at the Homesick Restaurant*)

47 Conveying character traits

Study this example again:

'He had straight, dark-yellow hair and milky blue eyes that made him seem dreamy and peaceful.'

Now look at this explanation of the way the writer achieves her effect. Do you agree with it?

"We get a clear picture of the impression this man makes because of the writer's carefully-chosen adjectives. She describes his eyes vividly as *milky blue*. Milk is associated with innocence and childhood. Using an unusual expression like *milky blue* emphasises the gentle, trusting qualities of the man. Choosing adjectives such as *dreamy* and *peaceful* strengthens the impression the man gives of being accepting and placid."

Choose one of the other examples from exercise 46 and try to write about it in the same way.

48 Writing your own description

Each of us is unique. No one has exactly the same face, hands, hair, body or voice as anyone else. Even identical twins are said to have different ears!

Choose a friend to describe. Don't try to describe everything about him/her. Concentrate on a few special characteristics which convey your friend's uniqueness. For example, he/she may have beautiful, well-shaped hands, a melodious voice, sparkling eyes. Try to link physical characteristics to character traits.

Remember, use adjectives and colour images selectively. Don't overdo them. Use clauses etc. to make your writing more mature.

Write about 75 words.

FEEDBACK

Read your description aloud to your group. Listen carefully to the feedback. (Criticisms should be positive!) Are there any changes you would like to make after hearing the comments?

Someone I admire

49 Model description

Read this article which was sent to a teenage magazine running a series called 'Special Friends'.

How did the writer meet Simon? As you read, underline any words you don't understand.

COMPREHENSION CHECK

1 What impression does Simon make?
2 Why was he unhappy at school?
3 How do you know Simon is a determined person?
4 Why does the writer value Simon's friendship?

My special friend

I'd like to describe my friend Simon. Simon is a complex mixture of frankness and reserve. He is small, slight and rather studious-looking. His gentle, golden-brown eyes are hidden behind a large pair of horn-rimmed glasses. Simon is very neat and particular in everything he does. Even his books and pencils are always arranged in perfect order on his desk!

I admire Simon because he used to be painfully shy. He's never been interested in sport or smart clothes and he often shops in secondhand shops. The other students used to think he was scruffy and called him 'ugly duckling'. One day, however, he decided he wasn't going to let his shyness crush him. He had to try to be himself. He began to open out and make friends.

Simon is a very trustworthy and straightforward friend. When I was worried about an operation I had to have, he helped me talk through my fears. I gradually got the confidence to ask the doctors for a proper explanation. I learned from Simon that it is better to face your fears than to hide them.

I know I'm really a lucky person because I have a dear friend on whom I can always rely.

FORMAT

A good description shows what the person is like by giving

- key details about appearance
- examples of behaviour
- reasons why this person is unusual or valued.

Underline the key phrases which provide insight into Simon as a person and as a friend.

What comments can you make about the structure of the sentences? Think about clauses, descriptive vocabulary and expressing reasons.

Beginnings and endings
What sentence is used to begin the article?
How is the article brought to a conclusion?

50 Comparing two styles

The following description was written by a student, Gary, as a first draft. What would you like to change to make the style more mature?

Gary showed his work to his partner. They discussed how he could improve his style. Are the changes an improvement, do you think? Why/Why not?

I am 16 years old and I would like to describe my father. My father is a nice man. You can talk to him. He will not get angry. My friends like him. He's tall and big and not very fat. He is about normal size. He's got brown eyes, black hair and a nice face. His black hair has some white hairs in it. He makes a lot of things at home. He made a cabinet for me. It is for my CD's. The cabinet is made from pine. I like my cabinet very much. It is very nice. I look after it all the time. He has made me a good desk. The desk is for my computer. He always wears a grey suit to work. He doesn't like his suit. It is not comfortable for him. He always likes jeans. He wears jeans a lot.

My father's a friendly, approachable person who is popular with all my friends. He's a genial-looking, tall man of medium build with dark brown eyes and coal-black hair, streaked with grey. He's very practical and confident with his hands. He made me a pine cabinet for my CD's, which I treasure, and an attractive computer desk. He has to dress formally for work in a smart suit, but he prefers casual dress and feels most comfortable in jeans.

51 Rewriting with more sophistication

Try to rewrite the following description in a more mature style.

My friend is a good person. Her eyes are big. They are green. They are nice eyes. She has short hair. It is very, very short. The colour is blonde. She smiles a lot. She has a nice smile. She shows her white teeth. Her clothes are nice. Her style of her clothes is different from other people. She looks at other people's clothes. She can see their character from their clothes. She is a very good student. Her work is always good. She gets high marks. She is kind. She helps me do my work too.

When you have finished, compare your draft to someone else's. What differences can you find, and what similarities?

52 Writing from notes

A Have you heard of Joseph Lister? Write down any facts you know about him.

B Now try to write the following description of Joseph Lister in full. You will need to change some words and add others.

I want/describe Joseph Lister. He be/surgeon who/be born/1827. In those days/many patients die/after operations because their wounds/become/badly infect. Lister wonder if/bacteria/air/which make/meat decay/also make/wounds septic.

Lister decide/clean/everything which touch/patient's wounds/carbolic acid. Carbolic acid/destroy/all germs. As result/these precautions/patients recover quickly/operations. The rate/infection/fall dramatically.

Lister develop/safe, antiseptic operations/which be/major medical advance. He receive/many awards/his work. I admire him because/he be dedicate/unselfish. He take/great personal risks/make this discovery. Surgery/use to be/highly dangerous. People be/terrify/surgeon's knife. Lister change/all that. Modern surgery be/life-saver.

Vocabulary
bacteria   organisms which cause disease
septic   badly infected
decay   go bad, rot
precautions   actions taken to avoid danger

Exam-format questions

Writing

1   Write an article for your school magazine or newsletter describing a person whose work has brought benefits to many people. In your article you should:

- say why you admire this person
- describe the work he/she has done
- explain how people have benefited.

Write about 200 words.

2   Write an article for a teenage magazine describing someone you are close to. In the article you should:

- describe the person's special qualities
- give examples of his/her behaviour
- explain why the relationship is important to you.

Write about 200 words.

3   You have joined a pen friend organisation. You receive this letter from your pen friend.

Dear ...

Thank you for your lovely letter telling me all about your home, your family and your school. I was just a little bit disappointed, however, because you didn't explain what I really want to know which is ... what makes YOU tick! Tell me what makes you happy or sad. What do you want to achieve in your life? What are your most important goals? Please hurry! I can't wait to hear from you.

Best wishes,

Chris

Write Chris a letter of reply, describing your approach to life and your personal goals. Write about 150 words.

Oral assessment

Becoming happier

1   Many young people say they are unhappy and feel negative about their lives. Why do you think this is? How could they develop a more positive approach? Try to explain your views.

You might consider such things as:

- the opportunity to enrich your life by doing more things which bring pleasure e.g. learning a new skill, developing a hobby, or simply learning to take more enjoyment from the people and things around you

- the advantages (or disadvantages) of planning your life and setting goals

- the value of role models in inspiring young people and giving them someone to look up to

- the value of getting involved in community projects which bring a wider perspective on life.

You are free to consider any other ideas of your own. You are not allowed to make any written notes.

2 Choose a topic

Choose one of the topics below and talk about it for five minutes. Be prepared to answer questions from the examiner. You may take a minute or two to write some brief notes before you begin.

1 'When you look at the lives of pop stars and other famous people, you see that achieving both happiness **and** success is an impossible dream.'

2 '100% literacy should be the goal of every government in the world.'

3 My hero

EXAMINER'S TIPS

I Use a special combination of visual recall (look, say, cover, write, check method), speech sounds, spelling patterns and spelling rules to **learn new spellings**.

2 When you learn a language, it helps to have a good memory. Improve your memory by:
- highlighting key ideas
- studying new vocabulary regularly and memorising it
- reading through your class notes frequently
- drawing pictures to illustrate words or concepts
- linking new words to words you already know
- using new words and phrases in your speech and writing
- learning something by heart because it means something special to you (e.g. a poem or pop song).

3 Find time each week to **organise your course notes**, to make it easy to find work from previous lessons. A lot of the work you'll be doing is sequential. This means you'll often have to look back at notes you made earlier.

4 Draft your written work two or three times. If you can't think of what to write, get something down on paper anyway. If you have nothing written, you have nothing to change. Show your written work to a friend. Listen to advice about improvements you could make.

5 Be prepared to work in groups and to be an active participant, but take responsibility for working alone at times too.

6 **Practising your English outside class** will help your progress. Here are some ways to do this.
- Get an English-speaking penfriend.
- Watch or listen to English programmes, films, videos, pop songs, etc.
- Make an arrangement with a friend who also wants to learn English, and practise speaking together once or twice a week.
- Read widely in English: books, magazines, newspapers, etc.

EXAM STRATEGY

7 When answering multiple-choice questions, make sure you read all the alternatives before ticking the answer you think is correct.

8 When you **describe a person**, remember that a physical description won't be enough to get the best exam marks. You will also have to describe character and give reasons, examples and evidence to support your views.

Unit focus

In this unit you have produced short answers to questions on detailed reading texts. This is practice for Papers 1/2, Part 1.

You have listened to a discussion and answered multiple-choice questions. This is practice for Paper 3, Part 3.

You have developed skills for **writing about yourself** and for **describing a person's appearance and qualities**. This is practice for Papers 1/2, Part 3.

You and Your Community

Home town

1 Interview: Introduction

'Home Town' is the title of a regular feature appearing in a national newspaper. It aims to give personal insights into famous people's home lives, so the interviewees are encouraged to talk as openly as they can.

Imagine that you are involved in writing or being interviewed for a 'Home Town' article. You will need to divide into two groups: Group A (Journalists) and Group B (Interviewees).

2 Group A: Journalists

You are going to interview one of your classmates about their home town and family life.

You need to achieve an insightful, revealing interview which really gets below the surface of your interviewee's life. Asking your interviewee for personal anecdotes, their opinions and attitudes will get the in-depth interview you are looking for.

Tick off any points you would like to raise in the interview.

Neighbourhood and home life

- [ ] some good points about the neighbourhood and its atmosphere
- [ ] a favourite family activity
- [ ] a happy family memory
- [ ] a special quality of his/her parents
- [ ] a value he/she has learned from his/her family

Personal information

- [ ] his/her pet hates
- [ ] a challenge or problem he/she is proud of overcoming
- [ ] the strangest experience he/she has ever had
- [ ] his/her personal goals

What else would you like to find out? Add any other points to the lists.

BEING FLEXIBLE

You obviously can't know how your interviewee is going to answer. Be prepared for 'dead end' answers. If your question leads nowhere, have an alternative up your sleeve.

Examples:
How does your family usually celebrate holidays/birthdays/religious festivals?
What are your brothers and sisters like?
What do you quarrel about?
Tell me about your own bad habits (!)

If your interviewee has left home, change your questions to the past tense. Or your interviewee may prefer to talk about his/her life now. Let him/her decide.

GETTING GOOD DESCRIPTIONS

Remember to use open questions.

Examples:
What is/are your ...... like?
What do you ...... about ...... ?
How do/does ...... ?
Tell me about ....
Tell me more about ....

Explore the answers you get by asking *Why?*, *In what way?*, etc.

3 Group B: Interviewees

Before being interviewed, spend a few quiet minutes thinking about your home life. Visualise the street you live in, your house, your parents, your brothers and sisters, things you enjoy doing at home, what you like about your locality. If you have moved away from your home town, you can talk about the way you live now. You decide.

DEALING WITH PERSONAL QUESTIONS

Personal questions can be intrusive. You have the right to avoid answering a question if you prefer. You can say things like
That's personal, I'd rather not say, if you don't mind.
I can't answer that.

BEING FLEXIBLE

If you are flexible when answering questions, it will help the interviewer. For example, you can say *I'd rather not answer that but I can tell you about my ....*

You can adapt a question by saying *I'm afraid I don't know much about that, but I can tell you about my ....*

GETTING MORE TIME

If you need more time to think, you can say
Let me think about that for a moment.
or
Well, let me see.

4 Honest feedback

Did you both feel the interview was successful? Why/Why not? Remember, interviewing and being interviewed are real skills which even professionals have to develop. Don't be afraid to say what you would change next time round.

After the feedback, it is useful to record your decisions like this:
Next time I'm taking part in an interview, I'll ....

5 Reading

You are going to read a magazine article about Diane Modahl's home town. Diane is a successful British athlete who grew up in a suburb of Manchester, a large city in the North of England.

As you read, number the following events in the order in which they happened.

a She began to compete internationally.
b She decided she wanted to be an athlete.
c She joined an athletics club.
d She got married.
e She moved from Longsight to Withington.

HOME TOWN

Diane Modahl's six older siblings all live within a ten-minute drive of their parents' house in Withington, a suburb of Manchester. It is the place where Modahl
5 lived from the age of 11 until the age of 24, when she married and moved to Sale – 20 minutes away by car. But every Sunday she and her husband, Vicente, like the rest of her siblings, return to Withington for a huge
10 Jamaican lunch of marinated chicken, rice with peas, and fried potatoes. It is a family tradition and they all relish it.

In Modahl's mind Withington stands for happiness. Up until the age of 11 she had
15 lived in Moss Side and Longsight. She remembers little about these places except, with fondness, the sports days her father used to organise for the children in the neighbourhood. Her father, who worked in
20 the pastry department of a food factory, was, she says, "like the Pied Piper", knocking on everybody's doors and encouraging them to take part. "The first prize for the races would be a chocolate bar, which really inspired me
25 then."

Her mother, an auxiliary nurse, "is a very ambitious, enthusiastic and positive lady", and Modahl suspects it was mostly due to her desire to make "a step up" that the family
30 moved from their three-bedroomed council house in Longsight to a very large five-bedroomed Victorian house in Withington, an area which "tended to be white middle-class".

35 Although their father stopped organising sports days once they moved there, Modahl and her siblings loved the place – the big cellar, the attic, the large kitchen. "All of us five girls had had to share one room before."

40 Modahl made friends with two girls living opposite. "I do remember always being different from them. But if they were racist, it was inadvertent. They'd ask rather silly questions, like did I burn in the sun, and
45 what kind of make-up could I use? Colour and race never came up in Longsight, but there were more black people there. I was bemused by people's reaction to me in Withington, but there was never any blatant
50 name-calling and I never felt uncomfortable. Although my brothers and sisters always accuse me of being naive, I think it was just ignorance and curiosity."

Modahl joined a nearby athletics club
55 and with "hundreds of other children" would go on Thursday evenings to train. "We did high and long jumping, hurdles, running, middle-distance sprinting, everything. The atmosphere was fun and I made lots of new
60 friends. When at 19 I decided I wanted to be an athlete, Withington became ideal for training. I felt safe there."

When she started making trips to compete abroad, she never felt homesick
65 because home had given her such a strong sense of confidence. "I was nervous, but I knew I could run well so I relished the thought of packing my bags, putting my spikes in my luggage and going. But it was
70 always nice to get back."

Whereas before her marriage Modahl would never have contemplated leaving her home town, since meeting Vicente she now feels "the sky's the limit". She says she's
75 more mature. "I wouldn't hesitate to move to Norway, where he comes from. We're thinking of it and it's an exciting thought. He and I rely on each other totally. We both want each other to achieve our ambitions.
80 Now we have our first child, we have to set a standard and tone for our family. I think my parents would be disappointed if they felt one of us was being held back and tied to them."

6 Discussion

In general, what do you think of the journalist's interview skills? Have you gained insights into the factors which have shaped Diane's personality? Why/Why not?

7 Detailed comprehension

Try to answer the following questions in full sentences.

1 What evidence is there that her father had a good sense of fun when Diane was very young?
2 Why was the new house in Withington such a contrast with their home in Longsight? Give two examples.
3 How did Diane feel about competing abroad after she decided to become an athlete?
4 How did she react to the remarks made by the girls who lived opposite her in Withington?
5 Using information from the article, write a paragraph of about 70 words explaining how Diane has changed since she married.

VOCABULARY

Find words in the text that mean the same as:

a puzzled
b brothers and sisters
c soaked in liquid and spices before cooking
d represents
e not deliberate
f delighted in
g thought about, considered
h open, obvious
i a person in a fairy tale

8 Describing Diane

From what Diane says in the passage, what kind of teenager do you think she was? Circle the appropriate adjectives, checking in a dictionary if necessary.

shy   rebellious   uptight   academic

hot-tempered   single-minded   good-natured

sociable   sporty   aggressive   timid

highly-strung   adventurous

9 Describing Diane's family

Can you pair up adjectives of similar meaning from the following lists? Using a dictionary and checking with a partner will help clarify unfamiliar items. When you've made the pairs, tick those that describe Diane's family. What clues in the text help you decide? Be prepared to justify your decisions!

exuberant   ordinary
critical   welcoming
close-knit   supportive
go-ahead   dynamic
reticent   reserved
hospitable   judgemental
down-to-earth   high-spirited

10 Colloquial words

Diane uses some colloquialisms (informal words and expressions). You can often guess their meaning by analysing the context in which they are used.

For example, the family's move to Withington is described as '*a step up*'. Does Diane think the move was an improvement in their social position or not?

Before going abroad, she looked forward to '*putting my spikes in my luggage*'. Are spikes things you wear, eat, or read? What would be essential for Diane to take with her when she competes?

With your partner, underline the colloquialisms in the following passage. Then try to work out their meaning from the context.

I can't lend you any money, I'm afraid. I'm broke. I've spent all my savings getting the car I bought repaired. It was advertised in our local paper and it seemed fine, but I think I was really conned by the owner. After a few days oil leaked non-stop from the engine and the starter motor went on the blink. The brakes were a bit dodgy too. In the end, I had to get quite stroppy with the seller, almost telling him he was a crook, before he agreed to give me a hundred quid towards repairs.

11 Translation

What colloquialisms do you use in your own language? Can you think of any direct equivalents in your language for the colloquial words in the text in exercise 10?

12 Discussion

A   Diane describes her mother as '*a very ambitious, enthusiastic and positive lady*'. Could Diane herself be described like this? Why/Why not? How far do you think children acquire their parents' characteristics?

B   Diane attributes a lot of her present success to her close-knit family. How far do you think early family life influences your chances of success later on? Apart from your family, where else can you find support and encouragement to help you achieve your goals?

C   What do you think of Diane? Do you admire her? Why/Why not? In your own culture, can you think of someone who has done well against the odds and who you find inspiring? Share your ideas with your partner.

13 Idioms

Can you work out the meaning of the following common sayings about family life from their context?

1   I gave the job to my nephew rather than my neighbour's boy. After all, *blood is thicker than water.*

2   She gave the police evidence against him, even though he was *her own flesh and blood.*

3   My job doesn't pay much but it does *keep the wolf from the door.*

Favourite places

14 Discussion

Most of us have one or two places nearby we especially like visiting. When you want relaxation and pleasure, where do you go? Do you head for wide, open spaces, relishing the thought of glorious sunsets, freedom and natural beauty? Or do you prefer urban environments and the intimate atmosphere of coffee bars and social clubs?

15 Reading and vocabulary

Read about the way one student likes to spend her time. What does she do? Does the place sound inviting? Would you like to go there? Why/Why not?

When I've got some free time, I love visiting our local market. It's a large, outdoor market by the seafront. Even if I'm not going to buy anything, I really like the light-hearted, bustling atmosphere and the cheerful sounds of stallholders calling to each other.

I'm usually tempted by the brightly-coloured array of fruit and impressed by the gorgeous cloth on sale. As the market is quite near the seafront, the pungent, fishy odours mingle with the fragrant smells of herbs, plants and vegetables. There's a second-hand stall I browse through too, unable to resist the chance of finding something valuable. I once bought a wonderful old Chinese candlestick for just 50p! When I'm at the market I forget all about my everyday problems. I can just relax, unwind and enjoy the sights and scenes around me.

Read the text again and underline the descriptive phrases. Then group them according to

Size and location: ....

Atmosphere: ....

Smells: ....

Sounds: ....

Colours: ....

Emotions: ....

Opinions: ....

16 Writing

Now close your eyes and imagine yourself in a favourite place of your own. Are you alone, or with family or friends? What are you doing? Let the sights, colours, sounds and smells of the place wash over you. Think about the way you feel when you go there.

When you're ready, try to write down your ideas on paper. Be prepared to make one or two drafts before you get the description just right. Use a dictionary to help. Don't forget to explain why this is one of your favourite places.

DESCRIPTIVE PHRASES

To help complete your writing, choose from the descriptive words and phrases below. Don't forget, however, the importance of correct collocations (word combinations). Check with a dictionary or a partner that the words you have chosen are appropriate for what you are describing.

Smells
fragrant   perfumed   sweet-smelling   scented
fresh   pungent   smoky

Sounds
cheerful sound of talk and laughter   peaceful
not a sound   noisy   silent   sound of birds calling

Colours
colourful   vibrant   bright   shining   rich
gorgeous   glowing   radiant   glorious   soft
muted

Atmosphere
light-hearted   bustling   tranquil   intimate
sophisticated   safe   warm and friendly
awe-inspiring   cosy   invigorating   eerie   lively
civilised   comfortable   appealing   relaxing
dimly/well lit   mysterious   unspoilt

Where is it?
off the beaten track   right in the centre of town
only five minutes away   isolated
hard to get to but worth the effort

Expressing feelings
When I'm there I ...

... feel close to my family or friends/revel in the solitude/enjoy my own company.

... relax and unwind/forget my everyday problems.

... feel excited/happy/contented/secure/exhilarated.

... experience the beauty of nature/find it spiritually uplifting/marvel at the wonderful things people have created.

17 Reading aloud

Everyone sees things differently, so it can be nice to share your thoughts and feelings with others and to hear why they might enjoy going to a favourite place. Without writing your name on the paper, drop what you have written into a box. The papers can then be shuffled and you can take turns in selecting one and reading it aloud to your group.

18 Showing enthusiasm

Listen to the following descriptions of places. Notice how the most important words which show strong, definite feelings are stressed.

1   What an AMAZING place! It would make a GREAT change from life in the city.

2   What a LOVELY place! I'm sure I'd appreciate the special ATMOSPHERE.

3   What FUN! It would be a SUPERB place to relax on holiday.

4   How FASCINATING! My friends and I LOVE wildlife. We MUST go there.

5   How INTERESTING! Now I'll see it through NEW EYES!

Practise saying the sentences to your partner. Make sure you sound enthusiastic. Stress the important words which show your attitude.

19 Order of adjectives

Study this sentence from the text in exercise 15.
*I bought a **wonderful** old Chinese candlestick for just 50p.*

Which type of adjective comes first: opinion, origin or age?

A sequence of adjectives before a noun usually has a certain order in English:

personal opinion/judgement, size/height/shape, age, colour, origin, material, purpose (what it's used for).

Put these adjectives into the sentences according to the rules above.

1   I've lost a bag. (sports canvas red)
2   We stayed in a house. (three-bedroomed Swedish quaint)
3   The new boss is a woman. (friendly Egyptian middle-aged)
4   I want to buy a jacket. (leather good-quality black)
5   I've bought a coat. (warm tweed winter).
6   Thieves stole a teapot. (oriental silver priceless)
7   On holiday I enjoyed trying the food. (Indian vegetarian tasty).
8   How do you remove coffee stains from a rug? (silk Chinese expensive).

20 Developing a more mature style

Using too many adjectives before a noun is confusing. Three is usually enough. You can 'break up' a long description by adding a clause instead. This creates a more mature style.

Examples:
Adjectives + noun + **with** (extra details)
*He decided to wear a cool white cotton shirt **with short sleeves**.*

Adjectives + noun **made of** (material)
*He was wearing an amazing, long, purple cloak **made of velvet and silk**.*
(Note that commas are sometimes used between adjectives in longer sequences.)

Adjective + noun + **which** (a variety of information)
*She was wearing an Italian gold watch **which looked very expensive**.*
*He has a reliable old scooter **which he doesn't mind lending to people**.*

PRACTICE

Combine each group of sentences into one longer sentence. Use the correct adjective order and a clause where appropriate. When you've finished, compare your answers with a partner. Do you both agree that the order sounds natural and the style is elegant?

1 He gave her a box. The box was made of wood. It had a picture of a famous story on the lid. It was Russian. It was an unusual box.
2 She was wearing a brown suit. It was wool. It looked too warm for the weather.
3 The television is portable. It's white. It's Japanese. It has a hundred channels.
4 It's a frying pan. It's copper. It's heavy. It's French. It has a lid.
5 Someone's taken my mug. It has my name on it. It's blue. It's a pottery mug. It's used for coffee.
6 He has lost a coat. It's polyester. It's a school coat. It has his name on the inside.
7 Rosanna decided to wear a long dress. It was green and white. It was made of silk. She had bought it in America.

What do teenagers want?

21 Discussion

A Have you ever campaigned to make your neighbourhood a better place to live in? What did you do? Were you successful? How proud do you feel of your achievement?

B How would you like to improve your neighbourhood for teenagers? Would you like to see improved facilities for education and training, more varied sports and leisure amenities, or better-lit streets and safer public areas? Discuss your ideas in your groups.

22 Before you listen: Vocabulary check

You are going to listen to a discussion between two officials, John and Pamela, about the best way of converting a disused warehouse for the benefit of local teenagers.

Before you listen, make sure you know the meaning of these words and phrases:

* maintenance
* facilities
* wear and tear
* drain on resources

* budget
* voluntary
* premises

23 Listening for gist

Listen to the conversation for general meaning first, and find answers to the three questions.

1 What facility does the woman want? *Study centre*
2 What facility does the man want? *U club*
3 What does Pamela say which shows she is changing her mind?

She used "maybe I should....."

24 Detailed listening

Now listen for detail and try to decide whether the following statements are true or false.

1   Pamela has thrown away inappropriate applications.
2   The study centre would be open at weekends.
3   The public library is easy to get to.
4   The staff at the public library are over-worked.
5   There is no proof that parents would prefer a study centre to a youth club.
6   They both agree that a study centre is more economical to run than a youth club.
7   The supervisor would work on a voluntary basis.
8   The premises are in the middle of a residential street.
9   The case in the newspapers influenced Pamela's attitude to the youth club.
10 John and Pamela will make the final decision about the use of the premises.

25 Follow-up

Whose views do you sympathise with – John's or Pamela's? Why?

IDIOMS

People sometimes say *I'm digging my heels in* or *I'm sticking to my guns* when they refuse to change their minds, despite pressure. Could these idioms be applied to John or Pamela? Why?/Why not?

26 Persuading: Stress and intonation

In their discussion, John and Pamela use the following polite phrases to persuade each other to listen to their point of view. Listen again and tick each one as you hear it. Notice how the words in capital letters are stressed. Do the phrases generally have a rising or a falling pattern?

☐ Do you REALLY think it's a good idea ...?

☐ (That) sounds all right in THEORY, but in PRACTICE ...

☐ I take your POINT, BUT ...

☐ (That's) all very well, BUT ...

☐ That's true, BUT ...

☐ Look at it THIS way, ...

Practise saying these phrases aloud to each other. How could you complete each one?

27 Role play: Spend, spend, spend

Your family has won £10,000 in a competition. You all took part in the competition, so you're having a family conference to discuss how to spend the money.

In groups of three or four, choose from the roles below. Your aim is to persuade the family that your ideas for spending the money are best. Use the phrases from exercise 26 to show you're listening to what they have to say but that you want to express a different opinion.

MUM

You think it is important to spend the money on something sensible and practical which will bring lasting benefits. You want to spend it on new furniture, curtains, carpets, and a new washing-machine.

DAD

You want to save the money for the future. Eventually the family will need money to move house, for the children's education or for retirement. It is silly to rush into spending the money without being sure of the best way to use it. A good investment account will earn high interest on the savings so the money will be worth more in the future.

DAUGHTER

You want the family to build a swimming pool in the garden. There is no swimming pool near your home and you are a keen swimmer. It would be a good way for the whole family to get exercise and to cool off after school/work in the summer.

SON

You think the money should be used for an exciting holiday of a lifetime that would be impossible to afford otherwise. You want the family to have a safari holiday in Kenya. You've always wanted to see wildlife in its own habitat, and everyone would learn so much from it.

Living with a foster family

28 Pre-reading discussion

Children and young people whose own family are in difficulties sometimes live with a 'foster' family. This is usually arranged by social workers. Not every family can become a foster family: the family must be suitable. Although some foster children are fostered for many years, eventually it is hoped that they will return to their parents' home.

You are going to read a magazine article about a boy of 14, Craig, who lives with a foster family.

Would you be keen to have a foster brother or sister? How would you feel about it? Share your ideas in groups.

29 Reading for gist

Now read the article for general meaning. Why is Craig being fostered? Is he happy?

Rita and Alan Dawson, both 42, from Kent, already had three children when they heard about a child at their daughter's school whose father had died and whose
5 mother was having difficulty coping. Rita and Alan, an architectural technician, decided to foster him, and now have four children under their roof – Lucy, 15, Craig, 14, Michael, 13, and Daniel, 11.

10 'When I heard about Craig, it struck a chord. Instead of sending a few pounds to an anonymous charity, we could give a child a home and really make a difference. So when Alan came home from work, I said "How do
15 you fancy another child?" And he said – and this is the truth – "Well we'd have to get an extra car seat for the car ..."

'We chatted to the kids and asked what they thought. My daughter knew Craig
20 vaguely and I suppose she was the most apprehensive. Because Lucy's the eldest, and already has two brothers, I think she would probably have preferred a puppy, but we talked about it and agreed to go ahead.

25 'After talking to Craig's mother and to the social workers, it was decided he would come and stay for half-term, to see how we got on. In February 1995, his mum brought him round and that was the first time I met
30 Craig. He's been here ever since.

'Craig was extremely brave that first night – he had his own room, though the boys all get on so well now they share one. I went into him and said, "I always kiss my
35 own children goodnight – do you want me to kiss you goodnight, too?" And he said he did. He's very outgoing and affectionate.

'You have to tread carefully as a foster parent. I've never tried to be his mum – he's
40 already got a mum whom he loves very much and sees regularly. All we're doing is giving him a home: the child has to feel he's part of the family without forgetting that his real family is elsewhere.

45 'There's a lot of red-tape involved in fostering – our private life was gone over with a fine-tooth comb – and we had a high turnover of social workers. But we now deal with a fostering liason officer who's brilliant.
50 We didn't get any financial help for the first nine months, so things were a bit tight, but it's sorted out now and we feel very settled.

'Our families thought we were taking on a bit much, though people have been helpful
55 and supportive, even if they doubted our sanity. A friend came round once when all the kids were here. Doors were slamming, the phone was ringing, one child was asking for money, another was looking for
60 something. After 15 minutes my friend said, "I've got to go – I can't stand this!"

'We've had our rocky moments. Craig came to us with different rules and tastes but he's adapted. For example, he never goes out
65 now without telling me where he's going. And I've always expected the children to help clear up after meals but, at first, Craig thought he was being punished when I asked him to help. He's obviously been

70 through a lot – we've sat down and cried together at times – but he's not difficult. I think a lot of people assume that if children need to be fostered, they must be troublemakers, but children are put into care
75 for any number of reasons.

'I now feel as though we're a family. And I'm so proud of my three children because they've had to share their mum and dad, but they've stuck together with Craig.

80 'The head of Lucy and Craig's year at school has been wonderful. When I felt as if I were banging my head against a brick wall, she'd listen, and she'd keep an eye on the children's behaviour so if she felt something
85 was worrying them, she'd ring me and we'd deal with it.

'We were finally approved as foster parents in May 1996, 15 months after Craig first came to us. It was a great moment.

90 'It is hard work, and sometimes I fantasise about being alone on a desert island, but only for about two minutes. It's been easier because Craig is such a lovely boy. We've told him he has a home here as
95 long as he wants one. He's happy, and we're happy to have him. No one can say what'll happen in the future but I feel we'll always know Craig – I hope so.

'Once, after a bad day, I told him, "You're
100 here because we wanted you. You don't owe us anything – we wanted you." We'd certainly do it again. Oh yes, like a shot.'

28/10/01

30 Vocabulary *ex book*

Match these words from the text with their definitions.

1 coping *E*
2 anonymous *A*
3 apprehensive *D*
4 liaison officer *F*
5 slamming *G*
6 adapted *C*
7 punished *b*

A unknown, not unusual
B treated harshly for doing something wrong
C person who makes contact between different people or groups
D nervous, worried
E managing to deal with a difficult situation
F fitted in to a new situation
G banging

31 Post-reading discussion

Share your views on the following questions in your groups.

How do you think people reading the magazine article would feel at the end? Would they feel

a saddened? (It is depressing to think children's natural parents cannot look after them.)

or

b positive? (The story is an example of human kindness and warmth.)

AUTHOR'S MAIN AIM

Do you think the MAIN aim of the article is to

a explain how to foster children?
b tell the reader what fostering children is like from the foster mother's viewpoint?
c describe how it feels to be a foster child?
d convey the viewpoints of everyone involved in the fostering process?

STRUCTURE

Which is the best description of the structure of the article?

a It is a mixture of long and short sentences. There are several short paragraphs.
b The sentences are mainly long and complex. The article is composed of a few long paragraphs.

STYLE

Is the style chatty, technical, formal or neutral?

32 Comprehension check

1 How many children of their own do Rita and Alan have? *3*
2 How did the children's parents approach telling them they wanted to become foster parents to Craig?
3 Who has Rita found particularly helpful in supporting her decision to foster?
4 What difficulties has Craig faced since living with the foster family? Give two examples.
5 Describe in about 50 words Rita's attitude to being a foster mum.

33 Further discussion

A Rita says some people assume foster children are troublemakers. Where do you think this idea comes from? What helps us decide that someone is or is not a troublemaker?

B In some countries, such as Zimbabwe, fostering arrangements are made informally by relatives. In other countries, such as The Netherlands, a child is not considered to be fostered unless he or she is placed by an official agency

What arrangements are made in your country to foster children? What are the advantages and disadvantages of formal versus informal arrangements?

34 Colloquial language in context

With a partner, study these colloquial phrases and idioms from the text. Try to work out their meaning from the context.

1 Rita and Alan have four children *under their roof.*
2 There's a lot of *red tape* involved in fostering.
3 Our private life was gone over *with a fine-tooth comb.*
4 We've had our *rocky moments.*
5 I felt as if I were *banging my head against a brick wall.*
6 We'd certainly do it again. Oh yes, *like a shot.*

35 Spelling: Doubling consonants when adding suffixes

Suffixes are word endings, such as

-ed -ing -er -est -ish -y -able

Adding a suffix can change a verb tense, make a comparative or superlative form, or change nouns into adjectives, etc.

Look at these verbs from the magazine article with their endings:

chat**ted** slam**ming** adapt**ed** send**ing** ask**ing**

Notice how the final consonant of *chat* and *slam* has been doubled, but not with the other verbs. Can you say why?

The rule for adding suffixes to ONE-SYLLABLE WORDS is:
Double the final consonant if the word ends in ONE VOWEL + ONE CONSONANT.

Examples:
cut **tt** cutting
sun **nn** sunny
spot **tt** spotty
red **dd** reddish
big **gg** bigger
wet **tt** wetter wettest

Exceptions are one-syllable words which end with **w**, **x** or **y**.
Examples:
buy buying
few fewer
box boxing

If a one-syllable word ends in either
TWO vowels + one consonant
or
one vowel + TWO consonants
we do NOT double the consonant.

Examples:
n**ee**d needing needed
w**ai**t waiting waited
ada**pt** adapting adapted adaptable
dou**bt** doubting doubted
ta**lk** talking talked

PRACTICE

Look carefully at the one-syllable words in the sentences below. Check the pattern of the ending (one vowel + one consonant, one vowel + two consonants, or two vowels + one consonant). Add suitable suffixes to complete the words, doubling the final consonant where necessary.

1 When I arrived home I could hear the phone ring _ing_ .

2 Yesterday was the hot _test_ day of the year.

3 Ibrahim has stop _ped_ smoking.

4 We really enjoy _ed_ our day out yesterday.

5 That's the sad _dest_ news I have ever heard.

6 Let's visit the new shop _ping_ centre.

7 Stop chat _ting_ and do some work!

8 The baby is already walk _ing_ .

9 We are send _ing_ our son to boarding school.

10 I bought these apples because they were much cheap _er_ than the other ones.

11 Zena got tired of wait _ing_ and left.

12 He is always ask _ing_ for money.

13 Don't go look _ing_ for trouble.

14 Our school has a new swim _ming_ pool.

15 We went through a rock _y_ time when our foster child first arrived.

36 Adding suffixes to multi-syllable words

There are some longer words in the article which double the final consonant when adding a suffix:
prefer**ring**   forget**ting**
Others do not: punish**ed**   foster**ing**

Do you know why?

The rule for adding suffixes to WORDS OF TWO OR MORE SYLLABLES is:
Double the final consonant if the last syllable is stressed and it ends in one syllable and one consonant.

Examples:
forGET forGETTING forGOTTEN
preFER preFERRING preFERRED

So, we do NOT double the final consonant if the stress is on the first syllable:

FOSter FOStering FOStered
PUNish PUNishing PUNished
LISten LIStening LIStened

or if the last syllable contains TWO vowels before the consonant:

expl**ai**n expl**ai**ned

PRACTICE

Add suitable suffixes to complete the words in these sentences, doubling the final consonant if necessary.

1 Patrick reGRET _ed_ leaving his job, but it was too late.

2 Smoking is not perMIT _ed_ .

3 The accident ocCUR _ed_ last night in thick fog.

4 I REAson _ed_ with him about his aggressive behaviour.

5 He has comMIT _ted_ a serious crime.

6 The earthquake HAPpen _ed_ in the evening.

7 She exPLAIN _ed_ the beGIN _ning_ of the story to them.

8 I've always preFER _ed_ travelling by train.

37 Look, say, cover, write, check

Understanding how grammar and pronunciation work helps you understand English spelling. You can also reinforce your understanding by using a visual strategy. Learn these commonly misspelled words through the 'look, say, cover, write, check' method. Why not ask a friend to test you when you are confident you have learned them correctly?

beginning   preferred
occurred   swimming
occurrence   shopping
happening   travelled
happened   dropped
permit   development
permitted

38 Words from different languages

Liaison is a French word which has come into English. English has a fascinating history of borrowing words from a vast number of languages. Many words came from invaders, colonisers and international trade.

With your partner, try to match the common 'loan' words in the box below with their language of origin. Use a dictionary to check the meaning of unfamiliar words.

Arabic _____	Italian _____
Aztec _____	Japanese _____
Chinese _____	Latin _____
French _____	Norwegian _____
Greek _____	Persian _____
Hindi _____	Spanish _____

Can you guess why the word might have come from that language? Think about the climate, way of life, food, etc.

Check your pronunciation of the words with your partner. Finally, use each word in a sentence of your own.

COMPARING LANGUAGES

What English words do you use in your own language? What words in your language come from other languages? Share your knowledge with your group.

athlete   cuisine   bungalow

chocolate   patio   ski

tea   sofa   caravan

opera   villa   karate

Welcoming an exchange visitor

39 Reassuring your guest

In order to learn more about other cultures, many young people take part in exchange visits with students of their own age. They take turns going overseas to stay with each other's families. By doing so, they improve their understanding of another culture and way of life, improve their skills in a foreign language and have a pleasant holiday at the same time.

Imagine that your family is going to take part in an exchange visit. Your guest, who you have not met before and is about your age, is coming from overseas to stay with you for three weeks. How do you think he/she might be feeling? Nervous, excited, apprehensive?

In a letter, how could you put your guest at ease and make your home and your local area sound inviting? Make a few notes under the following headings.

Paper mache notes

Positive things about my home and family

....

....

Enjoyable things to do together

....

....

Exciting places to visit

....

....

What aspects of your home life or area would you NOT want to draw attention to (if any)? Why?

....

....

BEGINNINGS AND ENDINGS

How would you like to begin your letter? Look at some sentences students have used and choose the appropriate ones. Which sentences are unsuitable. Why?

a I am very sorry that this is my first letter to you.
b I wish to write you a letter to inform you about my background.
c It is my generous attitude which invites you to my home.
d What a pleasant surprise to hear from me in this friendly letter.
e This is a quick line to welcome you to my home.

How would you like to close the letter?

f It will be a great joy for me on the day I see you.
g My friend, we are all waiting for you.
h We can't wait to meet you.
i Surprisingly, you will enjoy your life with me.
j I am happy I wrote you this letter today.

Homework 31/10/01 Wednesday do in th paper

40 Model letter

Now read this model letter. Underline the phrases used to welcome the visitor.

Dear Jacob,

I'm really pleased you're coming to stay with us soon. My family consists of my mum, dad and my older brother Matthew and my pet dog Rufus. We're an easy-going, ordinary family and my parents are very approachable. They let us do more or less what we like as long as we tell them about it first.

We live in a three-bedroomed Victorian terraced house with a small front and back garden. We live about ten minutes walk away from the town centre which has a wide choice of modern shops, three cinemas, lively clubs and a weekly market. We also have a superb new swimming pool in town, so I hope you'll bring your swimming things. If you enjoy history, I'll show you our museum. It has some fascinating information about the history of my town.

I've made a list of the most interesting things to do and see in the area. I heard you like football so I've booked two tickets to see a big match while you're here. I got my driving licence last month and dad has promised to let me use the car. We can explore the countryside and perhaps even camp for a night or two. The countryside won't be as spectacular as Kenya but it's very peaceful and we might even see some wild ponies.

Good luck with your trip!

Best wishes,

William

COMPREHENSION

1 What is William's family like?
2 What kind of environment does he live in?
3 What has he planned for Jacob's visit?

FORMAT

1 Do you think the letter sounds inviting or off-putting? Why/Why not? Underline the phrases which show that the writer has considered the feelings of his guest. Does he give reasons for the plans he is making? What are they?

2 Does William plunge straight into the topic of the exchange visit or is the beginning indirect? Do you think his approach is a good one? Why/Why not?

3 The letter has three main paragraphs. Do they follow each other in a smooth and natural way, or do they seem awkward and unconnected? Why?

4 Underline the opening and closing sentences of the letter. Are they appropriate? Why/Why not?

5 Overall, the letter is fairly short. Do you get a good enough picture of what the holiday is going to be like for Jacob? Why/Why not?

41 Achieving a suitable tone

In pairs, read the following sentences taken from students' exchange visit letters. If you were the recipient, which would make you feel at ease? Which might worry you? Put a tick against the sentences you like and a cross against the others.

As you work, discuss how any inappropriate expressions could be made more suitable. Correct any structural errors.

1 It'll be lovely to see you.
2 Unfortunately my father died seven years ago so you will not be able to meet him.
3 We're all looking forward to meeting you.
4 The food here will be rather distasteful for you.
5 At least when you are in the house try to behave with respect to my parents.
6 You'll be very welcome.
7 My friend, you can come and enjoy it but my family is very strict.
8 You'll soon feel at home.
9 The place itself is safety, you do not need to be afraid when walking, in case of thieves.
10 I would like to tell you that my parents are very good and they don't like people who drink too much.
11 Mostly, we will visit our countryside every day because here that is the only worth visiting place.
12 Mum and Dad always listen to our problems before giving their own point of view.
13 My family are selfishness and want someone to do things for them but I know such a thing will not inconvenient your visit to me.
14 We're going to have a wonderful time together.
15 We can go cycling through our beautiful countryside and have great parties on the beach.
16 As I already told you, this is a very small place, so don't think about hotels, theatres, cinemas and so on.
17 We can promise you the best time of your life.
18 Don't take chances if you cannot swim my friend, you will not survive.

REWRITING

Choose three of the sentences above which don't sound right and rewrite them to make a more appropriate impression. Try them out on a partner. Does he/she agree that they sound more inviting?

42 Correcting mistakes

This letter is from Jacob, who is writing to thank William for his holiday. Can you find the mistakes and correct them? The mistakes are to do with:

- prepositions
- tenses
- spelling
- vocabulary
- grammar
- missing words
- punctuation
- paragraphing
- articles

There are also two sentences in the letter which are inappropriate in tone. One of these can be deleted. You'll need to write a different sentence for the other one.

Finally, rewrite the whole letter correctly.

Dear William,

It is a great honour for me to write you this letter. Thank you for your kindness in the visit I make to your family last month. I am haveing many happy memorys of your family especially your mother. She is the best cooker in the world? I was very surprised of your town. It is extremely pleasant and not so industrial that I expected. I also liked your neighbours and I not forget familiar university students. I enjoyed the activities we done and I send you the best photographs of our camping trip in my next letter. Please come to a holiday in my family. Our house is standing in a lake. My father will let you to borrow his little boat. Beaches here are wonderful and now is becoming summer so we can go swimming which I know you enjoy. In cloudy days we can visit huge shoppings which are very popular for tourists. I'm expecting your letter with a cheerful heart.

Love,

Jacob

---

43 Sentence completion

Most of us find some aspects of our home life less than wonderful. You might wonder how a complete newcomer will fit in. If you want to give a realistic idea of your home life and still sound welcoming, it's a good idea to balance a negative idea with a positive one.

Try to complete these sentences positively.

1 Even though he is a nuisance at times, my little brother .....
2 Despite being too dangerous for swimming, our local river .....
3 Although we're a long way from the bright lights of the city, ...
4 My parents are a tiny bit strict yet .....
5 You'll probably find our way of life just a little strange at first, but .....
6 We don't have a perfect house but .....

REASSURANCE

When English people are trying to reassure someone about something, they sometimes use expressions like '*a tiny bit* awkward', '*just a little bit* difficult'. What do you say in your language?

44 Surprise party: Tone and register

You recently arranged a surprise party for your parents' wedding anniversary. You went to a lot of trouble to make the party a success. Unfortunately, your cousin was ill and unable to attend.

Which of the following would you say to your cousin? Why?

1 Where were you? Everyone expected you to come.
2 Why didn't you arrive? You should have been there.
3 It was such a shame you couldn't make it.
4 You disappointed us very much.

45 Re-ordering

The following letter describes a surprise party. It is written to a relative who missed the celebration. First, re-order the sentences and decide on the correct sequence of paragraphs. What overall impression do you think the letter will make on the recipient?

Dear Gillian,

a   As you know, Mum and Dad didn't know anything about it.
b   Just before the end, Uncle Steve let off lots of fireworks in the garden.
c   She had decorated the house beautifully.
d   Perhaps the video I'm sending you of the occasion will be a little compensation.
e   However, everyone understood that you were still feeling weak after the operation.
f   So you can imagine their surprise when, instead of going to the Blue Fountain, we arrived at Auntie Susan's house.
g   Hope you feel better soon.
h   No-one looked tired or seemed inclined to go early.
i   It was a great shame you couldn't come.
j   Although most of the guests must have been over 50, the party went on until the early hours.
k   Despite the fact that we all missed you, we had a lovely day.
l   This was a wonderful way to round off the occasion.
m   Once again, I know how disappointed you were not to be there.
n   Just a short letter to let you know about Mum and Dad's anniversary party.
o   They assumed I was taking them to a restaurant to celebrate.

Lots of love,

Linda

46 Writing

Your cousin went to live abroad with her family when she was only two or three years old. Her parents have asked if she can stay with your family for a holiday. You have never actually met before. Write a letter to your cousin in which you

•   introduce yourself
•   describe your family and background
•   tell her about enjoyable things to do together
•   describe interesting places to visit.

Write about 150 words.

INTERNATIONAL OVERVIEW

The 'top' five languages in the world, based on estimates made in 1992, are:

Approx. number of first language speakers

1	Mandarin Chinese	726 million
2	English	427 million
3	Spanish	266 million
4	Hindi	182 million
5	Arabic	181 million

However, at least another 350 million people speak English as a second language.

English is used as an official or semi-official language in over 60 countries in the world. It is well-established in a further 20. It is used as an international medium of communication for business, science, technology, medicine, sport, international competitions and advertising.

Do you find any of the figures in the above table surprising? If so, why?

Do you think it is right that English should become the language of international communication? Do you think it could disadvantage the development of local languages?

Is English used as an official or second language in your country? If so, why? Do you think this is a good thing?

Exam-format questions

Writing

1   The following note from your headteacher appears in your student newsletter.

> Some new students will be joining us next term. They and their families are new to this area and I have decided to put together a "Welcome" pack telling them about the school and neighbourhood. I would like to include articles about local places which you enjoy visiting. Please submit your articles by 10th December.

Write an article aimed at the new students. In the article you should:

- describe ONE local place of interest
- say why you enjoy visiting it (the atmosphere, scenery etc.)
- explain why you think the new students will enjoy it too.

Write about 200 words.

2   You are interested to read the following announcement.

> The Queen's Trust Newsletter wishes to hear from individuals or community groups about a project they have been involved in which has resulted in improved facilities for their school or neighbourhood. We have a number of prizes which will be given for the best entries.

Write an article for the newsletter describing a project you have been involved in. Explain why the improvement was needed and how it has benefited your school or neighbourhood.

The following may give you some ideas, but you are free to make up ideas of your own. Write about 200 words.

"We've started a clean-up campaign to get rid of litter in our area."

"I've raised funds to help provide food and shelter for homeless people."

"Our school raised money to make a recreation area for the students."

"Our swimming pool was going to be closed down but we persuaded the officials to keep it open."

"We were given a safe crossing on our street after we campaigned about the dangers."

Oral assessment

1   **Improving neighbourhoods**

What improvements would you like to see in your neighbourhood? Discuss your ideas with the examiner or your partner. Try, in particular, to think of specific improvements which would benefit people of all ages.

You might consider such things as:

- reducing noise, litter or pollution
- places of entertainment and relaxation
- expanding sports facilities
- the development of parks and pleasant, open spaces for everyone to enjoy
- improved transport facilities.

You are free to consider any other ideas of your own. You are not allowed to make any written notes.

2   **Choose a topic**

Choose one of the topics below and talk about it for five minutes. You will be asked a few questions about it when you have finished. You may take a minute or two to write some brief notes before you begin.

1   What makes me really annoyed is .....

2   The things I would change about my life if I could are .....

3   'Upbringing has nothing to do with the kind of person you become.'

4   If I had one day to spend exactly as I liked I would .....

5   My most cherished possession is .....

1   Enlarge your understanding of tone and register by listening as much as possible to English people speaking. Notice the words they use to express their feelings in different situations (breaking bad news, expressing pleasure, complaint, reservations or annoyance etc.).

Think also about the 'music' in their voices, the different intonation patterns that are used to show feelings, and try to imitate it. Listening to English radio plays (if you can) is a delightful source of tone, register and intonation, as is watching television dramas or going to the English-speaking theatre.

Joining a drama club and putting on English plays is an exciting and fun way to extend your spoken English skills.

2   Spelling and the grammatical system go hand in hand. Understanding how words are spelled will help you understand more about grammar and vice versa. Knowledge about grammar will expand your range of strategies for word-building (turning nouns into adjectives and so on) and for identifying the logic of irregular-looking spellings.

3   Proof-read your work for mistakes. You can do this during the writing process when you feel like a break from composing, and at the end. Use the dictionary as a spell-checker when proof-reading. Your dictionary is your friend. The more you use it, the quicker and more efficient with it you will become.

4   If you use a computer to help you learn English, there are many interesting and entertaining spelling programs you can use to back up your learning.

5   Some kinds of dictionary are a brilliant fund of information about the history of the English language. Have fun browsing through a dictionary, investigating the numerous 'borrowings' from a huge number of other languages.

EXAM STRATEGY

6   Reading comprehension questions don't always have to be answered in your own words. You can answer some questions by using words from the text.

Unit focus

In this unit you have taken part in an interview about yourself, your neighbourhood, and your family. This is practice for Papers 5/6.

You have listened to a dialogue about a community project for teenagers and answered true/false questions. This is practice for Paper 3, Part 3 and Paper 4, Part 2.

You have practised detailed reading skills. This is practice for Papers 1/2, Part 2.

You have developed skills for **writing about yourself, your family and background and places of local interest**. You have studied tone and register and learned how to **welcome and reassure** an overseas guest. This is practice for Papers 1/2, Part 3.

Is sport always fun?

1 Note-taking and summaries: Sharing ideas

In this unit you will be learning how to take notes and write summaries. To help you, the skills will be broken into small stages.

In some exercises, you will be asked to read a text, take notes on it and then join your notes into a connected summary. This is because note-taking practice is treated as one of the stages in learning to write a summary. In Paper 2 of the exam, different texts are used for note-taking and summary questions.

TAKING NOTES

With a partner, tick off the aspects of note-taking you find most challenging.

- [ ] reading quickly and absorbing a lot of information
- [ ] deciding what to select from the text
- [ ] finding some words and phrases of similar meaning, where possible
- [ ] presenting notes clearly so they can be followed by someone who has not seen the original text

In the exam, your notes don't have to be all in your own words. However, it's a good idea to try to find SOME words and phrases of similar meaning rather than copying out chunks of texts. This is particularly important when you are asked to write 'guided notes'.

SUMMARISING

Summarising involves the note-taking skills in the list above. However, summaries, unlike notes, must be presented in connected grammatical prose. Your exam summary must not be longer than 100 words. You MUST use your own words wherever possible.

What difficulties, if any, do you find in

- connecting ideas grammatically and in your own words?
- keeping to a strict word limit of 100 words?

2 Discussion

Which sports on your school curriculum do you particularly like? Why?

3 Quiz

Work with a partner to complete the quiz, about what you have learned from doing sport at school or college. (If you've left school, look back at your experiences.)

Sport at school has taught me ...

(Put a ✓ in the box for Yes, and a ✗ for No.)

		MYSELF	MY PARTNER
1	to enjoy healthy competition.	☐	☐
2	self-confidence.	☐	☐
3	self-discipline.	☐	☐
4	to enjoy team work.	☐	☐
5	to improve my concentration and coordination.	☐	☐
6	how enjoyable exercise is.	☐	☐
7	to think positively about carrying on with sport in adult life.	☐	☐
8	ways to relax and unwind when I feel tense.	☐	☐
9	how to approach sport safely, e.g. using the right clothing and equipment.	☐	☐
10	to appreciate fair play and the need for rules.	☐	☐

4 Is sport always fun?

How far do you agree with these comments about sport at school?
Work with your partner to rank them from **0 (disagree totally)** to
3 (agree completely).

		MYSELF	MY PARTNER
1	*"I hate sport at school. It's so competitive and only slim, fit children can do well."*	☐	☐
2	*"I don't mind things we can do at our own pace like swimming or gymnastics, but I hate being forced to take part in races."*	☐	☐
3	*"It's usually too hot or too cold to enjoy being outside."*	☐	☐
4	*"I dread the time when we get picked for the team. I'm always the last one to be selected."*	☐	☐
5	*"There's so much standing around on the playing field waiting for something to happen. Sport is plain boring!"*	☐	☐
6	*"At my school we're forced to do the traditional sports our parents did. Why can't we do more up-to-date activities?"*	☐	☐

5 Pre-reading discussion

'Sports day' in many schools is a competitive event in which all children take part. Parents usually attend to watch their children perform. Do you have a similar event in your school? Do you enjoy it? Why/Why not?

6 Predicting content

Predicting content is part of getting the right mental attitude to reading.

You are going to read an article in which the writer criticises the sports day at her son's primary school. What specific things about sports day do you expect the writer to criticise? Tick as many of the following points as you think could be relevant.

☐ the value of the prizes

☐ the competitive aspect of the day

☐ the bad effect competitive sport has on some children

☐ the skills of the teachers

☐ her child's poor performance

☐ the time of year sports day is held

☐ the fact that sports day takes time away from academic subjects.

☐ the young age of the children taking part

7 Reading with concentration

Now read the article as fast as possible, trying to absorb as much information as you can. This means reading fast any sentences which are easy to understand. Read more slowly the sentences which are difficult or which you think contain key ideas.

Try, where you can, to work out the meaning of unfamiliar words from the context. Use a dictionary if this technique doesn't help AND the word seems important to the key meaning. However, don't worry too much about each word. **You don't need to understand every word to understand a text well.**

1 One afternoon in the last week of term, I saw three children from my son's school in tears being comforted by teachers. That morning, my 11-year-old had stomach pains and had been retching into a bowl. Talking to other mothers, I heard about other children with stomach-ache or difficulty sleeping the night before.

2 What caused so much distress? Sports day – not sports day at a highly-competitive independent school, but at a large village primary. For the children who can fly like the wind, it causes no problem. For those who are poorly coordinated, overweight or just not good at sport, it is a nightmare. Even for those who enjoy running, but who fall half way down the track in front of the entire school and their parents, it can prove a disaster.

3 Why do we put our children through this annual torment? Some may say

competition is character building; or it's taking part that's important, not the winning; or that it's a tradition of school life. I just felt immense pity for those children in tears or in pain.

4 Team games at the end of the "sports" produced some close races, enormous enthusiasm, lots of shouting – and were fun to watch. More importantly, the children who were not so fast or so nimble at passing the ball were hidden a little from everyone's gaze. Some of them also had the thrill of being on the winning side.

5 I wish that sports day could be abandoned and replaced with some other summer event. Perhaps an afternoon of team games, with a few races for those who want them, would be less stressful for the children and a lot more fun to watch.

8 Comprehension check

Try to answer these questions without looking back at the text, if possible.

1 What symptoms do children who are afraid of sports day show?

2 Where was the sports day held?

3 Why do some of the children who like running still find sports day traumatic?

4 What does the writer feel for young children who are upset by sports day?

5 How did the children feel about the team games played after the races?

6 What alternative to sports day does the writer suggest?

FINDING THE MAIN IDEAS

Match the following main ideas to the relevant paragraphs (1-5) of the article.

A How team games produced a positive atmosphere on sports day.

B The reasons why sports days are still a part of school life.

C An alternative to the traditional sports day.

D The explanation for the children's illnesses and fears.

E The physical symptoms that fear of sports day produces.

9 Checking predictions

How many of the points you ticked in exercise 6 were mentioned in the article?

What did the writer say which you did not predict?

10 Choosing a headline

Reading the title or headline of a text you are going to summarise is important because it gives an overall idea of what the text is going to be about.

Which of these headlines do you prefer for the article you have just read? Be prepared to explain your choice.

Sports day torment

It is time that sports were banned from the school curriculum

Sports Day

How one school has upset many of its pupils

It is essential that protests are made about the unfair ways young children are treated on their school sports day

Mum raps sports day   *Complain*

11 Note-taking practice

CHECKING KEY WORDS IN AN EXAM QUESTION

Underline the key words in this exam question, which is based on the article. You are asked to do five things. What are they?

Read the following newspaper article about a school sports day. Then write a set of notes based on the article, outlining the reasons for having a sports day, the negative effects sports day can produce on children, and a way sports day could be improved. You should write under headings, number points and use your own words as far as possible.

UNDERLINING RELEVANT PARTS OF THE TEXT

Re-read the article and underline the parts which are relevant to the question. When you've finished, compare your underlined sections with your partner's. Do you both agree on what is relevant?

MAKING NOTES IN YOUR OWN WORDS

Make notes from the text under the three headings indicated by the question. Try to find some words and phrases of similar meaning.

In pairs or threes, compare your notes.

Check the **content**: *Story*
Do you need to add anything or leave anything out?

Check the **language**: *What do they use*
Have you managed to avoid copying out chunks of text? Have you managed to find some words and phrases of similar meaning?

Check the **presentation**: *the view*
Are your notes orderly?
Do you have clear headings?
Are your points numbered?

Pose — written language in its usual form as opposed to poetry

lifts — to bring from a lower to a higher level

12 Comparing two summaries

Summarising requires you to write in grammatical, connected prose. The following two summaries, based on the article, were written by students. Analyse them by answering these questions.

1 Which summary 'lifts' from the text? *notes. form*
2 Which summary uses the student's own words as far as possible?
3 Which summary uses two linking words incorrectly?
4 Both summaries have one mistake in common. What is it?
5 Which summary seems to show the best overall understanding of the text? Why?

SUMMARY 1

Many reasons are given for having a sports day, such as the competition is character building, or it's the taking part that is important, not the winning, or that it's a tradition of school life. Moreover, sports days can be a nightmare for those who are poorly coordinated, overweight or just not good at sport. Despite for those children who enjoy running but fall down on the track in front of the entire school it can prove a disaster. It is said that sports day should be abandoned and replaced by an afternoon of team games with a few races for those who want them but I think that would spoil a nice summer event.

SUMMARY 2

Sports days at school are said to be valuable because they're a school custom, the competition is healthy, it develops character and the main point of the event is on the enjoyment of playing. However, sports days can be traumatic, especially if the pupils are not slim, agile or capable at sport. Even the confident, athletic ones can be very upset if they fall over before a large audience. An afternoon of team games, with a few races for those who are interested, should be offered in the summer instead of sports day. I believe most parents would prefer this to a competitive sports day.

Enjoying sports safely

13 Compound nouns

Like *sports day*, many compound nouns are a combination of two nouns (or a gerund plus a noun, e.g. *running shoes*). By avoiding the need for a preposition, as in 'a day of sports' or 'shoes for running', compound nouns can help you write more concisely.

Some of these words can follow the word *sports* to make common compound nouns. Write **sports** in the spaces as appropriate.

____ ✓ ____ bag
____ ✓ ____ car
_____ child
____ ✓ ____ centre
____ ✓ ____ club
_____sometimes_ drink
_____ enjoyment
____ ✓ ____ equipment
_____ hobby
____ ✓ ____ instructor
____ ✓ ____ man
____ ✓ ____ person
_____ time
____ ✓ ____ woman

PRACTICE

Form compound nouns by writing suitable words from the box alongside these words. In each case more than one combination is possible.

1 swimming _____ 5 skating _____
2 football _____ 6 leisure _____
3 hockey _____ 7 cricket _____
4 fitness _____

match 2,3,7		bat 3,7	
costume 5		shorts 2	
players 2,3,7		team 1,2,3,7,5	
programme 4,5,6		centre 4,5,6	
rink 5		boots 2,3	
hat 1		trunks 1	
stick 3		field 2,3,7	
pool 1		shirt 2,6	

What other compound nouns do you know? Make a list with a partner.

14 Pre-listening discussion

Do you ever go to a sports centre? What facilities do you use? Do you enjoy it? Why/Why not?

If you don't go to a sports centre, would you like to visit one? Why/Why not? What facilities do you think you would see there?

15 Listening to a recorded announcement

 You are going to hear some recorded information about facilities available at a sports centre. Listen first for general meaning and try to complete the list of compound nouns, putting one word in each space.

1 open-air swimming _pool_   6 cheap-rate _ticket_

2 coin- _return_ locker system   7 sports centre _is £16 6 your members_

3 _Changing_ rooms   8 application _form_

4 _badminton_ court   9 reception _desk_

5 _table_ tennis   10 keep-fit _classes_

Now listen again and complete the diary. How much does membership of the sports centre cost?

Sports Centre Diary

Monday

A.M.   9-11 Swimming in the open-air pool

    (i)   Need ...._50 p coin - locker system_....

P.M.   (ii)   Sports centre...._is closed_....

Tuesday

A.M.   10-11.30 Badminton court open

    (iii)   Bring...._their own badminton racket_....

P.M.   Open for schools only.

Wednesday

A.M.   9-11.30 Table tennis

    (iv)   Ask supervisor for ...._bat & ball_....

P.M.   (v)   Gym ...._is open 2 - 4_....

    (vi)   Must wear...._indoor shoes_....

Thursday

A.M.   (vii)   Collect application form from...._reception_....

P.M.   (vii)   Senior citizens' ...._keep fit centre_....

16 Marking the main stress

 John and Ella are watching Poland and Finland play football. Ella is unsure about some things. Listen to the dialogue while you read. Why is the main stress marked in this way?

Ella: Is Poland playing in the blue and green?

John: No, Poland's playing in the yellow and green.

Ella: Did you say Finland was in the yellow and green?

John: No, I said Poland was in the yellow and green.

Ella: Is Poland playing France this season?

John: Poland plays France every season.

Ella: Did Poland win a few of their matches last season?

John: They won all their matches last season!

Now practise reading the dialogue in pairs, putting the main stress as indicated. Why is a different word stressed in each answer?

PRACTICE

With a partner decide where the main stress falls in the following dialogue and mark it. Then practise the dialogue together.

Chris: Were you surprised about Kelly's behaviour on the field last night?
Helen: I'm never surprised about Kelly's behaviour!
Chris: Did you think the referee acted fairly?
Helen: No-one thought the referee acted fairly.
Chris: Is anybody from your family going to see the game tomorrow?
Helen: Everybody's going to see the game tomorrow.
Chris: Do you think the match will be as exciting?
Helen: I don't think any match could be as exciting.

17 Analysing headlines

To save space in headlines, and to be dramatic, newspapers invent unusual word combinations like **TRAGEDY BOAT**. Such 'compound nouns', although very creative, can be difficult to understand. This is particularly true if several nouns are strung together:

BOMB HOTEL HORROR PROBE

Underline the key words in the following newspaper report. Make sure you understand the meaning of *collision* and *compensation*.

to crash — *to provide with a suitable payment for some loss, damage*

Crash woman rejects deal

compound nouns
A female student, who was seriously injured when she was involved in a collision with a Kuranda bus in October, today rejected the compensation offered by Kuranda Bus company.

How does the headline convey the key elements of the story? What compound noun is used? Do you think this is an invented compound or one in normal use?

VERB TENSES

As in many headlines, the present simple tense is used. Why is this, when the report describes the rejection in the past tense?

VOCABULARY

Why do you think the headline refers to *crash* and *deal*, when the report uses *collision* and *compensation*?

ARTICLES

The report refers to *a collision* and *the compensation*. Why does the headline not use the articles?

18 Expanding headlines

Read the following headlines and answer the questions.

COMA BABY HOPE: US SURGEON TO OPERATE

1 Try to read COMA BABY HOPE backwards. Does this provide clues to understanding? *No*
2 How is the future expressed? Why? *people will read it*
3 Why is the colon used? *So it can see clearly*
4 Try to rewrite the headline as a complete sentence. *US surgeon to operate*

TRAIN BLAZE: CHILD FOUND 'UNHURT'

5 Why is the compound *train blaze* used rather than 'big fire on train'? *It look more interesting "train blaze"*
6 How is the passive voice of the present perfect tense conveyed in the headline? *So people will read it*
7 Why, is 'unhurt' in inverted commas, do you think?
8 Rewrite the headline in full. *The Child found 'unhurt. Train blaze"*

19 Noun or verb?

The following short words are common in newspaper headlines. Sometimes they are used as nouns, and sometimes as verbs. Choose one word from the box to complete each pair of headlines.

AID	ARM	CUT	HEAD	JAIL	VOW

1 REFUGEES TO GET FRESH __Aid__
2 CHARITY SHOPS __vow__ HOMELESS
3 JUDGE TO __Jail__ MURDER INQUIRY
4 CRASH VICTIM DIES OF __cut__ INJURIES
5 BABY'S __ARM__ SAVED IN MIRACLE OP
6 POLICE CHIEF __vow__ S CITY POLICE
7 FATHER __Jail__ S REVENGE ON KILLER
8 PRESIDENT BREAKS ELECTION __head__.
9 GOVERNMENT TO __cut__ WORKING HOURS
10 MORE EDUCATION __aid__ S ON WAY
11 JUDGE __AID__ S TRAIN ROBBER
12 CONDITIONS IN WOMEN'S __vow__ S 'SHOCKING'

20 Comparing languages

How does the newspaper language of your own language compare with English? Do you find any similarities? Or do you feel it is plainer?

children treated badly at home

21 Discussion

What do you think has happened to the sports person in the picture?

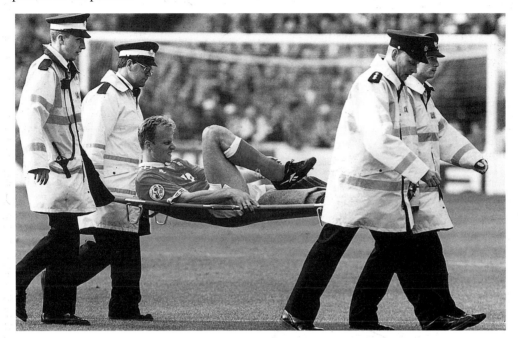

How can you get hurt when you play sport? If you are hurt, what should you do?

Have you ever suffered an injury whilst taking part in sport? How did it happen? What helped you recover?

22 Re-wording

When you write summaries, you need to use your own words without altering the meaning. For example:

If you carry out weight training, you would be well advised to do this in a gym under expert supervision.

could become

You should do weight training in a gym under the care of a qualified supervisor.

In groups of two or three, try to rewrite the following sentences about sports injuries, using your own words where you can. Can you also make the sentences more concise?

1   Many acute injuries to the body are accompanied by bleeding, swelling and pain.
2   In the first 24 hours, ice (or alternatively a packet of frozen peas) should only be used for short periods of ten minutes at a time.
3   Ice should never be applied directly to the skin because of the danger of burns.

4   In the early stages when there is a great deal of swelling and pain, you would be well advised to rest the injured area.
5   Nevertheless, you must begin gentle movement and exercise of the injured part as soon as possible.
6   Where possible, it is important that any exercise of the injured area is carried out under the supervision of a physiotherapist.
7   Your doctor may prescribe painkillers or anti-inflammatory tablets when your injury is painful or the swelling is marked.

23 Writing a short summary

Read the introduction to a leaflet entitled 'Avoiding Sports Injuries'. In your own words, write a paragraph of about 45 words explaining how you can avoid getting injured when you play sport. Approach the task in the methodical way you have done earlier in the unit.

When you have finished, ask a partner to check that you have:

*   kept to the question set
*   used your own words where possible
*   left out unnecessary words and details
*   left out opinions of your own
*   connected the summary grammatically
*   kept to the word limit.

Avoiding Sports Injuries

Active sports are becoming ever more popular. Whether for relaxation and as a way of reducing stress, or for weight control, or to improve health and fitness, greater numbers of people of all ages are taking part in various active sporting pursuits.

However, as more people take part, sports injuries are becoming more common. Fortunately, these injuries are seldom too serious, and if treated properly and promptly, get better quickly – never to return. Nevertheless, if you are planning to start a fitness programme, you need to be aware of the ways injuries can be prevented in the first place.

You need systematic and sensible physical preparation to get fit for sport. Besides training for strength and stamina, you should ensure that you get proper rest. It is essential never to try to train when you are tired, as tiredness itself can cause injury. It is also vital to use an appropriate technique when doing sport. Not only is it obviously very helpful in achieving success in your chosen sport, but it can also greatly reduce the chance of sustaining an injury.

Protective equipment, such as helmets, gum shields, shin pads and other items, including comfortable and supportive footwear, will improve your performance and help prevent unnecessary injury.

24 Expressing warnings

You have just read some warnings in written language. When we speak, warnings are expressed very directly.

In pairs, read the following mini-conversations giving warnings about the possible dangers of sport and physical exercise.

1 *A:* I've just started to play cricket.
   B: Take care to use protective shin pads. They can stop you getting a nasty injury.
   A: Thanks. I'll remember that.

2 *A:* My brother is only three but he wants to learn to swim.
   B: Make sure he wears armbands, even in shallow water. He could easily lose coordination.
   A: You're right. I'm glad you told me.

3 *A:* We're going sailing in Hinton Bay on Saturday.
   B: Watch out for rocks in that area. You can easily run aground.
   A: That's true. I'll tell the others too.

Warnings
Take care to/Be careful to (take precautions)
Make sure you (take precautions)
Watch out for/Look out for (unseen danger)

Responses
Thanks. I'll remember that/I'll do that.
That's true. I'm glad you told me.
You're right. I will.

PRACTICE

Create mini-conversations with a partner around the situations below, using the following pattern.

Student A: Talk about plans.
Student B: Give a warning.
Student A: Show you've understood the warning.

1 start jogging/need good running shoes to protect feet
2 lift weights at the gym for first time/proper supervision from instructor
3 hill walking alone/tell someone where you are going
4 swimming in sea on holiday/jellyfish sting you
5 mountain biking in a new area/lots of rain recently, ground muddy and slippery

Learning cricket

25 Pre-reading discussion

Do you play or watch cricket? What do you like or dislike about it? If you don't play cricket, would you like to learn? Why/Why not?

26 Predicting content

You are going to read an article about a project which sends instructors to primary schools to teach young children to play cricket. What points might you expect to find in the article? Complete the list.

1 *Difficulties young children have learning a complicated game*

2 ....

3 ....

4 ....

5 ....

27 Vocabulary check

Before you read the article, match these words and phrases with their meanings.

1 refining individual technique	A	tuition given in an intensive way
2 concentrated instruction	B	improving each person's skills
3 tarmac	C	sports instructor
4 coach	D	hard surface for playground, road etc.

28 Reading with concentration

Read the article as quickly as possible but with full concentration. Adapt your reading speed to your comprehension of what you are reading. Don't worry about trying to understand every word.

CRICKET is not the easiest sport to introduce to youngsters. The traditional game demands time and patience and a high level of skill, something that small children do not usually possess. They like action and non-stop involvement compressed into short periods of the primary school day.

The London Schools' Cricket Project has met these difficulties head-on. Desperately keen that more youngsters should be introduced to the sport, it sends coaches to hundreds of primary schools to give concentrated instruction and supervision of Kwik cricket.

The William Davies School in Forest Gate, East London did not have the most cheerful of January afternoons last week to introduce youngsters to England's traditional summer game. The sun may have been shining but a sharp wind cut across the playground. With 30 pupils eager for exercise, it did not seem a suitable day for refining individual technique.

Yet, what was remarkable was the amount of individual tuition that was possible by one coach, while still keeping the interest of the rest of the class. During bowling practice, the youngsters would deliver their balls and then run across the tarmac to swap places with their partners. In this way, not only did they keep warm but they also got more exercise.

Vic Griffith, the coach, said: "I always try to get their attention, to get them to focus on me and, while they are in the cold, to get them to move up and down. They should have as much enjoyment and exercise as possible."

At this co-educational school, he is preaching, if not always to the converted, at least to the interested. Ninety-five per cent of the 250 pupils come from the ethnic minorities, particularly the Indian sub-continent.

Gill Gordon, the head teacher, said: "They know far more about cricketers than footballers and their fathers will often play cricket with them on the park. They support England against Australia or the West Indies, but when England are playing India or Pakistan, they sometimes don't know where they are."

She has always welcomed the Project's suggestion to send in a coach for five sessions a year. "Cricket teaches teamwork and the discipline of learning a game, with its rules and need for fairness."

The Project has a budget of about £100,000 for this year to help pay for two full-time and ten part-time coaches to tour the London schools. This total includes £5,000 from Tesco – the supermarket chain – plus a further £5,000 from the government, and funds from charitable and cricket trusts and donations from the schools.

Oliver McClintock, the deputy coordinator of the Project, says: "We are not only creating the players of the future. We are also creating the parents and paying public of the future."

The hour-long session ended with 25 minutes of Kwik cricket, which allows everyone to have a go, either hitting Griffith's deliveries across the playground to everyone's delight or missing the ball.

One pupil, Bilal Hassan, 9, said: "I like whacking the ball a long way." He was bowled by one ball, that may have turned on the tarmac. "The ball went wonky," he said.

29 True/false comprehension

Are the following statements true or false?

1. Traditional cricket is an ideal game for young children.
2. Secondary schools have been involved in the project.
3. The coach tries to keep children as active as possible.
4. William Davies School is a multi-cultural school for boys and girls.
5. The parents of the children have encouraged their interest in cricket.
6. The headteacher is disappointed with the benefits the children have got from the game.
7. A number of organisations have contributed money to the project.
8. The project hopes to make an impact on cricket in the future.
9. Not all the children get a chance to hit the ball during the session.

30 Checking predictions

How much of what you expected to read about was actually mentioned in the article?

31 Writing a headline

With a partner, write a headline for the article and suggest a suitable picture. Refer back to the guidelines earlier in the unit to help you.

32 Post-reading discussion

Which sports would you love to learn at school? Explain your views in your group.

33 Making notes

Write a set of notes based on the article about Kwik cricket. In your notes, describe the aim of the project, the best approach for teaching cricket to young children and the reasons why schools support the project.

Refer to the approach suggested in exercise 11 and apply that method here. When you've finished, ask your partner to check the following.

Content: Is it all relevant? Should anything be left out?

Language: Where possible, have you found some words and phrases of similar meaning?

Presentation: Are your notes under clear headings? Are the points numbered?

34 Correcting a connected summary

Study this exam question.

> Read the article about Kwik cricket and then write a summary describing the aim of the project, the best approach for teaching cricket to young children and the reasons why the William Davies school supports the project.
>
> Your summary should not be longer than 100 words. Use your own words as far as possible.

Here is one student's attempt to answer the summary question. Some of the information in the summary is unnecessary, making the answer too long. Cross the unnecessary information out.

The aim of the project is to encourage young children to take up cricket. One of the project's coaches is Vic Griffith, who gives instruction to children in schools. He explained his approach to teaching cricket to young children. He believes the best approach is to get the children's concentration, keep everyone active and involved and let all the children have some time to hit the ball. The project has a budget of £100,000 which pays for the coaching. According to the headteacher, Gill Gordon, who is head of William Davies School in Forest Gate, East London, the project links with the interest children's families, who are largely Asian, already have in cricket. It is popular because it introduces children to the idea of team work and the mental attitudes required to learn a game successfully.

When you have finished, compare your version with your partner's.

35 Rewriting a summary

Now rewrite the summary correctly. Make sure you keep within the word limit.

36 Expressions of measurement

The article says the children learn cricket in an *hour-long* session. This is a more concise way of saying 'a session which lasts one hour'. Similarly, we can say a note which is worth ten pounds is a *ten-pound note*, a hotel graded as being worth three stars is a *three-star hotel*, and a walk which is five miles long is a *five-mile walk*. Notice how the plural *-s* is not used in the hyphenated words.

PRACTICE

Rewrite each of these sentences using a number + noun form.

1 She uses a fitness video which lasts for fifty minutes.
2 He made a cut which was six inches deep.
3 Ali got a contract worth a thousand pounds.
4 They ordered a meal which consisted of six courses
5 I need a coin worth ten pence for the phone.
6 The drive to work takes ten minutes.
7 Tanya gave birth to a baby weighing seven pounds.
8 I'd like a bag of sugar weighing two pounds.

Boxing in schools

37 Pre-reading discussion

A Boxing used to be popular in many schools, especially in poor areas, but it became less popular some years ago. Can you suggest why?

Work in pairs to discuss the following questions.

- Is boxing more dangerous than other school sports? Why/Why not?
- Is being encouraged to take up boxing after leaving school a good idea?
- Does professional boxing have an attractive image?

B Do you think a 'non-contact' method of teaching boxing (where no actual physical contact takes place and children learn using punch pads) makes the return of boxing more acceptable? Why/Why not? Could the skills which you acquire from boxing be learned from doing any other sport?

C Whose opinion on whether boxing should return to schools do you think is the most important?

- the pupils
- the teachers
- the Boxing Association
- the medical profession

D Pilot schemes
A 'pilot scheme' means trying out a new idea on a relatively small group. In Liverpool a number of boys have taken part in a pilot scheme to learn boxing. Is this a good idea? Why/Why not?

E Would you like to learn boxing at your school? Explain your views to your partner.

38 Vocabulary check

In the article you are going to read about boxing, you'll find these words. Try to match them with their definitions.

1	reversing	A	doubtful
2	winning converts	B	feeling of personal worth
3	bottom of the trough		
4	self-esteem	C	persuading people to support the idea
5	starting from scratch		
6	sceptical	D	lowest point
		E	beginning at the very beginning
		F	turning back

39 Predicting the writer's intention

Look at the headline of the article and check that you understand it. What do you think is the writer's MAIN intention in writing the article? Write one point and compare it with your partner's.

....

40 Reading with concentration

Read the article through quickly with maximum concentration. Use fast and slow speeds. (Remember: this means reading the easier sentences fast, and the difficult or more important ones more slowly.) Work out meanings from context. Don't worry about understanding every word.

Boxing shapes up for a come-back

In the gym of Croxteth Community School, Liverpool, 50 boys have completed a course on boxing that is seen as a pilot for its return to state schools.

The boarded-up houses and high-rise flats in Croxteth are typical of the kind of deprived area where boxing once flourished. Now a new generation is taking up the sport, despite widespread national criticism.

The Schools Amateur Boxing Association has developed the Kid Gloves scheme, a non-contact version of the sport where outside coaches teach a range of basic skills. Instead of chins, the blows land on punch pads.

Chris Andrews, assistant secretary of the SABA, said the scheme was regarded as a way of reversing the decline in boxing in state schools which began 20 years ago.

Safety fears and the poor image of professional boxing had accelerated the sport's demise. Concern was exacerbated by incidents such as the death of the professional boxer Bradley Stone. But the Croxteth example was winning converts further afield. Mr Andrews said the idea was particularly well received in the north-east.

"The interest shown so far has been enormous," he said. "I believe that boxing will come back into schools. The last five years have seen the bottom of the trough. The arguments now being advanced are getting through to those in education."

A video has been produced to promote boxing in schools, and a bid has between made for a Sports Council grant.

He said: "I think there is a genuine recognition that there are aspects to boxing if it is controlled and properly run that really are very beneficial for children. This scheme takes away the dangers. I hope boxing can be promoted throughout the country in a more co-ordinated way." Such an idea horrifies such groups as the British Medical Association and the British Safety Council, both critics of the idea.

Dr Jeffrey Cundy, the joint author of the BMA's last report on boxing, published in 1993, accepted that the scheme in Liverpool was non-contact, but he was still opposed. He said: "We feel that children should still not be introduced to boxing, because they will then be encouraged to take up an activity which is uniquely dangerous when actual contact takes place."

He added: "There is a whole range of sports which will teach the discipline that comes from boxing without the dangers. We see this reintroduction in schools as an unhealthy development".

At the 800-pupil Croxteth school, Steve Stewart, head of PE, said boxing had helped to improve self-confidence, self-discipline, self-awareness and self-esteem in those taking part. Everybody could get involved and, because all were starting from scratch, the improvements could be quickly seen.

Certificates were presented to the pupils at the end of the course by Paul Hodgkinson, a local boxer who is a former world champion. Next year, the course will be repeated and if possible girls will be allowed to take part following requests from them.

"If I was sceptical before I started, I am not now," said Mr Stewart. "We are not showing boxing as glamorous, nor are we trying to push youngsters to local boxing clubs. The boys can go to local clubs if they want to, but we wouldn't start one in the schools."

Gerry Thompson and Tony Curry, both 12, have enjoyed the boxing sessions and say they will both join a local boxing club. "I thought it was brilliant," said Gerry. "I would rather be a professional boxer than a footballer. It's more enjoyable."

Summary writing 100 words

41 Audience awareness

The article comes from an educational newspaper for teachers. How do you think the content shows awareness of the writer's audience? Write two points.

1 ....

2 ....

42 Multiple-choice comprehension

Choose the best answer to each question.

1 The Kid Gloves scheme uses a non-contact style of boxing because
  a the children prefer this method.
  b boxers have recommended it.
  c it is a much less dangerous form of boxing.
  d it reflects a trend in professional sport.

2 The Schools Amateur Boxing Association wants to promote boxing in schools because
  a children asked for it to return to the curriculum.
  b it helps children defend themselves if attacked.
  c they think it has many benefits if done properly.
  d children have never been injured while boxing at school.

3 The British Medical Association disapproves of the scheme because
  a it is not being taught properly.
  b the pilot scheme used only 50 pupils.
  c pupils might start contact boxing later.
  d no first aid is available if injuries occur.

4 The attitude of the head of physical education at Croxteth school is
  a pushy – all children should be made to do it.
  b impressed – all the children have gained.
  c disillusioned – boys' progress is too slow.
  d neutral – boxing is no better or worse than other sports.

5 Which statement best sums up the views of the two boys who were on the pilot scheme? It was
  a interesting, but I don't want to do it again.
  b a nice change but not as good as football.
  c superb – I want to take it up in my spare time.
  d disappointing – it wasn't like real boxing at all.

43 Writing a for and against summary

Write a summary, based on the article, explaining why boxing was withdrawn from the curriculum and outlining the points for and against the return of boxing to state schools. Use your own words as far as possible. Write about 100 words.

APPROACH

Approach your summary methodically: check key words in the question, underline relevant parts of the text, write notes in your own words and then connect them into a summary. You may need to make a few drafts before your summary is 'polished'.

When you have finished, ask your partner to check you have:
- included the relevant points
- put the points in the right order
- left out unnecessary details, examples, names of people, jobs etc.
- left out personal opinions and ideas of your own
- used suitable connectors
- used the appropriate number of words.

44 Vocabulary: Using fewer words

In the article, houses which are closed up and secured against entry are described as *boarded-up*.

The following words are also taken from the article. With a partner, choose the correct one to replace the words in italics in the sentences.

flourished	unique
exacerbated	conference
deprived	scheme

1 The town is *poor and lacks basic facilities*.
2 Interest in science *began to grow and do well* after the arrival of the new teacher.
3 Their financial problems were *made worse* when he lost his job.
4 We attended a *formal, organised meeting*.
5 The carving I bought on holiday is *the only one of its kind*.

Now put each word into a sentence of your own.

45 Redundant words

Extra words, which repeat what we have already said, often slip into our speech. Such repetition usually goes unnoticed in everyday conversation. In fact, the repetition is sometimes helpful. However, when we write we should write concisely and try to avoid 'redundancy'.

Example:
The children stood patiently in a round circle and listened to the coach.

Round is unnecessary because a circle is always round.

With a partner, decide which words are redundant in the following sentences and cross them out.

1 When did you first begin to learn basketball?
2 Aysha bought new summer sandals for the children's feet.
3 He has some priceless old antiques in his house which are so valuable that it is impossible to say how much they are worth.
4 We received an unexpected shock on our return from holiday.
5 She was upset that the vase was broken as it was very unique.
6 Betty wasn't very helpful when I asked for some scissors to cut with.
7 He had to repeat himself many times, saying the words over and over again, before he was understood.
8 Since starting to play squash, Jeff has been unhealthily obsessed with winning every game.

46 Spelling: Adding suffixes to words with a final -e

In the boxing text you saw these words with suffixes:
reversing (reverse + -ing)
improvements (improve + -ment)

Notice how the final *-e* of *reverse* is dropped before the suffix, but the *-e* is kept in the word *improvements*.

Can you explain why?

SPELLING RULES

A final **-e** in a word is usually dropped when adding a suffix beginning with a **vowel**:
*dance   danc**ing***
*educate   educat**ion***

So the **-e** is usually kept when the suffix begins with a consonant:
*hope   hope**ful***
*care   care**less***
*improve   improve**ment***

There are some IMPORTANT EXCEPTIONS to the above rule.

The **-e** is usually kept before the suffix **-able**:
*notice   notic**eable***

The **-e** is usually kept when it follows another vowel:
*see   see**ing***
*canoe   canoe**ist***

PRACTICE

Read this newspaper report about the teaching of traditional dance in schools. Add the correct suffixes to the words in brackets. Check your spelling with the rules above.

Choose from the following:

-ative	-ment	-ing	-tion
-ion	-ity	-ish	-ivity

More and more pupils are learning dance as part of their physical (educate) programme. It is a wonderful way of (have) fun and an (excite) way of keeping fit. Dance allows all pupils a chance to express their (create). Even the youngest pupils can learn simple (move) to music which act as an (introduce) to more complex traditional dance. Older pupils who lack (motivate) when it comes to competitive sport find traditional dance very (stimulate). Secondary school teachers say (participate) in such an enjoyable activity needs no (encourage).

Schools (achieve) a high standard may be selected for the Schools Dance Festival held each year. The festival is a wonderful (celebrate) of traditional dance. Last year, the (style) costumes, great (diverse) of dances, (imagine) approaches and wonderful music made the evening particularly special.

DISCUSSION

Do you (or would you) enjoy watching or taking part in traditional dances? Explain your views.

47 Word building

Homework

Below are the root words of ten words taken from articles you have read so far. Working with a partner, choose a suitable suffix from the box to add to each word. Sometimes more than one is possible.

-ing	-ion	-ly	-ment	-ness

1 time   *timing   timely*
2 concentrate   *concentration   concentrating*
3 refine   *refinment refining*
4 exercise   *exercising*
5 welcome   *welcoming*
6 involve   *involvment   involving*
7 ache   *aching*
8 state   *statment   statly*
9 unique   *uniquely   uniquness*
10 aware   *awareness   awarement*

Make sure your spelling is correct by checking with the rules for keeping or dropping the final *-e*.

Give each new word a grammar label (*noun, verb, adjective* etc). Refer to a dictionary if necessary.

Now use each word you have made in a sentence of your own.

48 Look, say, cover, write, check

Use the 'look, say, cover, write, check' method to learn these words, which are among those most frequently misspelled.

amaze   amazing   amazement
argue   arguing   argument
become   becoming
excite   exciting   excitable   excitement
welcome   welcoming
shine   shining
invite   inviting   invitation
surprise   surprising
imagine   imaginary   imaginative   imagining
immediate   immediately

INTERNATIONAL OVERVIEW

Work with a partner to test your knowledge of these sports across the world.

1 Which are the three most popular (widely played) sports in the world?
   a   swimming
   b   basketball
   c   table tennis
   d   angling
   e   football (soccer)
   f   bowls

2 Which are the two most dangerous sports in the world?
   a   motor racing
   b   bullfighting
   c   motorcycle racing
   d   boxing
   e   skydiving

3 Which are the two safest sports in the world (fewest injuries per hour)?
   a   bowls
   b   weightlifting
   c   angling
   d   table tennis
   e   swimming

Diet and fitness

49 Pre-reading discussion

Sport itself cannot make you fit. You have to get fit for sport. A healthy diet is an important part of getting and staying fit.

Discuss with your partner what, if anything, you do to make sure you eat a balanced, healthy diet.

50 Predicting content

You are going to read a magazine article about Sheila, who lost a lot of weight and got fitter. Using the headline and picture to find clues, what particular things do you think she might mention in the article?

Write four points.

AUDIENCE AWARENESS

Who do you think this magazine is MAINLY aimed at – the medical profession, children, teenagers, women, young men or elderly people?

What kind of language and style do you expect the writer to use? Do you expect to find a chatty style with lots of phrasal verbs? Or will the article be formal and use many specialised terms?

WRITER'S INTENTION

What do you think the writer's intention is?

☐ to make people identify with Sheila and decide to lose weight too

☐ to make people try harder to keep to diets and fitness programmes

☐ to promote a particular diet and fitness programme

51 Vocabulary check

The following words connected with food and fitness are used in the article. Can you explain their meaning?

- nibbles/nibbled
- snack on
- packed lunches
- sluggish

52 Reading

Read the article quickly and tick off these points as the story develops.

☐ Sheila's misery about being overweight

☐ family lifestyle

☐ work patterns

☐ after work habits

☐ starting the fitness programme

☐ success on the programme

☐ Sheila today

I WENT DOWN FOUR DRESS SIZES!

Staff nurse Sheila Auckland was so busy with her career and raising a family that she never noticed as her weight crept up – until the day she had to buy a size 18 skirt!

HILARY TALBOT reports.

It was a wedding invitation two years ago that finally made Sheila face the fact that she was overweight and didn't like it. "I was trying to find something to wear but nothing in my wardrobe would fit. I remember panicking because none of my skirts or suits met in the right places," she recalls. Sheila solved the immediate problem by rushing out and buying a white pleated skirt that fitted – but it was a size 18. "Until then I'd kidded myself that either I didn't have a problem at all or I wasn't bothered. The skirt proved my weight had got out of hand and suddenly I couldn't stand it."

For Sheila, a mum, wife and nurse who works shifts, the idea of going on a diet seemed inconceivable. "My husband Paul and our two sons adore food and cooking, and entertaining is part of our social lives. I couldn't imagine giving it all up.

"I've always loved having people round and we've got a large extended family so there always seemed to be some excuse for a celebration party or weekend barbeque.

"There were always cakes in the cupboard for the boys, and because we've got Sky TV it's like a football stadium in the sitting room when there's a big match. Half-time meant drinks, nibbles, tea, cakes, or whatever else I'd conjured up. And at work, patients were always giving us boxes of biscuits and gorgeous chocolates, so there was no shortage of things to snack on. I even nibbled food that came round on the trolley!"

Sheila realises now that her weight dramatically reduced her energy levels and even her enthusiasm. As a staff nurse she has a lot of responsibility and pressure is part of the job. But there's also an awful lot of lifting and carrying. "I used to go home, cook a meal and then slump in a chair. That would be it. I was always exhausted and I used to wish that I could wake up from a night's sleep and not feel as though I needed another eight hours."

Although Shelia was extremely unhappy with her weight no one ever mentioned it to her. No one, that is, until her sister Janet plucked up the courage. "Janet waited until I was relaxed one evening and then plunged in. She'd read that Rosemary Conley was starting up diet and fitness classes and persuaded me that we should both give them a try." Shelia wasn't exactly thrilled but felt she ought to go. After the very first class she was hooked.

"I lost weight immediately and never put so much as a pound back on. In a year I'd got rid of four stone." Shelia made sure she did quite a lot of swimming and walking and kept clear of chips and crisps but didn't really feel she had to be on a diet as such in order to maintain her new slimline figure. And that, she feels, is the key to the success of this eating and exercise plan. "You don't have to deprive yourself of all the nice things and you never feel hungry."

It's hard to believe Shelia ever lacked energy or enthusiasm. She now seems able to cram two days into one – working, cooking, making up three packed lunches a day, cycling to work as well as starting a Bachelor of Science nursing degree.

"I've got all my old enthusiasm back and just don't feel sluggish any more." And even though she doesn't need to lose any more weight, Shelia still goes to the diet and fitness classes, mainly for the exercise sessions. "Having started off stumbling about at the back, Janet and I are always in the front row now and love the workouts."

Shelia has found a new lease of life as well as a new shape but she doesn't hesitate when naming the biggest boost to being slim. "When I was unhappy, Paul was unhappy too. Now I've got my self-esteem back we're happier than ever."

53 Post-reading discussion

A In your culture, how do you define a healthy diet? Is slimness admired?

B Do you think encouraging people to diet can be harmful? Is pressure to be slim really about being fit for a healthy, sporty life? Or is it more about looking like the fashion models in magazines? Can slimming articles make people obsessed with dieting and body image?

Discuss your ideas in your group.

54 Writing a summary

Write a summary of the article. Contrast Sheila's eating patterns, emotions and attitudes before she lost weight with her lifestyle now. Explain why she feels the diet and fitness programme is particularly suitable for her. Try to use your own words as far as possible. Write about 100 words.

APPROACH

Approach the summary in the methodical way you have done previously. When you have finished, compare your version with your partner's. Is your summary:

- relevant to the question?
- grammatically correct?
- within the word limit?

Have you:

- used your own words where possible?
- left out unnecessary details?

55 Vocabulary: Phrasal verbs

The following phrasal verbs were used in the article. Can you use them in an appropriate form in the sentences below?

| give up | pluck up | start up |
| conjure up | plunge in | make up |

1 He's trying to _____ an after-school judo club for children in the village.
2 She knew mentioning the topic would be unpopular but she decided to _____ anyway.
3 Antonio decided to _____ doing overtime and see more of his family.
4 He _____ the courage and asked Jane to marry him.
5 Although she didn't have much food in the fridge, Sally was able to _____ a delicious meal.
6 They _____ food parcels for people whose homes had been damaged in the flood.

Exam-format questions

Oral assessment

The importance of fitness

In some countries many people are becoming overweight and suffer from lack of exercise. Why is this happening, do you think? What can be done to raise people's awareness of the importance of fitness and a healthy diet? Discuss your ideas with your examiner or partner.

You might consider such things as:

- ways to develop a more energetic lifestyle in general, such as walking or cycling rather than using buses or cars
- the increased consumption of snack foods such as crisps and chocolate bars which are eaten quickly and do not satisfy hunger for long
- the fact that playing computer games and watching videos and TV can result in a lack of exercise
- the fact that in some countries children have less freedom to play outside than in the past
- the fact that increased use of washing machines and vacuum cleaners is reducing effort spent on keeping houses clean and comfortable.

Notes and summary writing

1   Read the following magazine article and then write notes outlining the reasons why children may fear learning to swim and the best methods of overcoming the fear of swimming.

Fear of swimming

To what extent can you force children to cope with situations they find scary?

A concerned parent writes:

How seriously should you take a child's fear of the water? My son has a weekly swimming lesson at school which, for us, has become a nightmare scenario. His initial reluctance to swim has developed into a fear that seems little short of a phobia. We feel very strongly that it is important that he learn to swim, but each week, as the day of the lesson dawns, our son gets into a real state, which is emotionally exhausting for all of us. Should we give in to his strongly-held reluctance to swim or, as we have been doing, force him to go ahead with his lessons?

A Professor of Child Psychiatry replies:

This little boy's fear of water is a very natural and healthy response, but on the other hand, children are much safer if they are able to swim.

A lot of children find group swimming lessons difficult to cope with for various reasons. School pools can be cold and noisy, with lots of people shouting and splashing, which is very off-putting for someone who doesn't feel in control of the situation.

So it is easy to see why this could be a nasty experience. Fear or dislike of group lessons is understandable given the situation, so these parents first need to teach their son to like water, probably in a pool which is warm rather than cold (presumably he doesn't have a problem in the bath, so the fear is probably not of water *itself*).

Choose a smallish, quiet pool, where the water is warm. Take it slowly and base it around having fun rather than focusing on getting on with swimming. He should get used to going underwater – it is much easier to start swimming while submerged.

His parents should not continue exposing him to repeated traumatic experiences, so they should speak to the teachers and see if they can take him out of his lessons until he feels that he is ready to re-join the class.

It really is not helpful to force him; his parents should work on his reluctance to swim outside the context of school and build up his confidence and skills.

A tutor at a swimming school replies:

I would suggest that this little boy would benefit from one-to-one tuition.

Obviously something is happening in school – maybe someone has ducked him or splashed him in the pool and he doesn't like it. His parents should try to find out if something specific has happened to cause this problem.

In a situation like this, pushing him won't help at all, but they mustn't give up on him. Solo lessons should help. Perhaps the parents should take him swimming at the weekend and make sure it is fun, or get a teacher just for him.

It might be a good idea to leave the school lessons for a while. At the pool, they should forget the swimming aspect and just encourage him to enjoy the water.

At the swimming school we get a lot of adults who have been put off at a young age by being ducked or splashed, being taught to swim with a rope tied around the waist or a pole pushing them so, perhaps unsurprisingly, they have given up. Of course, there are people with a real fear of water, but they are more unusual.

We find that the main thing is helping individuals to become accustomed to getting their face wet. Bearing this in mind, perhaps bathtime would be a good time for the boy's parents to try this. They should also get him to put his mouth in the water and blow bubbles, and pour water over his head starting at the back so that it is not too startling. A lot of people really hate getting their heads wet, but if he can surmount the problem in a non-threatening environment such as the bath, he will be off to a good start.

At the pool, wearing good goggles might make a difference to him; it really is worth investing in a decent pair.

At our children's weeks, I advise parents of children who are petrified of water not to put the pressure on and to be happy with whatever their children can actually achieve in the water.

2 Read the following article about insomnia and then write a summary of the article explaining the causes and effects of lack of sleep. Write about 100 words. Use your own words as far as possible.

Insomnia
In search of the big sleep

Our bodies depend on sleep to keep a number of delicately balanced systems running smoothly. Without it these systems become subtly off-key, which can eventually lead to more serious consequences. Although the odd broken night never hurt anyone, some sleep experts are now saying that even just an hour of missed sleep, night after night, can cause ill health.

WHAT CAUSES INSOMNIA?

Persistent low-level fatigue is extremely common since one in three of us has problems dropping off or sleeping through the night. The cause can lie in surrounding factors, such as an uncomfortable mattress or noisy neighbours. Some insomnia is temporarily caused by stress brought on by a forthcoming special event, such as an exam or getting married or pressure at work. How you feel can notoriously affect sleep, too. Anxiety, anger or resentment can all stop us from dropping off and one of the prime symptoms of depression is early morning waking.

Sleep apnoea, a common disorder in which lapses in breathing cause a shortage of oxygen which in turn disrupts sleep, may need treating (for more details see our feature next month). Shift work, partying until the small hours and jet lag can also disrupt the body's internal clock that tells us when to stay awake and when to sleep (doctors call this sort of insomnia 'circadian rhythm disorders').

Too much food, tea, coffee, cola or other stimulants can also be culprits. Physical illness such as pain from arthritis can be a factor, too, as can drugs such as those used to treat chronic illnesses like high blood pressure and asthma.

Some of us simply need to make sure that the bedroom is a calm, pleasant place conducive to sleep and avoid daytime naps. And last but not least, anxiously lying awake worrying about not sleeping can cause what the doctors call psychophysiological insomnia.

KNOCK-ON EFFECTS

Whatever the cause, fatigue can have devastating effects on all aspects of our lives. It is thought to be a principle factor in around 10 per cent of the road accidents in Britain, for example. And new US research offers some clues as to further effects of this disturbance to the body's natural rhythms. Perhaps the greatest risk could be the effect on the immune system. The research shows that loss of sleep can slow down the action of cells which are involved in fighting off infection and even protecting us against more serious diseases such as cancer.

What isn't known, however, is whether one or two broken nights can have a long-term effect. People who suffer from long periods of stress, for example after a bereavement, seem to be more vulnerable to illness, which suggests that lack of sleep may be a factor.

American research also suggests that lack of sleep can make you want to eat too much! In one survey of hospital nurses, nine out of 10 who worked night shifts put on weight. The weight gained ranged from 2.25kg to a massive 44kg. The nurses, it was discovered, nibbled to stay awake and keep going. And, although food didn't actually lift the symptoms of fatigue, it gave them the illusion of staying awake. Nurses on the overnight shift gained more than those on the evening shift, suggesting that the greater the disruption in sleep patterns, the greater the tendency to overeat and thus gain weight.

SLEEPING AND AGEING

Lack of sleep may even contribute to or speed up the ageing process. During sleep the body produces a hormone which is vital for growth and cell renewal. Without enough sleep this rejuvenation time is lost. It comes as no surprise that the period in life when we sleep most – as babies and toddlers – is the period of greatest growth.

One thing is certain: sleep is important and we could do worse than add a new resolution to the rules for living a long and healthy life – don't smoke, eat plenty of fresh fruit and vegetables, exercise regularly and ... make sure you get enough sleep!

EXAMINER'S TIPS

1 Before you start to read

Many students say they find it hard to 'get into' a newspaper or magazine article. The following strategies will help you get into reading more easily.

Ask yourself:

* What is this text likely to be about?
* What do I already know about the topic?
* Who is this writing for? (young people, the general public, children, specialists in a profession, people with a particular hobby?)

This will orientate you to the likely style (technical, formal, chatty) and structure (long sentences and paragraphs, or short, simpler sentences and paragraphs).

Think about the author's main aim (to advise, warn, give technical information, entertain, give opinions etc). This will help you see the difference between the main points and background information.

Skimming headlines, subheadings and photos, diagrams or charts will also help to give you a quick idea of what the text is about.

2 Most students would like to read faster but still absorb what they read. Adjust your reading speed to your reading needs. You can skim read sentences which are easy to understand or less relevant. Slow down (as much as you need to) over the parts which are more complex or which contain key points.

Keep a pen or a highlighter with you to mark important parts of the text.

After you have finished reading, ask yourself:

* What were the main points of this text?

Make a short list. Check your list against the original text.

3 Summarising is a useful skill that can spill over into other areas of your life. It's a practical study skill for all parts of the curriculum.

When you summarise informally (plots of films, sports matches, social events), you are practising important intellectual and sequencing skills. Use these opportunities to improve your skills.

4 Feel proud of your progress with summarising. You are achieving in a tricky area which uses all your language resources and intellectual abilities.

Summarising is very challenging but don't be afraid of it. Tell your unconscious mind that you enjoy it, and as you become more at home with the skills you really will become more expert.

EXAM STRATEGY

5 Exam summary questions are usually 'guided'. You are asked, for example, to *outline the advantages and disadvantages/trace the history of/explain the importance of* something.

a Underline key words like those above in the exam question.

b Look carefully at any headline, pictures, charts or sub-headings to get a general idea of what the text is about before you start to read.

c Read quickly with as much concentration as possible.

d Underline or highlight key words and phrases.

e Make a rough draft of the key words and phrases in connected prose. Use your own words as far as possible.

f Count the words. Make corrections to the grammar and spelling as required.

g Write a final draft in no more than 100 words.

h Proof-read your summary for mistakes.

6 When you answer the exam note-taking question (Paper 2 only), use the above method as far as **d**. Try to use some words and phrases of similar meaning to those in the text, to show understanding. Don't copy big chunks of text.

Present your notes clearly, using headings and numbered points. If bullet points are given, write one point for each bullet.

Your notes should be presented so that they can be followed by someone who has not seen the original passage.

Although a word limit is not given, your notes must be brief and concise.

Unit focus

In this unit you have learned the strategies you need to **summarise and take notes** from a text. This is practice for Papers 1/2, Part 2.

You have also practised listening to a recorded announcement and completing a diary. This is practice for Papers 3/4, Part 2.

4

Transport Issues

Fear of flying

1 Pre-reading discussion

A Which do you feel is the safest mode of transport in your country? Which is the least safe? Give reasons for your views.

B Study the chart showing fatal accidents by mode of transport in Great Britain. Which two modes of transport are the least safe? Do you find the figures surprising? How do they compare with what you thought about your own country?

C Many people say they are afraid of flying. At the same time we are told air travel is the safest form of transport. Is fear of flying reasonable?

2 Making notes

With a partner, look at the picture of an aeroplane on page 61 and read the information in the boxes. The information shows the steps which are taken to make aeroplanes as safe as possible.

After reading, try to complete the notes below.

PRE-FLIGHT CHECKS

a Made _____ flight.

b 4 types of maintenance procedure:

'A' checks – frequent, minor checks.

'D' checks take place every _____ years; involve _____.

LOCATION OF EQUIPMENT

c Black box _____.

d Fire extinguishers _____.

e _____ and other instruments in cockpit.

f Baggage carried in _____.

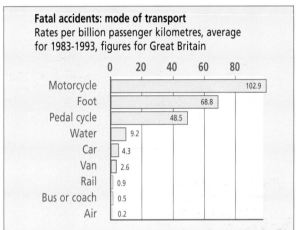

Fatal accidents: mode of transport
Rates per billion passenger kilometres, average for 1983-1993, figures for Great Britain

Mode	Rate
Motorcycle	102.9
Foot	68.8
Pedal cycle	48.5
Water	9.2
Car	4.3
Van	2.6
Rail	0.9
Bus or coach	0.5
Air	0.2

g _____ inside the wing.

h Oxygen masks _____.

i _____ under seats.

j Chutes located _____.

MATERIALS USED

k Material used for fuselage (body frame) is _____.

l Surfaces inside the plane made from _____.

OTHER SAFETY FEATURES

m _____ fold up to reduce air resistance.

n _____ if one set of controls fail.

Pre-flight checks
All aeroplanes undergo a comprehensive external and on-board inspection, conducted by the flight crew, before every flight. If anything is faulty, engineers are called in. In addition, aircraft have to undergo strict maintenance procedures known as A, B, C and D checks. 'A' checks are comparatively minor and are made at frequent intervals. 'D' checks take place approximately every five years – depending on the type of aircraft – and may involve the entire plane being stripped down to its basic air-frame.

The rudder makes the plane turn to the left or right. It can split into two so that if one set of controls fails the plane can still fly.

If the plane crashes, details of the flight are recorded in the black box. This is usually located in the tail fin, part of the plane which is likely to survive after a crash.

Fuel tank inside wing.

The interior surfaces are made from fire-resistant material.

All seats have life-jackets underneath and oxygen masks above.

Fire extinguishers are normally located in the galley and near the toilets.

Stand-by radios and other instruments are located in the cockpit.

The fuselage or body frame is made of special light-weight aluminium alloys and plastic composites.

The undercarriage or main landing wheels fold up inside the plane during flight to reduce air resistance.

All passenger doors contain chutes which open in an emergency landing and allow everyone to slide to the ground.

Baggage is carried in an unpressurised compartment beneath the passengers.

3 Vocabulary check

Before you read, check the meaning of these words.

- aviation
- lifespan
- rigorously
- obsolete

4 Reading with multiple choice

Read the text on page 63 carefully and then try to choose the best answer to each question.

1 The period of time a plane may be expected to function is decided by
a its age.
b the amount of time it has spent flying.
c its cost.
d the total number of journeys it has made.

2 The Ageing Aircraft Programme (AAP) has resulted in
a much stricter requirements for old aircraft.
b more economical arrangements for airlines.
c increased risks for passengers.
d wider use of obsolete technology.

3 The Chicago Convention was set up in 1947 to ensure that all countries operated to the same standards of air safety. The Convention is
a working well and has raised standards across the world.
b unsatisfactory because some countries have better safety records than others.
c raising the cost of air travel because there are extra regulations to be met.
d widely disliked by several countries and likely to be abandoned.

4 Scheduled flights are more expensive than charter flights because
a more modern aeroplanes are used.
b safety standards are higher.
c fewer tickets are sold and so flying costs are higher.
d only a few tour operators are allowed to sell tickets.

5 Most air crashes are the result of pilot error. Pilot error has been linked to
a passenger power and misuse of the auto-pilot.
b management pressures and lack of stimulation.
c impatience and lack of knowledge.
d fatigue and inadequate training.

5 Post-reading task

1 What qualities do you think air crew need to have? Would you agree that flight attendants need the same qualities as pilots? Write down your opinions.

....

....

....

2 What specific factual things could you point out to someone who is afraid of flying?

Example: *The flight crew inspect the plane before every flight.*

Note down some further ideas.

....

....

....

6 Language study: Logical reasoning

A Study these opening sentences of the article again with a partner. Underline the words you think are used to express reasoning.

Air crashes often make front page news because they involve a high number of deaths. As a result, many people tend to forget that flying is one of the safest forms of travel.

The writer uses *because* to express reason and *as a result* to express consequence. Can you replace *because* and *as a result* with words of similar meaning? Use commas if necessary.

B Here are two more sentences from the text. Study them carefully and underline the words which express a logical connection. Notice where commas are used.

If the disaster rate remains constant, more planes will crash and more people will die.

If a plane is found to be safe, then it is judged fit to make so many thousand more trips before being re-examined.

C Which word in the following sentence is an alternative to *because*?

These planes are safe and likely to be in service for many years to come as they are economical to run.

How safe is air travel?

Air crashes often make front-page news because they can involve a high number of deaths. As a result, many people tend to forget that flying is one of the safest forms of travel. There is only a one in two million chance that a flight on an airline registered in western Europe will end in a serious accident.

The skies are more crowded than before, with some 14 million commercial aircraft departures each year across the planet. This figure is predicted to rise to 22 million by the year 2010. If the disaster rate remains constant, more planes will crash and more people will die. The challenge for the world's aviation authorities is to prevent this happening.

Aircraft lifespans

The main stresses on an aircraft come from pressurisation of the cabin, and take-off and landing, not from the length of the flight. The lifespan of an aeroplane is determined by the number of trips it has made, not by the hours it has flown.

Manufacturers rigorously test their planes on the ground. This procedure simulates the stresses of flight. Based on the findings, each model of aircraft is only allowed to fly a predetermined number of trips that is known to be safe. In some cases, this may be 60,000 flights.

Once a plane has reached its limit of trips, engineers examine the plane for cracks or other weaknesses. If the plane is found to be safe, then it is judged to be fit to make so many thousand more trips before being re-examined.

Any problem found must be corrected before the plane is allowed to fly. In some cases, where the fault is thought to be severe or the engineers have found something which they don't yet understand, all planes of that type may be grounded. This happened in 1979 when a DC10 crashed in Chicago after an engine detached itself from the wing. The fault was later traced to incorrect maintenance and the ban was lifted.

'Ageing aircraft' programme

Many aircraft of certain types, such as the Boeing 737 and the DC9, may be up to 30 years old. These planes are safe and likely to be in service for many years to come as they are economical to run and have not been made obsolete by new technology.

Aviation authorities always tried to ensure that old planes were examined regularly, but they tightened up regulations with the introduction of the Ageing Aircraft Programme (AAP) following an incident in 1988 on an Aloha Airlines flight to Hawaii where the roof of the plane was ripped off in flight at about 6,000 metres. The plane subsequently landed safely.

The AAP obliged manufacturers to put one of their old aeroplanes that had made a high number of trips under all known stresses. These findings then formed the basis for a new set of laws for old aircraft.

Chicago Convention

In 1947 all countries with a significant international air transport industry signed the Chicago Convention which laid down standards for air safety. These regulations are constantly updated in response to the latest available information.

In theory this means that all countries operate to the same standards; in practice this is not so. Airlines from North America, Western Europe, the Middle East and Australasia have better safety records than those from other countries.

Charter flights

Charter flights make up nearly half of all air travel in Western Europe. Many people think they are cheaper than scheduled flights because they use older aeroplanes and are less safe. This is not so. Charter airlines often use newer aircraft and have a slightly better safety record than scheduled airlines.

Charter flights are cheaper because the airlines sell their tickets wholesale to the tour operators. Scheduled airlines only expect to sell 60 per cent of their seats on any one flight and fix their prices to allow for this.

Pressures on pilots

Strains on commercial pilots can be considerable, and most air crashes are the result of pilot error.

Airlines run tight schedules and a delay on one flight can seriously affect later flights. So, although pilots are duty bound to make sure that their plane is completely airworthy before take-off, they are under pressure from their managers to pass the plane fit as quickly as possible.

Passenger power can also affect a pilot. Recently a group of passengers refused to fly on an Excalibur Airways DC10 from Manchester to Orlando, Florida. A series of delays, including an aborted take-off, had convinced them that the plane was unsafe. Experts argue that the delays occurred precisely because the airline did not want the plane to take off until it was passed as completely safe. They say further shows of 'passenger power' are more likely to compromise safety than guarantee it. Airlines do not like to generate bad publicity and the threat of passenger revolt may tempt them to persuade their pilots to fly unsafe planes.

Boredom is also a major problem. Planes are flown on auto-pilot for most of the flight, and there have been reports of pilots falling asleep on long-haul routes. Pilots fear that tiredness could become an even bigger issue if proposals to allow pilots to work longer hours with shorter rests between periods of duty are accepted.

7 Completing a text

Read this information about the dangers of using electronic equipment during a flight. With a partner, try to fill the gaps with words expressing reasoning and logical connection.

Many airlines are concerned about passengers using laptop computers, personal stereos and camcorders _____ this kind of electronic equipment can seriously disturb the controls of an aircraft in flight. Radio waves from these electronic devices can confuse an aeroplane's on-board computers. _____, the auto-pilot can disconnect, compasses can fluctuate and there can be a loss of communication with the ground.

More than 100 such incidents have been reported worldwide. Some experts believe the use of personal electronic equipment caused the 1991 air disaster in Thailand in which 223 people were killed. _____similar disasters are to be avoided, _____ airlines need to ask passengers not to use such equipment, especially during take-off and landing.

8 Spelling and pronunciation: The letter *g*

The letter **g** is a hard sound in words like *glass, great* and *peg*. The phonetic symbol is /g/.

gu in words like *guard* and *guest* is also pronounced /g/.

(In a few words like *extinguish*, **gu** is pronounced /gw/.)

Notice how **g** is pronounced in *Egypt, giant* and *generous*. This is sometimes called 'soft g' and the phonetic symbol is /dʒ/. What other words do you know which sound like this? *grand*

RECOGNITION

Almost all the words in the list are taken from the information you have just read. Listen to the words on the tape. Mark them **g** if you think the g sound is hard, pronounced /g/. Mark them **s** if the g sound is soft, pronounced /dʒ/.

1 engineer	g	**7** oxygen	s
2 rigorously	s	**8** apology	g
3 challenge	s	**9** regulations	g
4 figure	g	**10** registered	s
5 passengers	s	**11** significant	g
6 guarantee	g	**12** ageing	g

PRACTICE

/g/ and /dʒ/ are voiced sounds. If you place your fingers on the spot where your vocal chords are, and say the sounds, you will feel your vocal chords vibrate. Practise saying the words in the list clearly to your partner. Does he/she think you are pronouncing the words correctly?

9 Spelling patterns

Did you notice how all the /dʒ/ sounds in exercise 8 were followed by either the letters *e, i* or *y*? Look back at the word list and circle this spelling pattern for each soft **g** word.

But hard **g** sounds are also sometimes followed by *e* or *i*, as in the words *get, tiger* and *girl*.

10 Vocabulary

Choose a word from the list in exercise 8 to match each of the following sentences.

1 She should offer one for breaking your vase. apology
2 We breathe this gas. oxygen
3 He or she is trained to repair machines. engineer
4 The people who pay to travel on a plane, train or boat. passengers
5 It's worthwhile but sometimes difficult too. challenge
6 To promise that something will happen. guarantee
7 A word with a similar meaning to rules. regulation
8 Another word for number. figure
9 The aircraft should be checked in this way if a fault is suspected. rigorously

What do you notice about the sounds of the words in 1–5 and 6–9?

11 Odd word out

Circle the odd word out in each list. Can you say why it is different?

A hygienic gypsy vegetable gymnasium surgeon privilege changeable regard manager encourage

B grateful vague magazine guard Portuguese pigeon dialogue angry catalogue guilt guess

12 Look, say, cover, write, check

The following words can be problematic to spell. Read them first and check that you understand the meaning of each one. Then use the look, say, cover, write, check method to learn to spell them correctly. (See pages 6–7.)

When you feel you have learned them properly, ask your partner to test you. All the words are taken from previous exercises.

changeable	hygienic
passenger	Portuguese
privilege	fire extinguisher
baggage	vegetables
encourage	apology
rigorously	catalogue
guard	manager

Choose six of the words and put each one into a sentence to show its meaning.

What transport do you use?

13 Before you listen

What form of transport do you use to

- get to school or college?
- go shopping?
- visit friends?
- go to places of entertainment?

How satisfied do you feel with the forms of transport you use? Is there any form of transport you would prefer? Try to explain your views.

VOCABULARY CHECK

Before you listen, make sure you know the meaning of these words and expressions.

- get a lift from someone
- acid rain
- asthma

14 Listening for gist

You are going to listen to a discussion between two friends, Paolo and Linda, on the results of a survey. The survey was carried out to determine patterns of car usage by pupils in their school. Listen to the discussion first for general meaning.

15 Listening and note taking

Now listen again and try to complete these notes.

1 Average weekly number of car journeys:
   _____11-20_____.

2 5% make more than _car_ *traps a week*.

3 _____80%_____ admitted using a car when it was not necessary.

4 The school:
   a _buses route_.
   b has a train station only 5 minutes away.

5 Coming to school by train or bus is:
   a too expensive.
   b _inconvient_ (homes aren't near a bus stop or train station).

6 Parents' opinions of roads for walking or cycling: _dangerous_.

7 Reasons for not wanting own car in future:
   a effect on the environment.
   b _health concerned_.

8 When _buying a car_ they try to persuade them to get a small, fuel-efficient type.

16 Post-listening discussion

How do the results of the survey compare with your personal usage of the car?

Do you agree with Paolo and Linda that we should restrict car usage and use other forms of transport? How feasible would that be for you and your family? Share your ideas with your group.

17 Euphemisms

Paolo says pupils prefer to get lifts instead of walking. He comments that the reason is 'just laziness'. This is a very direct statement. If he were telling the school the results of the survey, he would probably avoid this remark because he could cause offence. He might prefer to use a euphemism like 'pupils prefer to take a relaxed approach to transport'.

MATCHING

hw.

Match the common euphemisms in italics with their meanings.

1 Her cardigan *had seen better days.* H
2 I need the *loo.* B
3 Discounts for s*enior citizens.* E
4 When is *the happy event?* F
5 He's *careful* with his money. G
6 The house *is in need of some modernisation.* A
7 She's *looking the worse for wear.* H
8 My grandfather has *passed away.* C

A requires repairs and decoration
B toilet
C died
D very tired, dishevelled
E old people
F the birth
G mean, not generous
H was shabby, perhaps had holes in it

18 Rewriting a school report

Look at this extract from a school report. The words in italics are euphemistic. Read it carefully with a partner. Discuss what you think the teacher really means for each subject. Then rewrite the report, trying to be more direct and less polite!

MANOR PARK SCHOOL END OF YEAR REPORT		
Name of pupil:		Christopher Higgins
English:	12%.	Christopher's handwriting *needs immediate attention.*
Maths:	5%.	Christopher's concentration *is not always adequate to the demands of* the subject.
Geography:	Nil.	Sadly, *I am obliged to request that Christopher no longer continues with* this subject.
French:	2%.	Christopher's influence on the other pupils is *not quite what one would wish for.*
History:	7%.	Punctuality *has been an ongoing issue for* Christopher this term
PE:	Nil.	Unfortunately, *Christopher's enjoyment of life does not include* PE lessons.
Science:	9%.	Christopher's handling of the laboratory equipment *has been a matter of some considerable concern* this term.

19 Vocabulary: Ways of walking

There are different ways of walking and different words for describing them. With a partner, match the styles of walking with the definitions.

1 limp
2 stumble
3 stagger
4 stroll
5 stride
6 plod

A to walk in a pleasant, relaxed way
B to walk slowly with heavy steps, as if tired
C to walk as if your foot or leg hurts
D to hit your foot against something and nearly fall
E to walk in an unbalanced way, as if you are drunk or going to fall
F to walk quite fast with long steps

20 Asking for a favour

Study this dialogue.

Joe: Dad, could you do me a favour? Would you mind giving me a lift to the sports hall? I've got a basketball game.
Dad: When do you want to go?
Joe: In about half an hour.
Dad: Oh, all right.
Joe: Thanks, Dad. Are you sure it's not too much trouble?
Dad: No, I need to go out anyway.
Joe: Well, thanks a lot. That's nice of you.

ASKING FOR A FAVOUR

Could you do me a favour?
Can I ask you something?
Would you mind giving me a lift?
Could you please ...?

CHECKING

Are you sure it's not too much trouble?
Are you sure it's all right with you?
Are you sure it's not too inconvenient?
Are you certain it's not too much bother?
I hope it doesn't put you out.
Are you sure it's OK? I don't want to be a nuisance.

EXPRESSING THANKS

Thanks, that's nice of you.
Thanks a lot. That really helps me out.
Thanks very much. I really appreciate it.

PRACTICE

Take turns asking for a favour in the following situations. Work in pairs. Try to sound a little tentative.

1 You need a lift to the cinema.
2 You need to be picked up from a party.
3 You need someone to post a letter for you.
4 You need someone to take a parcel round to a friend's house.
5 You need to borrow a tennis racquet.
6 You need someone to pick up your jacket from the dry cleaner's.

Nature under threat

21 Pre-reading discussion

Do you own a bicycle? How often do you cycle and where do you usually go to? If you do not own a bicycle, would you like one?

In pairs work out the advantages and disadvantages of cycling as a form of transport. When you have finished, compare your ideas with other pairs and add any new points to your list.

ADVANTAGES

It doesn't pollute the environment.

....
....
....
....
....
....

DISADVANTAGES

You can get knocked off and hurt.

....
....
....
....
....
....

22 Predicting content

You are going to read a leaflet asking people to join a sponsored cycle ride. ('Sponsored' means that the people taking part will have asked 'sponsors' to donate money to charity.)

Look at the title of the leaflet and the pictures. What kind of people do you think will join the ride? What do you think the cycle route will be like?

23 Reading for gist

Skim read the leaflet quickly to get a general idea of the contents. There are three reasons the bike ride is being held. What are they?

1 ...... Fund raising ...... enjoyment ......
2 ...... health problems ......
3 ...... earn money ......
...... evcvt ......

bike to the
Sunday 21st May
future

Registration is now open for Bike to the Future — Friends of the Earth's annual sponsored cycle ride. So shake off those winter blues and sign up early for what promises to be another great May day out in the countryside!

Bike to the Future is the most popular event in Friends of the Earth's calendar. Year after year, people have written in to tell us how much they've enjoyed the route, the warm and friendly atmosphere, and the high spirits of their fellow cyclists!

This year, Bike to the Future will start near Hampton Court and take its riders through beautiful countryside to Eton. As ever, its gentle and undemanding 30 miles will be lined with refreshment stops, entertainments and lots of surprises. Bike to the Future is first and foremost a fun day out, but there's a serious message too. The route will highlight the threats to the surrounding area from new road schemes – passing through Chobham Common, which is affected by plans to widen the M3, and areas close to where sections of the M25 and M4 are also currently marked out for widening.

These are just a few reminders of the continuing threats to our health and environment from increased traffic and pollution due to unnecessary road schemes. The funds raised from Bike to

the Future will help sustain our campaign to halt unnecessary road schemes in favour of transport options which encourage less, rather than more, travel by road.

So help us get there! Register now for Bike to the Future to give yourself time to sign up as many sponsors as you can.

Above: Chobham Common has a rich diversity of wildlife.

Right: The ride ends within sight of Windsor Castle in the village of Eton.

ALL YOU NEED IS A BIKE

The route and all the practical details are taken care of by experts. It will be easy to get to the start and home again – British Rail is laying on special trains to take you and your bike to the start, and get you back to London from the finish. Marshals will guide you on the route, and first aid will be available for you and your bike if needed.

GOOD REASONS TO GET SPONSORED

Once you've sent us your entry form and fee, we'll send you an official sponsorship form so you can start signing up your friends and workmates. Whether you cycle on your own or in a team, there are loads of prizes for reaching fundraising targets, including Bike to the Future badges and T-shirts, cycle accessories and even mountain bikes!

There are also prizes for your sponsors. Anyone who sponsors you for £5.00 or more will automatically be entered in a prize draw.

THE MORE THE MERRIER

You're welcome to register on your own. However, it can be more fun in a group – and if you get together a team of ten or more, we'll give you a free Bike to the Future T-shirt. Your team-mates will also be able to order T-shirts at half price.

24 True/false comprehension

Are these statements about the cycle ride true or false? Try to spot answers in the text.

1 This is the first time the sponsored cycle ride has been held. *F*
2 The route will be strenuous. *F*
3 The day is primarily for enjoyment. *T*
4 The cycle ride celebrates the victory over plans to develop Chobham Common. *F*
5 Participants will help plan the route. *F*
6 Extra trains to and from London will be provided. *T*
7 Medical help will be available. *T*
8 Prizes are only available to the teams. *F, Sponsor*
9 Participants in teams of ten or more get a discount on the T-shirts. *T*
10 The ride finishes at Chobham Common. *F*

25 Post-reading discussion

Have you ever taken part in a sponsored charity event, e.g. a swim, a dance or a walk? Tell your partner what it was like.

26 Re-ordering an article

The following article in a school magazine puts forward the pros and cons of cycling.

Try to re-order it so that it is in a logical sequence. How do the words and phrases in italics link the text together?

THE PROS AND CONS OF CYCLING

a Cycling at night is *particularly dangerous,* especially along dark country roads as a motorist may not see you until too late.

b *Above all,* cycling is very cheap.

c Second-hand bikes are *not expensive* and you can learn to carry out simple repairs yourself.

d *Although* cycling has many advantages, there are some *drawbacks* too.

e *In the first place,* owning a bike frees you from dependence on your parents to take you to places.

f Cycling is an enjoyable, efficient and liberating mode of transport.

g Cycling can be *dangerous* on busy roads and you can be seriously hurt if you are knocked off your bike by a motorist.

h *In addition,* attending a cycling proficiency training scheme enables you to cycle more safely and prepares you for tricky cycling conditions.

i *On balance, however,* I feel that the personal enjoyment and freedom you get from cycling outweigh the disadvantages.

j Many of the dangers of cycling *can be eliminated* if you take sensible precautions such as using lights at night and wearing reflector strips.

k *Furthermore,* many roads are polluted by traffic fumes which makes cycling unpleasant and perhaps even unhealthy.

l It *also* removes the frustrations of hanging around waiting for a bus to turn up.

27 What makes a good argument essay?

A When you have re-ordered the article correctly, read it through or write it out in full to get a feeling of how the text flows.

B The text above could be described as 'even-handed'. Why, do you think?

C The last paragraph shows the writer's point of view 'on balance'. Is this a good way of rounding off an argument? Why/Why not?

D A good argument essay needs to be convincing. This means it should help the reader understand the issues. It should present strong, believable arguments. (Whether or not the reader changes his/her mind about the topic in the end is irrelevant.) Do you think the article 'The Pros and Cons of Cycling' achieves this? Try to explain how you feel to your group.

28 Presenting contrasting ideas in the same paragraph

'The Pros and Cons of Cycling' devotes separate paragraphs to the advantages and disadvantages of cycling. It then sums up at the end. An alternative to this approach is to consider contrasting ideas in the same paragraph.

The following extract comes from a composition about whether cycle helmets should be made compulsory. Circle the word that contrasts one idea with its opposite.

I recognise that a feeling of freedom is part of the pleasure of cycling. Nevertheless, in my opinion it is essential that cyclists are made aware of the dangers of not wearing a helmet.

Now rewrite the extract using a different linking word or phrase. Choose from: *although, however, but, yet, in spite of.* Make changes to the extract if you think it is necessary.

29 Presenting more contrasting ideas

Study these incomplete sentences from argument essays. Notice the use of a contrast word in each one. Then try to complete each sentence in an appropriate way.

1 Car accidents continue to increase *despite*
2 The government has launched a big safety campaign to encourage cyclists to take a cycling test. *Nevertheless,*
3 A new airport is planned for our area *in spite of*
4 I have always been a keen supporter of the private car. *However,*
5 It seems unfair to stop cars going into the town centre, *yet*

6 A good train service would help to reduce traffic on the roads. *On the other hand,*

7 Cycling is not encouraged in the town *although*

8 People are frightened of travelling by plane *even though*

9 The railway companies tell us train journeys are quick and comfortable *but*

10 I would always travel by sea rather than air *despite*

30 Language study: Linking words

Linking words have a variety of functions in an argument essay. They can be used to express opinion, show contrast, express consequence, give reasons, etc.

Working in pairs, try to add words or expressions under each of the following headings. Then compare your ideas with the rest of the group.

LISTING
First of all
Secondly
Thirdly

ADDITION
also
In addition
moreover

CONTRAST
but on the other hand
While
Wheras
however

REASONING
because
So that
the reason is

OPINION
We think As far as I'm
I feel In my opinion concerned
I believe In my view
To my mind

EMPHASIS
Above all
All of these
Over all

CONSEQUENCE
so
therefore
however

SUMMING UP
On balance

31 Brainstorming

Brainstorming is a group work activity you'll be using regularly to help spark off ideas on a topic. It's important because you can't write a convincing argument unless you have strong ideas to work with. Work in small groups to brainstorm ideas about the following topic.

Imagine that the local council is considering cutting down a small wood near a shopping centre to make a car park for the convenience of shoppers. Write down points for and against the idea. Take five minutes to do this.

Should St John's Wood be cut down to provide a car park for shoppers?

POINTS FOR	POINTS AGAINST
....	....
....	....

32 Text completion

A local student, Roland Chang, heard about the proposal to cut down the wood. He felt very strongly about it so he wrote to his local newspaper. Study his letter carefully with a partner. Then try to complete each gap with appropriate linking words from the choices given.

Dear Editor,

I was dismayed when I heard of the proposals to cut down St John's Wood to make a car park for shoppers. 1) _____ I agree that the town is short of car parks, this solution would be insensitive and improper.

2) _____, the wood is an area of natural beauty. There are many ancient trees of an unusual kind. I often go there for a picnic or just to relax at weekends. The wood is 3) _____ a vital habitat for birds, animals and insects. If the trees were cut down, many species would be lost.

4) _____ the wood is right in the centre of a heavily polluted part of town. The trees help to make the air cleaner 5) _____ they trap dust, smoke and fume particles in their branches and leaves. The council says it is worried about global warming 6) _____ trees help reduce the build up of gases that contribute to global warming because they feed on carbon dioxide. 7) _____ that area 8) _____ suffers from high noise levels from passing lorries and the railway line. The trees help reduce the noise levels and have a beneficial effect on the whole environment.

9) _____ cutting down the wood would be stupid, greedy and pointless. A car park may well attract shoppers to the town and increase the shopkeepers' trade. 10) _____ a unique and beautiful part of our heritage would be destroyed. I would be very interested in hearing what your other readers think.

Yours faithfully,

Roland Chang

1 However, On the other hand, In my opinion, Although, Because

2 In addition, In the first place, Nevertheless, Yet, But

3 on the contrary, without doubt, also, in my view, nevertheless

4 On the other hand, At the beginning, Furthermore, Also, Finally

5 secondly, not at all, because, however, such as

6 for example, yet, thirdly, even though, so

7 In addition, Despite, Therefore, Consequently, However

8 also, but, thirdly, last but not least, on the other hand

9 In the end, In my opinion, On the contrary, For instance, Furthermore

10 Alternatively, For example, After all, In fact, On the other hand

33 Discussion

Do you think the letter is too formal, too informal or about right? Try to explain why.

How does Roland show an awareness of his audience in the letter?

Obviously, Roland is opposed to the council's plans. How convincing do you think his argument is? Try to mention particular examples to justify your opinion.

34 Words often confused

These words, some of which are taken from Roland's letter, are often confused. Complete each sentence with the correct alternative.

1 council/counsel

a The _council_ meets once a month.

b The doctor may also _counsel_ you about your personal problems.

2 affect/effect

a The medicine didn't have any _effect_ on my cold.

b The new rules _affect_ all aircraft over 30 years old.

3 there/they're/their

a _There_ are plenty of pegs for the children's coats and lockers for _their_ shoes.

b They said if _they're_ going to be late they will let us know.

4 lose/loose

a You must be careful not to _lose_ your passport.

b Since I lost weight, my trousers have been too _loose_.

5 alternate/alternative

a I have to work on _alternate_ weekends.

b The last bus had gone so walking home was the only _alternative_

6 lightning/lightening

a The house was struck by _lightning_

b The sun came up, gradually _lightening_ the sky.

7 practice/practise

a He tries to _practice_ the guitar once a day. _practise_

b We have music _practise_ on Tuesdays. _practice_

8 past/passed

a Have you seen Harry in the _past_ few days?
Yes, I _passed_ him in the street on Saturday.

b Luckily, we all _passed_ our maths test.

INTERNATIONAL OVERVIEW

A Study the graph carefully. What does it show you about the world's production of bicycles compared with cars

(a) from 1950—1970?   (b) from 1970—1992?

Do you think car production will 'catch up' with bicycle production in the future? Why/Why not?

B What do you think are the reasons for the differences between car and bicycle production in the world? Think about

- the relative costs of car and bicycle production
- the cost of owning a car compared with the cost of owning a bicycle
- the restrictions some cities and/or governments place on car use to protect the environment.

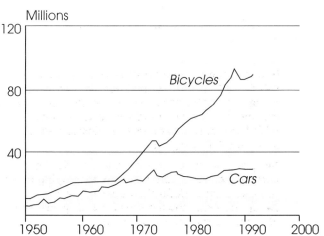

World bicycle and car production, 1950-92

A new motorway for Conway?

35 Pre-reading discussion

Study the photographs and try to describe them. How do you think the people in the cars are feeling? What causes traffic jams to build up on main roads and motorways? Is there any way of preventing them?

BRAINSTORMING

Divide into two groups. Group A should try to list all the advantages of motorways. Group B should aim to list all the disadvantages.

When you have finished compare your ideas. Can you add any new ideas between you?

MOTORWAYS – FOR AND AGAINST

ADVANTAGES	DISADVANTAGES
....	....
....	....
....	....

36 Reading a model text

Conway's council is supporting government plans to build a new motorway. This will link Conway to the capital and to some other large cities. Do you think this will be a good development for Conway? Who is likely to benefit? Who might be against the idea? Try to think of reasons for your opinions.

Now scan the text quickly. Are any of the points you thought of in the discussion noted here?

Dear Editor,

We are <u>delighted</u> that a new motorway is being planned for Conway because it will bring so many benefits to the town.

In the first place, Conway has suffered from the recession and many young people are unemployed after leaving school. The motorway will bring a much needed boost to business, as communications will be faster, cheaper and more efficient. Consequently, the businesses we already have will find life easier, new companies will be attracted to Conway and there will be more jobs for everyone.

Furthermore, we know a large number of people commute daily to the city. The present winding road is tiring, time-wasting and, above all, dangerous. The new scheme will not only mean a big reduction in time spent commuting, it will also provide a much safer and more relaxing journey. We don't think anyone ever feels nostalgic about traffic jams!

Many readers might be worried about pollution from increased traffic. On the contrary, pollution will actually decrease as so many new trees, especially chosen for their ability to absorb car fumes, will be planted.

Finally, the new motorway will also serve as a by-pass for the large lorries that now go through Conway town centre.

There is no doubt that the motorway will really put Conway on the map. If we want a bright future for ourselves and our children, we should all support it.

Yours faithfully,

The Conway Business Group

37 Comprehension check

1 Where does the text on page 72 come from? *Abk*
2 What are the writer's main points in favour of a new motorway?
3 How convincing do you find the argument? Give some reasons.

VOCABULARY

Here are some definitions of words in the letter. Try to find the words and underline them.

a a bad period in the country's economy *recession*
b something which helps and encourages
c routes linking one place to another
d to travel between home and work every day
e wishing something in the past would return
f a main road built to avoid a town

38 Analysing the text

Work in pairs to answer these questions. They will help you analyse the way the model argument is structured.

1 Underline the word in the opening paragraph which expresses emotion. Which word introduces a reason for the feeling? Underline it. An opening paragraph should grab attention. Does this paragraph do that? *delighted*
Yes, because it tell us the passage

2 Which words are used in paragraph 3 for emphasis? *Furthermore, above all, not only*

3 Paragraph 4 considers an opposing point of view. What is it? Which phrase is used to introduce a contrasting opinion? *on the contary*

4 *Finally* is used at the start of paragraph 5. Why? *It tells it is the last thing of the passage*

5 The last paragraph of an argument essay should not 'tail off', leaving the reader wondering what you really think. It should be firm and decisive. How does the final paragraph of this letter sound? *He is very convincing (sure)*

He is very sure what he talus

39 Putting forward an opposing viewpoint

homework 9/1/02

The Conway Nature Society held a meeting to discuss the letter from the Conway Business Group that appeared in the local newspaper. At the meeting, they drafted their own letter to the newspaper. Here is an outline. Read the points carefully and make sure you understand each one.

Are any of the points similar to the list of disadvantages of motorways you made earlier?

```
DRAFT LETTER

Dear Editor, We were horrified to hear of
the plans for a new motorway for Conway and
we are sure our feelings are shared by many
of your readers. We believe the scheme would
destroy the environment and cause untold
damage to wildlife. The motorway itself will
cost a great deal of money to build. It
would be better to use this money to help
local businesses by improving the rail
network. Commuters to the city would benefit
from a better train service. The idea that
the motorway will be more efficient is
completely unfounded. The new road will soon
attract extra traffic and eventually become
heavily congested. The suggestion that
planting trees alongside the motorway will
eliminate pollution is ludicrous. Trees can
help. They cannot make up for the destruction
of wildflowers and wildlife. Many of us cycle
or walk across the present road to get to
school or work. The new motorway which
replaces the old road will split the area
into two, making it impossible to get to the
other side on foot or by bicycle. Please,
people of Conway, don't stand by and watch
your environment being destroyed. We urge you
to support the Conway Nature Society campaign
by writing to your local councillor.

Yours faithfully,

The Conway Nature Society
```

40 Redrafting

Redraft the letter so that it flows more smoothly. Remember, you will need linking words to show connection or contrast between ideas. Add words to express personal opinion or emphasis where you think it is appropriate. Finally, make sure you use paragraphs.

When you have finished, show your work to a partner. Does he or she agree that your letter now flows more smoothly, has an appropriately formal tone and sounds more persuasive?

41 Relating to your target audience

Your letter or article should reflect the interest of those who are going to read it. These people are called your 'target audience'.

Study the extracts below. Decide with a partner whether each extract comes from

- a school magazine
- a letter to a local newspaper
- a letter to a magazine
- a personal letter
- a formal letter.

Decide whether the target audience in each case is

- school pupils
- elderly people
- the general public
- an individual the writer has not met
- a friend.

What key features helped you make up your mind? Underline them.

A

I think that's all for now about the good time we had at the party. Don't feel too left out! See you soon.

Love,

Tom

a personal letter

School pupils

B

Most of us already have problems getting to school on time. The proposed cuts to the bus service will make things even worse. I suggest we have an urgent meeting to discuss a plan of action in the Common Room next Wednesday lunchtime.

A school pupils

a school magazin

an individual the writer has not met

C

newspaper

I am writing to express my concern about your suggestion printed in yesterday's *Evening News* that the greenhouse effect has no scientific basis. Like many of the readers of this newspaper, I have no doubt that the greenhouse effect is a reality that is becoming steadily worse. *the general public*

D

Most people of our age will welcome the news, reported in your article 'Fair Dues At Last', that senior citizens will be able to travel free of charge at weekends.

elderly people   a formal

E

I would be grateful if you could contact me to discuss a mutually convenient time to meet.

formal letter

42 Writing a letter from outline notes

In your neighbourhood, there is a large open area called Antalya Place which is used by young people for ball games. Your council are proposing to dig up the area and plant a flower garden with benches for elderly people. Trees will be planted too. No ball games will be allowed.

Write a letter to the local newspaper giving your views. You should try to be even-handed in your discussion of the issues. However, your final paragraph should show clearly whether or not you are in favour of the proposal. Use the following outline to guide you.

PARAGRAPH ONE: INTRODUCTION

POINTS IN FAVOUR

1 Flower garden attractive. Would brighten up area. Flowers and plants provide a habitat for a wide variety of insect life.

2 Old people lonely. Have no meeting place. Garden would provide focal point for meeting each other.

3 Trees welcome. Provide shade. Reduce pollution and noise levels. Provide protection against wind.

POINTS AGAINST

1 Young people need opportunity to practise ball games. Most live in flats — no gardens or other space nearby.

2 Local football and netball teams are winning matches. Will be less successful if cannot practise. Morale and team confidence will sink.

3 Young people meet friends, have picnics, watch matches, enjoy themselves here. Without this area, boredom and resentment might set in. Vandalism might be a problem.

FINAL PARAGRAPH

Sum up and state opinions firmly.

43 Understanding a typical exam stimulus

The argument essay question often provides a stimulus in the form of comments. Study this example. What does the question ask you to do?

There are proposals to develop a river near your home. A marina would be built, and tourists would be encouraged to come and use the river for boating and fishing. Write an article for the school magazine saying what you think of this idea.

Here are some comments from local people. You can use these for ideas, or use ideas of your own.

'The development will create jobs which we need.'

'Engine oil and litter from boats will pollute the water.'

'The plants which grow in the water help to absorb pollution. Many of them will die if the river becomes developed.'

'The river is in a beautiful, relaxing setting. It's only right to encourage more people to benefit from the tranquillity of the area.'

'Local people use the plants in the river for raw material for making things, such as reeds for making baskets. We will lose a source of raw material if the river is developed.'

'If too much fishing goes on, the river will become over-fished and many species will die out, disrupting the sensitive ecology of the river.'

'Our area needs to become more modern and to progress. Developing the river will help us achieve this aim.'

44 Redrafting an exam answer

With a partner, study this answer to the exam question in exercise 43. What do you think are the strengths of the answer? What do you feel are the weaknesses? Write them down.

I think it is a good idea to develop the river because it will create jobs which we need in our area. Moreover, the river is set in a beautiful, relaxing part of the countryside. It is only right to encourage more people to benefit from the tranquillity of the area. Our area needs to become more modern and to progress. Developing the river will help us achieve this aim. On the other hand, engine oil and litter from boats will pollute the water. The plants which grow in the water help to absorb pollution. Many of them will die if the river becomes developed. Local people use the plants in the river for raw material. We will lose a source of raw material if the river is developed. If too much fishing goes on, the river will become over-fished and many species will die out, disrupting the ecological cycle. In my opinion, the river should be developed because there are more advantages than disadvantages in doing so.

STRENGTHS

....

....

....

WEAKNESSES

....

....

....

Try to redraft the composition above. Aim to develop a few points more fully, with more reasons and examples of your own. Remember to set out your writing clearly with paragraphing and logical connectors. The target audience is the readers of the school magazine, so try to link your answer in some way with their interests.

When you've finished, compare your version with a partner's. What are the main differences? Does he/she feel you have improved the original draft? How convincing is your argument and how well does it relate to the target audience?

Exam-format questions

Writing

1   There is a proposal in your country to raise the legal age for learning to drive a car by five years. Do you think this is a good idea? Write a letter to your local newspaper giving your views. You should write between 150-200 words.

The comments below may give you some ideas, but you are free to use ideas of your own.

"We live in a rural area without buses or trains. Learning to drive early is essential."

"Most of the accidents are caused by young people. They should wait until they are older to learn to drive."

"Your actual age is less important than your personal maturity. Some 17-year-olds are more mature and responsible than some people of thirty."

"There is too much traffic on the roads. Raising the age limit for learning to drive would help reduce traffic congestion and pollution."

"If young people weren't allowed to drive until they were older, they would get used to more environmentally friendly forms of travel like cycling."

"Young people need their independence. It's unfair to expect young people to go on being dependent on their family and friends for lifts."

"We have lots of traffic jams, pollution and an inadequate road system. Depriving young people of the right to learn to drive until they are older is not going to solve the real problems."

2   There are plans to build an airport near your home. Write an article for your school magazine outlining your views on the proposal. You should write between 150-200 words.

You may wish to write about:

- the possibility of creating more jobs
- the possibility of pollution and increased noise
- the effect on the landscape and wildlife
- the possibility of better communications for companies and individuals.

Oral assessment

1   Imagine that you are in charge of transport in your area. Discuss with the examiner or your partner the changes you would make to improve transport facilities where you live.

You are not allowed to make any written notes.

2   Give a short talk, of about five minutes, on the following topic.

'Is travelling by air really safe?'

Be prepared for questions at the end. You may take a minute or two to write some brief notes before you begin.

EXAMINER'S TIPS

1   **Writing an argument essay** requires the ability to think of relevant points in the first place. You can improve your understanding of controversial subjects by listening to or watching a current affairs programme once a week. Discuss matters of concern with your family or friends.

2   Take an active part in class discussions and school debates to practise thinking logically and giving your opinions orally. Even if you don't do this in English, it is still good practice. Offer to research a mini topic for your class and present your findings to everyone.

3   Improve your ability to write about controversial topics by reading newspaper and magazine articles which are opinion based. Examine them carefully to see how the ideas are linked and expanded.

4   Have patience with your writing skills and be prepared to practise them. Show your written work to someone you trust and listen to their comments.

EXAM STRATEGY

5   Use the composition stimulus wisely. It is there to help you understand the rubric and to stimulate your own thoughts. Choose a few points and expand them; don't just copy them out. Give reasons of your own to support your views.

6   Express your ideas clearly and link them coherently with appropriate linking words. Remember to show some audience awareness if you can.

7   There is often a **box-ticking question** on the Reading and Writing paper. The questions are written so that all statements seem possible – they cannot be answered from guesswork. Make sure your answers are based on information in the text.

Unit focus

In this unit you have learned to write a formal **argument composition**. You have learned to structure it so you write in favour, or against, or present both sides of a controversial topic. This is practice for Paper 2, Part 3.

You have listened to a discussion and taken notes on specific items of information. This is practice for Papers 3/4, Part 2.

You have read a detailed and a less detailed text and answered multiple-choice questions and true/false questions. This is practice for Papers 1/2, Part 1.

That's Entertainment!

Talking about entertainment

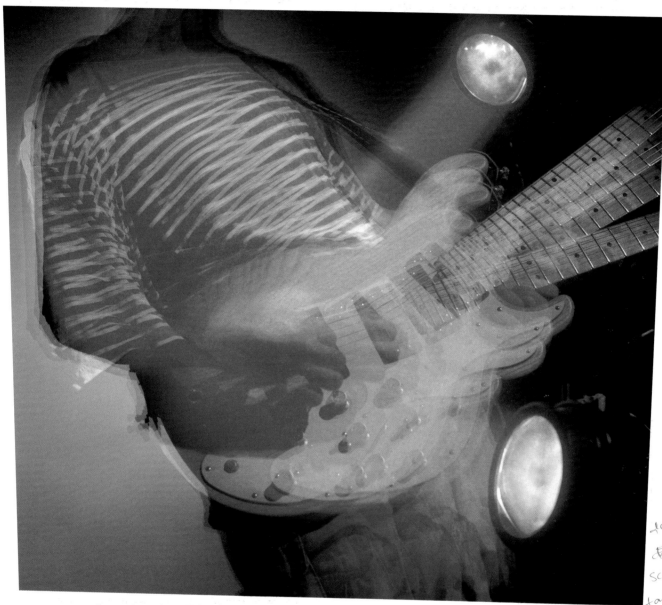

1 Introduction and discussion

A What kinds of entertainment do you like? Using the list below, tell your partner about the kinds of entertainment you most enjoy and why.

- Listening to music – pop, jazz, classical etc.
- Going to the cinema
- Reading a book or magazine for pleasure
- Going to a concert or live performance
- Going to the theatre
- Listening to the radio
- Watching TV or a video

B Have you ever been involved in entertaining people? For example, have you ever performed on stage or helped produce a play? Explain how you felt about it. If you've never done this, would you like to? Why/Why not?

C Would you like a job in the 'entertainment business'? Explain what sort of work, if any, you would like to do. Why would you like to do that kind of work?

2 Film vocabulary

As some exercises in this unit will require a working knowledge of film vocabulary, this exercise will help you be better prepared.

Complete the film review by choosing from the words and phrases in the box below to fill each space.

The Quick and the Dead

Sharon Stone deserves a(n) _Oscar_ for her superb _performance_ as Ellen, the tough and mysterious _heroine_ who rides into a small town in the Wild West. Ellen is on a quest for vengeance against Herod. Herod, _____ Gene Hackman, is entirely convincing in the _role_ of ruthless town boss. The hair-raising _plot_ becomes more violent when Ellen has to beat off the other outlaws in a quick draw contest. The final _cast_, however, leaves no one guessing who the real winner is. The other members of the _characters_ include Leonardo DiCaprio and Russell Crowe who are perfect as the brash, overconfident _genre_ typical of the Wild West. The film is _played by_ Sam Raimi who may be remembered for other _box office_ hits such as 'Darkman'. The _film_ is a welcome addition to the growing spaghetti western _____.

---

box office   cast   played by   heroine   Oscar   scene   plot
characters   directed by   role   performance   genre   film

Make a note of unfamiliar words in your vocabulary book, with a translation if necessary.

3 Film quiz

What we look for when we watch a film is very personal. To help you understand more about your preferences and attitudes to films, complete this quiz.

WHAT I WANT FROM A FILM

1 How do you choose a film you enjoy?
  a   Recommendation from friends. ✓
  b   By looking at film reviews in the newspapers, etc.
  c   Turning up at the cinema or video shop and making a choice on the spot.
  d   I've got my favourite actors – I'm prepared to see any film if they are acting in it.

2 The following comments are often made about films. How far do you agree with them? Mark each comment like this:
  Agree strongly ✓✓   Agree ✓   Don't agree ✗
  a   A lot of suspense should be an important ingredient. ✗
  b   Fast-moving action is essential. ✓
  c   The plot should contain many surprising twists. ✓✓
  d   It should be acted by big Hollywood stars. ✓✓
  e   It should have been made recently. ✗

  f   It should contain many emotional scenes. ✓
  g   It should make a serious point. ✗
  h   It should make you laugh. ✓
  i   It should contain many special effects. ✓✓

3 Tick the statements you agree with.
  a   There is too much violence in films today. ✓
  b   I prefer films which seem realistic and true to life rather than science fiction, horror or ghost movies.
  c   My favourite films are based on true stories.
  d   Seeing the film after you've read the book is usually disappointing.
  e   Too many films come from Hollywood. We should be watching films that are made in our own country. ✓
  f   I'm sick of hearing about films in which evil people commit terrible crimes. ✓

When you've finished the quiz, swap answers with a partner. Read your partner's answers carefully and pick out a few responses that interest you. Ask for more information in a friendly way, to show you're genuinely interested.

Examples:

May I ask why you think fast-moving action is essential/the plot should contain many surprising twists?

Would you mind telling me about your favourite actors/films that have made you laugh/films you've seen which are based on true stories?

What I'd like to know is why you prefer films that seem realistic and true to life/you don't like films about evil people.

Could you explain in more detail why you think suspense is an important ingredient/films should contain emotional scenes/films should make a serious point/more films should be made in your country?

Here are some more useful phrases for following up your partner's answers:

Something else I'd like to know is ...
Can you give me an example?
What exactly do you mean by ...?
Sorry, I don't quite understand why ...

You are going to hear a model conversation in which two students tell their teacher about two films they have enjoyed.

You can follow the conversation while you listen. (Turn to page 192.) Notice how the teacher asks for information and follows up the students' answers.

Later, when you want to write or talk about a film, you can look again at the model conversation for examples of what you can say about a film.

Which of these aspects of the films were mentioned by Carol and Sam? Check back in the conversation if you're not sure.

☐ characters
☐ genre
☐ hero
☐ message of the film
☐ plot
☐ reasons for recommending
☐ setting
☐ special effects
☐ suspense

You will need to include some or all these aspects of films when speaking or writing about films later in the unit.

Two main tenses are used by Sam and Carol: the Present Simple and the Past Simple.
Examples: *I was on the edge of my seat!*
Dundee confronts an angry bull in the bush.

Why are these two different tenses used, do you think?

Read the following statements. Tick the points which reflect Sam's view of 'Crocodile Dundee'.

a He thought it was very realistic and believable.
b It contained some spectacular stunts.
c It was interesting but told him nothing memorable about life.
d He preferred the Australian location to the American location.

Tick the points which reflect Carol's view of 'The Hand that Rocks the Cradle'.

e She identified with the family in the film.
f She was on the edge of her seat from tension.
g She thought the ending was very emotional.
h It showed how we are exposed to evil, even in our everyday life.
i It made her realise how much power a nanny can have.

Do you feel that Sam and Carol's appraisals give you an understanding of the background to each film? Why do their reasons and examples manage to convey the qualities of each film?

These forms are often used to give emphasis when we say how we feel.

So... that ... can be used with an adjective without a noun.
Example: *The film was so scary that I was on the edge of my seat.*

Such ... that ... is used with an adjective and a noun.
Example: *It's such an escapist film that I forgot all about my exams.*

In both cases you can leave out *that* if you wish to.

PRACTICE

Join these pairs of sentences using *so ... (that)*.

1 I was keen to see the concert. I was prepared to pay a lot for a ticket.
2 She was disappointed not to get the role of princess. She cried all day.

Join these pairs of sentences with *such ... (that)*.

3 The film took a long time to make. The director ran out of money.
4 The story was fascinating. The film company wanted to make a film about it. (Begin: *It was ...*)

10 Involving your listener

People can read film reviews for themselves, but when you talk about a film your listener is interested in **your** particular responses to a film.

Sentences like those below make your responses sound more personal and will engage your listener more effectively. Working with a partner, discuss how each of the sentences could end. Complete them appropriately, using a past tense.

Example: *The scene where the monster appears is so frightening that I jumped off my seat.*

1 The scene where the heroine dies is so sad that ....

2 It's such an intriguing plot that ....

3 The scene was so comical that ....

4 The scene when we find out who the murderer

   really is is so compelling that ....

5 The hero gives such a convincing performance as a blind man that

   ....

6 The gangster scenes are so violent that ....

Recommendations and reviews

11 Discussion

TV, radio and hi-fi systems are such a normal part of many people's lives that it seems strange to remember that at one time all entertainment was 'live'. The development of silent 'moving pictures' at the cinema was one of the first kinds of non-live entertainment.

As technology progresses, it becomes less and less necessary for people to leave their homes to enjoy music, films or concerts. Entertainment is not merely 'non-live', it is also becoming more home-based. For example, videos and CD players mean that new films and music concerts can be enjoyed at home. As a result, cinema and concert audiences in some countries have fallen.

It has been claimed that home-based entertainment has 'gone too far'. Some people think, for instance, that videos are a poor substitute for the excitement of going to the cinema or theatre. They say it's creating a lonely and passive society. What do you think?

With a partner, try to think of the advantages, disadvantages and dangers of home-based entertainment. Add your ideas to those below.

ADVANTAGES

It's convenient.

....

....

DISADVANTAGES

Films are less powerful on the video screen..

....

....

DANGERS

People can become more cut off and isolated.

....

....

12 Choosing a home video

Whether you feel that home videos are good or bad, it seems that they are here to stay.

In pairs, read aloud this short dialogue between a video store assistant and a customer who wants to choose a home video. Why do you think the customer didn't make a choice?

Customer: Excuse me, can you recommend a good video?

Assistant: What about a historical romance like 'Pride and Prejudice'? It's set in nice English countryside. It's got a really nice heroine and the historical costumes are really good.

Customer: Mmm, maybe … What have you got for young children?

Assistant: The 'Jungle Book' is a nice children's movie. The animation is very good.

Customer: Have you got any thrillers?

Assistant: 'Extreme Measures' is good. The acting is good too.

Customer: I'm not sure. What's this comedy 'Funny Bones' like?

Assistant: That's a good comedy. It's got some good characters.

Customer: Well … have you got anything with special effects?

Assistant: 'Mortal Kombat' is a good science fiction film with good special effects.

Customer: Actually, I think I'm going to leave it for today. Thanks for the help.

13 A wider vocabulary

You may not know all the films mentioned above, but try to replace 'nice' and 'good' with more precise, revealing adjectives from the box. Make an intelligent guess about the most likely adjective for that kind of plot/character, etc. There are more adjectives than you need, so think carefully before making a choice, consulting a dictionary if necessary.

Can you think of any adjectives to add to the groups in the box?

impressive	amusing	intriguing
striking	hilarious	absorbing
magnificent	witty	thought-provoking
stunning	sophisticated	engaging
superb	stylish	mesmerising
sumptuous	sparkling	convincing
dazzling	quirky	
glorious		
enjoyable	sad	appealing
satisfying	poignant	likeable
well made	heart-rending	attractive
skilful		
memorable		
tough	dramatic	
ruthless	gripping	
embittered	breathtaking	
revengeful	mysterious	
violent	spine-chilling	
bloodthirsty	atmospheric	

14 Collocations

You can describe a character as 'amusing' or 'convincing'. The plot of a film or an actor's performance can also be described in this way. However, some adjectives do not go with certain nouns. 'Ruthless', for example, can be used to describe a character but not a plot or performance.

Collocations, or word combinations, are based on conventional usage, not hard and fast rules. Look again at the adjectives in the box. Working in small groups, decide which adjectives can be used with each of the nouns below. Some adjectives can go with more than one noun. When you've finished, compare your lists with those of another group.

PLOT   CHARACTERS   COSTUMES

SETTING   SPECIAL EFFECTS   PERFORMANCE

Make a note in your vocabulary book of the collocations that appeal to you … and make a promise to yourself to use them!

15 Understanding the style of short newspaper reviews

Short film reviews in newspapers and film guides are written to be scan read by people in a hurry. They aim to outline the plot and give us a 'taste' of the film's atmosphere. To do this, reviews have developed a style and techniques of their own.

Read these eight short reviews and match them with descriptions 1-6 on the next page.

A

THE NEXT KARATE KID
HILARY SWANK, PAT MORITA

The wise old karate mentor Miyagi is brought together with the teenage granddaughter of his old war buddy, a man who saved his life 50 years ago. Julie Pierce is an aggressive, ill-mannered teenager who has been taking her anger out on the nearest person to her, usually her long-suffering grandmother. At school, Julie's rebellious attitude has meant that she has become the target for constant and violent harassment from the local gang of young macho men.
Enter Mr Miyagi, the first person to detect Julie's real potential and true personality and take the troubled youngster under his wing. Can she become the next Karate Kid?

B

POCAHONTAS
VOICES: MEL GIBSON, DAVID OGDEN STIERS, BILLY CONNOLLY

In 1607 a group of British adventurers, led by the greedy John Ratcliffe and soldier John Smith, arrive in the New World seeking gold and treasures. Smith meets a beautiful Indian girl, Pocahontas, and they are attracted to one another. She introduces him to her world but, as friendship blossoms, relations between the natives and the British deteriorate. When Smith is captured it's up to Pocahontas to save his life.

C

LITTLE WOMEN
WINONA RYDER, GABRIEL BYRNE, SUSAN SARANDON

Every 30 years or so there is a movie remake of the classic novel Little Women. Here's one for the Winona Ryder generation. Ryder – whose role here produced her second consecutive Oscar-nomination – gives her best performance to date in a role that follows in the small footsteps of the delicate, caring but often overwhelmed women she has come to specialise in.
But it's not until the second half of this sprawling, American Civil War-set tale that she takes centre screen. Before that she's just one of the gaggle of girls – including prim Meg, tragic Beth and precocious Amy – who cluck and fuss around their pillar of common sense mother, Marmee (Susan Saradon, excellent).
Only when the little women become big girls and each goes her own way in search of romance and fulfilment does the story blossom, giving Ryder room to shine as she becomes the centre of attention.

D

APOLLO 13
TOM HANKS, KEVIN BACON, BILL PAXTON

'Houston, we have a problem,' came the laconic words to Mission Control from 205,000 miles away. The crew of Apollo 13 was almost at the moon when an explosion in space caused them to lose oxygen, power and guidance. Suddenly, Jim Lovell, Fred Haise and Jack Swigert faced dying as no man had died before. With only four days to bring them back, there was no margin for error in a daring rescue attempt that defied all the odds.

E

THE MASK
JIM CARREY, CAMERON DIAZ

It's time for the retail release of the blockbuster that took Jim Carrey from zero to hero and made him one of the highest paid stars in Hollywood.
He plays meek bank clerk Stanley Ipkiss whose life changes big time when he finds an ancient, magical mask. When he puts it on he is instantly transformed into a suit-wearing apparition with a green head, huge eyes and enormous white teeth.
He has superhuman abilities and is a living, breathing cartoon character able to fulfil his innermost whims, wishes and desires – and exact revenge against those who have wronged him!

F

FREE WILLY 3
JASON JAMES RICHTER

Jesse (Richter), now 17, has landed a summer job tracking whales on a research vessel with his old mentor Randolph. They are trying to find the cause of a mysterious decline in the Orca population off the rugged North West Pacific coast.
Willy has also matured into a young adult and has a mate. Ten-year-old Max is on his first trip on his father's commercial fishing boat, but his happiness turns to dismay when he discovers his father's true business – illegal whaling. The whales being hunted are Willy, his mate and the rest of the J pod!

G

VOLCANO
TOMMY LEE JONES, ANNE HECHE

As well as the glitz, glamour, crime and pollution, Los Angeles is also the unwilling epicentre of virtually every natural disaster, including earthquakes, firestorms and mudslides. Now it is about to experience its most cataclysmic ever. A vent in the Earth's crust has unleashed an erupting volcano. An endless stream of fiery, deadly lava insidiously creeps across traffic-choked streets while wreaking havoc below ground in the labyrinth of man-made and natural tunnels. Seismologists Mike Roark and Dr Amy Barnes are caught in the middle of hell's inferno.

H

FIRST STRIKE
JACKIE CHAN

In the fourth instalment of the popular Police Story series, Chan portrays a Hong Kong police officer who is contracted by the CIA and a Russian intelligence organisation to retrieve a stolen Ukrainian nuclear warhead. From the snow-capped mountains of the Ukraine to a shark-infested water park in Australia, Chan pursues a rogue CIA agent. Along the way, he is attacked, assaulted, framed for murder and forced to defend himself any way he can. Everything within arm's reach becomes a weapon: ladders, brooms, tables, cars, stilts – even sharks!

1 This review starts with a string of nouns to convey the atmosphere of a well-known city.
2 This review tells us that the film is based on a novel.
3 This review starts with a brief history lesson.
4 This review starts with a quotation from one of the characters.
5 This review starts by telling us the film is the latest in a series about the police.
6 This review indicates that wildlife will be an important part of this film.

In film reviews, key words signal important information about character and plot. The result is a compressed style in which maximum information is conveyed in the most concise form.

1 Examine the opening sentence of the review of 'Pocahontas' and identify the use of key words.

In 1607 a group of British adventurers, led by the greedy John Ratcliffe and soldier John Smith, arrive in the New World seeking gold and treasures.

Tick the noun which implies the characters will exploit others. Underline the adjective that signals 'bad' with regard to one character. Circle the verb which suggests they went to the New World with only one purpose in mind.

2 Examine this extract from 'First Strike'.

From the snow-capped mountains of the Ukraine to a shark-infested water park in Australia, Chan pursues a rogue CIA agent. Along the way he is attacked, assaulted, framed for murder and forced to defend himself any way he can.

Tick, circle or underline the key signals which tell us:

a that the film has very different settings.
b that the film has a fast-paced, dramatic plot.

c that the CIA agent is not to be trusted.
d that Chan himself doesn't initiate the violence in the film.

3 Examine the use of key words in an extract of your own choice.

Choose a film you found particularly powerful and give a short talk about it to your class.

Remember your classmates will be interested in your personal reactions and opinions, so think carefully about why the film was memorable. It is essential that your reasons are clear and that you provide examples of scenes. Refer back to exercises 5 and 6 to help structure your talk.

Before you begin, make a plan.

INTRODUCTION

Mention the title and genre (and the director and stars of the film if you wish to).

Say why you have chosen to talk about this film. These reasons will be personal to you and will reveal something of your personality and attitudes. Looking back at your answers to the film quiz in exercise 3 may remind you of what you look for in a film.

PLOT, CHARACTERS AND SETTING

Your audience will expect a brief outline of what happens in the film, who takes part in the action and where it takes place.

Try to arouse the interest of your audience by describing the plot, characters and setting in a fresh and lively way. Re-reading some of the short newspaper reviews may provide interesting ways of opening your description.

Tenses

Remember that the plot and characters should be described in the present tense.

Clarity

Plots can be complicated, so keep your description short, giving most attention to the beginning of the plot.

CONVEYING THE QUALITY OF THE FILM

Say why you thought the film was powerful. Try to use vivid adjectives to convey the quality of the film. Aim to involve your listeners when you describe your reactions (exercise 10). Remember the importance of key words in signalling information (exercise 16).

Some points you may want to consider are:

*   the performance of the actors and their suitability for the roles they play.
*   the use of humour, suspense or special effects. (Provide examples of scenes.)
*   the underlying 'message' of the film.

RECOMMENDING THE FILM

Say why you recommend the film. Link your recommendations to your knowledge of your audience. Do they need to relax and laugh? Are they very interested in a particular genre such as science fiction, horror or westerns? Does the film raise topics that you have discussed in class (jobs, social problems, life in the future)?

ACTIVE LISTENING

In good communication, listening is as important as talking. Listen attentively to the speaker. After he or she has finished, make one positive comment about what you have heard and then ask at least one question seeking further information.

TAPING YOUR TALKS

You may like to give your talks in small groups, tape them and analyse the results. Check the clarity and vividness of the talk. Does the audience feel involved? Why? Listen for accuracy in the language – tenses, articles, collocations etc. How would you correct any mistakes?

Working in the film industry

18 Pre-reading discussion

A   Would you like to work in the film industry? What sort of work would you find most attractive? Acting, designing sets or costumes, writing scripts or directing? Why?

B   You are going to read about a young man who has built up a successful career as an animator. Looking at the pictures, what would you expect the films to be like? Would you like to watch one? Or have you already watched one?

C   What do you think are the challenges presented in making an animated film using puppets or models?

D   What kind of personal attributes do you think an animator needs? Tick from the list below.

- ☐ good at making things
- ☐ imagination
- ☐ ability to pay attention to detail
- ☐ single-mindedness
- ☐ a sense of humour
- ☐ enjoys working with technical equipment

Does the job of an animator appeal to you? Why/Why not?

19 Vocabulary check

Before you read, make sure you know the meaning of these words.

- eccentric
- villain
- Plasticine
- models
- wire
- phonetics

20 Reading for gist

Now read the article for general meaning. What did Nick study at the National Film and Television School? How many of the possible attributes listed in D above are mentioned or suggested by the text?

An interview with Nick Park

Philip Gray talks to Oscar-winning film-maker and animator, Nick Park, about his career and his amazing animations: Wallace, a slightly eccentric inventor, and Gromit, his ever-faithful dog.

'Your work is seen by audiences around the world, but what was it that first started
5 **off your interest in film-making?'**

'It all started when my parents bought a simple home movie camera, and I discovered that it had an animation button to build up films one frame at a time. As a keen photographer, my father was able to help me with the technical side of camera work, and I worked with Plasticine models right from the start.'

10 **'At what stage did you realise that your hobby would turn into a full-time career?'**

'I don't remember a great deal of formal careers advice about the film industry while I was at school. There seemed to be very little information available, and the fact that I didn't tell people about my interest in animation probably explains why I didn't have much advice. I certainly didn't find out that it was possible to take a degree in film-
15 making until much later.

But one of my teachers did find out about my films – my English teacher, Mr Kelly. By watching my films, and encouraging me to show them to the school, he was one of the important influences on my early career. By the time I was 17, one of my earliest films, 'Archie's Concrete Nightmare', had been shown on the BBC.

20 After completing a BA degree in communication arts at Sheffield Art School, I went on to study animation at the National Film and Television School, where I started work on the first Wallace and Gromit adventure, 'A Grand Day Out'. In 1985, I joined the Bristol-based Aardman Animations studio. 'A Grand Day Out' was finally completed in 1989, followed by 'Creature Comforts' and, of course, 'The Wrong
25 Trousers'.

85

Nick Park's art of animation

Nick's characters have been described as having too-close-together eyeballs and
mouths as wide as coathangers. Created from a recipe of ordinary Plasticine plus
American modelling clay, beeswax and dental wax, they are then formed around a wire
30 frame to give them flexibility.

The characters are actors and they perform in accurately modelled sets that have been
researched on location. Remarkable attention to detail extends down to the repeated
bone pattern of the wallpaper in Gromit's room.

The speech patterns of each character have to be broken down into phonetics, with
35 each frame matched to a portion of a particular work and animated with appropriate
body, face and lip movements. No wonder one 30-minute film takes so long to make.

**'With an Aardman Animations production team of nearly 30 people involved in 'The
Wrong Trousers', the list of credits reads like that of any other feature film. Can you
give any clues about your next production?'**

40 *'At the moment, we are hard at work on another Wallace and Gromit film. I can't give
too much of the plot away, but I can tell you that it will be another fast-moving thriller.
There will be a new villain on the scene, and I can promise some love interest for
Wallace. I have plenty of exciting projects planned for the future, including a full-length
feature film. As I have spent nearly ten years working with Wallace and Gromit, there
45 may well be some new characters in the film.'*

**'What advice can you offer to our next generation of film-makers as they prepare for
their college courses and careers?'**

*'Firstly, I think commitment is essential in this work. Any film-maker must learn to be
single-minded for those times when it is all too tempting to do other things. Setting up
50 with expensive equipment doesn't need to be a major problem. I started with a cheap
8 mm cine camera and one problem to overcome – the price of film.*

*Secondly, without good powers of observation, it is difficult to find sufficient
inspiration. Study examples of animation to see exactly how they have been created.
Many video players will operate frame by frame to show how the animator has
55 worked.'*

'Working hours must be very long during production. Can you find time to relax?'

*'It's all too easy to spend very long hours on this type of work, as it certainly isn't a
nine-to-five job. Filming sessions can be hectic, but I do find the time to relax
occasionally, and have even managed to keep a few weekends clear just to get out into
60 the countryside.'*

Decide whether the following statements are true
or false.

1 Nick's father played a large part in helping him
develop film making skills.
2 Nick decided early on in his school career that
he would take a degree in film making.
3 A teacher at school gave him the confidence to
aim for professional film making.
4 The animated film 'A Grand Day Out' took a year
to make.
5 'The Wrong Trousers' was his first film.
6 Matching his characters' speech to their body
language takes less time than you would
expect.
7 Nick is happy to talk freely about the story line
of his next Wallace and Gromit film.
8 In his next production, he intends to stay with
the successful formula he has worked out
rather than risk new developments.

9 If you want to learn this work, you have to be
prepared to invest in an expensive camera.
10 He has no difficulty limiting the length of his
working week.

Try to guess the meanings of these words and
phrases from the article.

1 frame *(line 7)*
2 influences *(line 18)*
3 wire frame *(line 29)*
4 on location *(line 32)*
5 list of credits *(line 38)*
6 powers of observation *(line 52)*
7 a nine-to-five job *(line 58)*
8 hectic *(line 58)*

Find two other places in the article where the word *frame* is used. Which of the above meanings (1 or 3) does the word have each time?

23 Spelling and pronunciation: The letter *c*

A Have you noticed that *c* is pronounced in different ways? Say these words from the text aloud to show the different ways *c* can be pronounced.

camera   advice   sufficient

Can you think of the reason for these differences?

B Study the following rules, underlining the letter(s) according to the rule.

1 *c* is pronounced /k/ before the vowels *a, o,* and *u*. This is called 'hard c'.

Examples: *camera   discovered   difficult account*

2 *c* is also pronounced /k/ before most consonants.

Examples: *actors   crackers   clues*

3 *c* is pronounced /s/ before the vowels *e, i,* or *y*. This is called 'soft c'.

Examples: *receive   cinema   exciting   icy*

4 Before the letters *ea, ia, ie, ien* or *iou, c* is usually pronounced 'sh'. The phonetic symbol is /ʃ/.

Examples: *ocean   conscious*

5 When double *c* comes before *e* or *i*, the first *c* is hard and the second is soft; so the pronunciation is /ks/.

Examples: *accept   accident*

PRACTICE

Put each of the following words into the correct group, according to its sound. Most of the words come from the text.

Hard c /k/
(as in *camera*)

Soft c /s/
(as in *cinema*)

Double c pronounced /ks/
(as in *accent*)

'Sh' sound pronounced /ʃ/
(as in *ocean*)

1 Oscar
2 career
3 eccentric
4 Wallace
5 scene
6 centimetre
7 Plasticine
8 action
9 comedy
10 discovered
11 efficient
12 advice
13 certainly
14 influence
15 communication
16 recipe
17 accurately
18 accident
19 particular
20 face
21 credits
22 delicious
23 cine
24 sufficient

With a partner, listen to each other saying the words aloud. Do you both agree that your pronunciation is correct?

24 Using words in context

Make up five sentences using words from the list above. Write them down and check your spelling. Then swap sentences with a partner. Read your partner's sentences aloud.

Examples:
1 *Yasmin built up a successful career as a make-up artist.*
2 *English shows the influence of other languages.*
3 *The telephone is an efficient means of communication.*

25 Spelling and pronunciation: The letters *ch*

Ch has three main sounds.

1 In some words, *ch* is pronounced /k/. Examples: *chemist   technical   school   Christmas*

2 In some words, *ch* is pronounced /tʃ/. Examples: *cheese   check   teacher   rich*

3 In a few words, *ch* is pronounced /ʃ/. Examples: *chef   machine*

PRACTICE: ODD WORD OUT

20/2/02

Listen to the three groups of words and cross out the odd one out in each group, according to the pronunciation of *ch*. Rewrite the word in the correct sound group.

Group A	Group B	Group C
chemist	church	chauffeur
architect	watch	chute
mechanic	search	champagne
headache	scheme A	sachet
chef C	match	chocolate B
technology	butcher	brochure

With a partner, practise saying each group of words. Do you know the meaning of each word?

26 More practice of *c* and *ch* sounds

Read this dialogue with a partner. Check each other's pronunciation.

Richard: Our drama club is putting on a production of 'Charlie and the Chocolate Factory' for the end of term.

Clare: That sounds exciting.

Richard: It is! The club is in charge of everything. We've chosen the actors, written the script, created the costumes, painted the scenery and even designed the brochure advertising it. The teachers weren't involved at all.

Clare: Sounds like a recipe for chaos to me!

Richard: Well, we've had one or two headaches but we've concentrated very hard on getting it right. There was one little slip, though. I play an eccentric character and I have to wear a big moustache. In our dress rehearsal the moustache fell off just as I was about to speak!

Clare: Never mind. I'm certain the audience will appreciate all the effort you've put in. How much do the tickets cost?

Richard: Actually, it's free but there's a collection at the end. Half the proceeds will go to the school fund and the other half will go to *Children in Crisis*, the school's charity.

Clare: Well, I really hope it's a big success.

27 Look, say, cover, write, check

Here are some words which often present spelling problems. Do you know what they mean? Can you say them properly? Use the 'look, say, cover, write, check' method to learn them.

delicious	succeed
special	success
influence	bicycle
chauffeur	conscious
technology	conscience
receive	except
confidence	

Reading for pleasure

28 Pre-listening discussion

It is sometimes claimed that reading for pleasure is now taking second place to watching videos or TV. What do you think? Would you rather watch a video than read a novel? What can you get out of reading novels that videos can't provide?

In small groups, make notes of the unique pleasures that reading offers.

Special things about reading for pleasure
Examples:
You can take it at your own pace.
You can do it almost anywhere.

....

....

29 Listening for gist

You are going to listen to a radio interview. Jonathan, a librarian, is concerned that young people are giving up reading because of television and videos.

A   Listen first for the general meaning and try to decide why Jonathan thinks videos are intellectually less stimulating than reading.

B   Strategies for interrupting
The interviewer has some difficulty interrupting Jonathan. Tick the phrases he uses to try to interrupt.

[handwritten: Advantage / children & 80hr TV / good & bad / disadvantage / violence / parents should]

☐ Just a minute …

☐ With respect …

☐ If I could just butt in here, …

☐ Excuse me, I'd like to say that …

☐ Hang on!

☐ But surely …

☐ If you don't mind my interrupting …

☐ If I could get a word in here …

30 Detailed listening

Listen again and answer the questions.

1   What are children not getting when they watch TV and videos rather than read? Give two examples. *[handwritten: children can't pay for books than quality of videos]*
2   What is the difference, according to Jonathan, between reading a novel and watching a film? *[handwritten: we can imagine the story]*
3   How, according to Jonathan, are children affected by watching violence on screen? *[handwritten: The crime rate (rouse) children get influenced]*
4   How can parents help their children to understand what they read? Give two examples. *[handwritten: Parents should show a good example to show their children - switch off TV]*

31 Post-listening discussion *[handwritten: - Parents should & let them join the library setion]*

A   Do you feel reading quality fiction helps intellectual development more than watching films and videos?

B   Do you agree with Jonathan that violence in films and on TV influences behaviour more than violence in respected novels? Try to explain your point of view to your group.

32 Dialogue: Interrupting each other

Lee and Michelle are having a discussion about violence on television. They keep interrupting each other.

Read the dialogue aloud with a partner. Use a suitable phrase for interrupting each time you see the word *interrupting*. Choose from the list above.

Michelle: I agree with Jonathan that people are copying the violence they see on TV and it's time something was done about it. TV programmes are much more violent than they used to be. The crime rate is getting worse too. Children are being influenced to think that violence is all right and …

Lee: (interrupting) … Children are very sensible. They can tell the difference between what happens on TV and what goes on in real life. It's rubbish to suggest that people watch a programme and suddenly become more violent. I don't think violent scenes in books are better or worse than violence on TV. There isn't that much violence on TV anyway.

Michelle: (interrupting) … Some of the cartoons they are putting on even for very young children are very violent. They don't help children understand the terrible effects real violence has. How it can destroy lives. TV makes violence seem exciting and …

Lee: (interrupting) … Violent behaviour comes from your background and the way you're brought up. It has nothing to do with the television set. TV doesn't make people behave violently. If you see violence in your home or around you in your real life, that's the example you copy.

Michelle: (interrupting) … Violent TV programmes will make children who are growing up in bad homes even worse. They're even more likely to commit aggressive acts. Jonathan said parents should help children read more, and I think they should say what their children are allowed to watch too. They'll know if their children will be affected.

Lee: (interrupting) … That would be a complete waste of time. In the first place, children don't want their parents interfering. Surely kids have the right to some privacy about what they choose to read or watch on TV.

Michelle: (interrupting) … It's not only children who are influenced. Mentally unstable people, for instance, might not be able to discriminate about what they watch. They might think violence is fun, or even learn how to commit a crime. They find TV incredibly powerful and …

Lee: (interrupting) … Most TV programmes are really boring! I lose interest after five minutes. Not that I want to start reading so-called good books instead. I get enough mental stimulation at school. What I want is more exciting TV and less boring programmes!

INTERNATIONAL OVERVIEW

Readers, writers and cinema-goers

A   The following countries of the world have the greatest number of library book loans per year. Can you put them into order from 1 (highest number) to 5 (lowest number)?

Germany   China
Japan   United Kingdom
Ukraine

B   Who do you think are the two most translated authors in the world? Choose from this list.

William Shakespeare   Mark Twain
Walt Disney Productions Vladimir Ilyich Lenin
Agatha Christie   Jakob & Wilhelm Grimm

C   Which country has the most cinema attendances per head per year? Choose from this list.

Hong Kong   India
United States   Ex-Soviet Union
China   Australia

D   Which country produces the most films per year?

United States   India
Germany   Brazil

Writing reviews

33 Pre-reading tasks

A   Do you enjoy reading novels? Do you prefer murder mysteries, romances, historical fiction or some other genre? Do you have a favourite author? What do you like about his/her books? Discuss your ideas with a partner.

B   Write down the title of a novel you've enjoyed. Imagine you've been asked to write a review of it for your school magazine. You've already learned a lot about the skills of reviewing from your work on films earlier in the unit. You now need to build on those skills and extend them into book reviewing.

C   The following questions may help you work out what made the novel memorable. Note down your answers.

1   **Plot**
Was the plot unusual at all? Was it gripping? Was it interesting but less important than   the characters?

2   **Setting**
What did you like about the setting – historical details, fascinating details of fast-paced city life? How was the atmosphere conveyed through the setting?

3   **Character(s)**
Did the characters feel 'real'? Did they change during the book and cope with new challenges? Did you identify with any of them? Why? Think of one or more examples in the novel which show this.

4   **Style**
Did you like the style of the novel? Why? Was it punchy and direct or leisurely and gentle?

5   **Audience**
Remember to think about your target audience. Why would these people enjoy reading the novel?

Keep your notes safely as you will use them later.

34 Reading model reviews

The following two reviews were written by students for the school magazine. One reviews a novel, the other a film. Notice how the writers try to slant the reviews to their audience.

GREAT EXPECTATIONS reviewed by Deepak Thandir

Have you ever liked the hero in a novel so much that you wanted everything to turn out all right for him? I felt like this when I read 'Great Expectations' by Charles Dickens. I'd like to recommend it for the school library because I'm sure other students will identify with the main character too. *A recommend book in the school library*

Set in bleak 19th-century England, the novel tells the story of a poor orphan called Pip, who secretly helps an escaped prisoner. His good turn has unexpected consequences and he becomes rich beyond his wildest dreams. I won't spoil the story by telling you how the plot twists and turns, but I can guarantee surprises in store! *Character, setting, story, plot*

In a style I found painfully direct, Pip shares his innermost thoughts and aspirations – even ideas he later becomes ashamed of. During the course of the novel, Pip changes a lot. He becomes more aware of his shortcomings and more compassionate. He pays a high price for self knowledge and, like me, I think you'll be moved to tears at the end. *The story about Pip, style*

One of the things I learned from reading the novel is how corrupting money is. Pip, for example, no longer cares about keeping promises he made when he was poor. The novel made me think about how the values of loyalty and integrity are more worthwhile than any amount of material wealth. *How have we learn moral massage. The things when the author learn the most,*

The novel provides a vivid and rewarding insight into 19th-century Britain. Students who have chosen English language and literature as a subject will find it particularly fascinating. *The advantage of reading this book Conclusion, audience*

NOTES

aspirations: hopes
shortcomings: personal failings
compassionate: feeling pity for others
corrupting: causing to become dishonest or immoral
integrity: honesty

COMPREHENSION CHECK

1 What is the title of the novel and who is the author? *'Great*
2 When and where is the story set?
3 Why does Pip become rich?
4 How does Pip change during the novel?
5 Why does Deepak think money is corrupting?

As you read this film review, try to work out the meaning of any unfamiliar words from the context.

Jurassic Park reviewed by Neena Gopal

introduction

Do you enjoy being so terrified during a film that you can hardly breathe? If so, then I would recommend that you watch 'Jurassic Park'. But be warned – it's not the best video to select when you are home alone!

The film is set on a remote island and centres around the work of a mad scientist who has, by experimentation, bred dinosaurs in his lab. He hopes to create a dinosaur theme park and attract visitors in big numbers. To test out the impression his project might make in the future, he invites some guests for a preview. *setting, plot*

The suspense is maintained throughout the film, and the timing of the dinosaur attacks is perfect too. Just when you think it's safe to open your popcorn, another rampaging monster appears! However, the director does his best to make sure the tension is mixed with humour. For example, in one special effect a baby dinosaur is hatched. He breaks out of his shell with such a cunning expression that I burst out laughing. *style, reason "why the film is enjoyable"*

The scientist in 'Jurassic Park' has interfered with genetics and caused a catastrophe. It made me think how scientific experiments, although they have the potential to bring many benefits, can also bring terrible consequences. *moral, what we have*

Try not to miss this film. It's well-made, entertaining and makes you think. However, if you're watching it at home, I don't think your younger brothers or sisters should see it. In my opinion, it's too frightening for children under ten. *audience* *opinion*

COMPREHENSION CHECK

1 How have the dinosaurs been created?
2 Why does the scientist invite people to see the dinosaurs?
3 Why is the timing effective?
4 Why is the scientist to blame for what happens?
5 Why is the film not recommended for children under ten?

35 Analysing model reviews

A The opening of each review begins with a question. Do you find this effective?

B Compare the way the story of the book/film is described in the second paragraph of each review. Underline the phrases which are used to introduce the description. How does Deepak skate over a complicated plot?

C The third paragraph of each review gives reasons why the book or film was found to be enjoyable. Quite different kinds of things were found rewarding. What are they?

D The fourth paragraphs explain what Deepak and Neena gained from reading the book/watching the film. Underline the phrases they use. Contrast what each student learned.

E Deepak and Neena recommend *Great Expectations* and *Jurassic Park* for different reasons. What are they? How do we know they are aware of their audience?

F Which review interested you more? Why?

36 Useful language for book reviews

Here is some typical language used by reviewers of novels. Which expressions would also be suitable for film reviewing? Tick those you'd like to use in your own reviews.

STYLE

It's beautifully written.
It's got a style of its own .
A subtle, poetic style that ...
An elegant style which ...
It flows beautifully.
Its light, chatty style ...
Its crisp, punchy style ...
Its leisurely style ...

SETTING

It's set in ...
It's set against the powerful background of ...
The historical details are superb.
It's a wonderful re-creation of ...
Set in the midst of ...
It has a marvellous sense of time and place.

RECOMMENDING

It's worth reading because ...
You'll be delighted/enthralled/intrigued/riveted by ...
It's hard to put down.
It's a real page turner.
It's a winner from the first sentence.
It's well worth the paperback price of ...
It's a masterpiece.
It's the best I've read yet/the best I've ever read.
It's compelling ...
It's not to be missed.
It's a classic.
You'll be moved to tears.

37 Criticising a film or a book

If you are writing a review under exam conditions, try to choose a film or book you found powerful. You'll remember it better and find more to say. However, you might still want to add a comment or two about what you didn't like.

Examples:
The performances were excellent, but the ending was very depressing.
The main character looked too old/too young for the part.
The slapstick comedy delighted me but it wouldn't be to everyone's taste.
The characters were engaging but the plot was too far-fetched at times.
The photography was sumptuous although the special effects were surprisingly bland.
Although I enjoyed the nineteenth-century setting, the story was too sentimental for my taste.
The violent and bloodthirsty ending spoiled the story for me.
The plot was intriguing but the characters were not really believable.

38 Effective openings for book reviews

When writing an opening paragraph, remember that you should:

*   immediately involve the reader.
*   make the reader want to read on.
*   convey the novel's special qualities.
*   use a concise style.

In small groups, read the following opening paragraphs A–F of book reviews written by students. Try to rank them from most to least effective, using the points above. Correct any structural errors as you work. Discuss the reasons for your choices.

A
I want to try to explain to you about a very good novel I recently read called 'The Sphinx'. Extremely, the writer did his best for this book and I couldn't leave any single moment in the book without reading it.

B
As long as I have been chosen to write an article for the school magazine this month then I decided to write you about a book I read last weekend and I think you will really injoy. I read 'The Buried Treasure' by Mary Dickson. It is about buried treasure on an island and the plot will really make you surprising.

C

Last week I read one of the most gripping and moving books ever, 'The Bellmaker' by Brian Jacques. In the novel, animals are given human personalities and motives. However hard-hearted you are, this compelling tale of how a courageous group of animals band together to defend their kingdom against the evil schemer, Foxwolf, will bring a tear to your eye.

D

If you've been recently bored and willing to read a long and emotional book I recommend you read 'Kofi's Dream'. It's a book about how a boy who lives in Asia and wants to help the dozens of people in it. His dream tells him about a worst than AIDS disease which is going to come to the country and how to save people attained of this disease.

E

Have you ever wanted to be the hero in a novel? No matter how you reply you'll love reading 'Dark Eye'. The hero is a likeable but naive trainee police cop who is on a hunt for a gang of ruthless criminals in the underworld of New York. The suspense is great and the writing is just perfect.

F

The book I really liked and want to describe for my school magazine is 'Weather Eye' by Lesley Howarth. I could read it over and over again. I think the book has already sold a million of them which is very scarce. I want to tell you about Telly (the character in the book) and the strange and unusual things that happened to her after her accident in which she nearly died.

39 Writing an opening paragraph

Write the opening paragraph for your own review of a novel you have enjoyed. You may find it helpful to refer to the notes you made for exercise 33.

Remember: Aim to convey the 'flavour' of the novel and to make the reader want to find out more. Try to be concise, choose revealing adjectives and avoid unnecessary words.

40 Writing a review of a thriller from prompts

Do you enjoy reading novels in which the plot is tense and unexpected and you can identify with the hero of heroine? If so, then you might enjoy *The Kidnapping of Suzy Q* by Catherine Sefton.

Try to build up a complete review of it from the following prompts.

THE KIDNAPPING OF SUZY Q

'The Kidnapping of Suzy Q' / Catherine Sefton / be / most thought-provoking / atmospheric / novel / have read. It be / set / modern urban Britain / it tell / story / through / eyes / courageous heroine / Suzy. One day / she be / making / ordinary trip / supermarket / buy groceries / when / supermarket be / raided. In the confusion / bungling criminals / kidnap Suzy / she / be standing in / checkout queue.

The criminals / keep / Suzy / captivity. Suzy recount / ordeal / graphic / painful detail. I be / impress / Suzy's courage / determination / refusal / panic / give up. Several incidents / novel / reveal / Suzy's ability / cope / when / she be / threatened / them.

The story / make / think / ordinary life / be / dramatically changed / a fluke incident. It be / also / inspiring / make / me realise / inner strength / ordinary people can have / cope with / disaster.

The novel be / skilfully written. Catherine Sefton's style be / crisp / witty / characters be / strong / convincing. The plot be / intriguing / never predictable. If you like / spine chilling / tense novels / you find this / hard / put down.

41 Writing a film review based on a dialogue

The Internet is the global electronic highway which gives us access to information on a worldwide scale about every imaginable subject. People who have the right passwords can use a computer to 'tap into' the Internet. What do you think are the advantages and the dangers of this form of accessing information?

Here is a conversation between two friends about the film 'The Net' which is based on the Internet. Why not read it aloud with a partner? Then try to write a review of the film for your school magazine. Before you begin writing, make a plan of the points you want to include and their order.

Fatima: I saw 'The Net' last night and I would definitely recommend it.

Joanne: Is that the one about crime and the Internet?

Fatima: Yes. It's very exciting. It's about a computer analyst called Angela who spends her days ironing out 'bugs' in computer games and her nights chatting with other cyber-jockeys on the 'Net'.

Joanne: Sandra Bullock plays Angela, doesn't she? I thought her performance in 'Speed' was really powerful.

Fatima: She gives a very convincing performance in this too. She plays an intelligent but lonely person whose main contact with people comes through computerised communication. She's rather cut off and isolated from real people. Her life changes dramatically when her fun and games on the 'Net' at night lead her to *being embroiled with a different kind of 'net', murder, corruption and conspiracy on an international business scale.*

Joanne: Sounds like the sort of tense, action-packed thriller I like.

Fatima: Yes, and it makes you realise that the Internet can mean trouble for ordinary people. There's a chance your confidential records can be seen by the wrong people. In the film, for instance, the criminals delete Angela's real identity and give her a false one. Then she discovers that it's impossible to convince the authorities who she really is.

Joanne: So she has to fight against the odds to clear her name? I think I'd like to see that. I admire gutsy heroines.

Fatima: Maybe your social studies teacher would agree to show it in class. It's interesting to discuss how face-to-face contact with people gets less necessary as we can communicate more and more through computers. It's inevitable that some people are going to end up cut off and isolated from real people.

Joanne: That's a good idea. I might be able to persuade him!

Exam-format questions

Writing

1 Write the review of a video you have enjoyed and wish to recommend for the new video club mentioned below. Your article should be suitable for publication in the school magazine. Write about 200 words.

Competition!

Calling all students! Form Six is starting a video club for all students. We want to hire videos which we can show to students on Tuesdays after school. The headteacher is inviting you all to submit video reviews based on videos you want to recommend for the club. All entries will be published in the school magazine. The panel judging the entries will be made up of the headteacher, the head of English and two student representatives.

We are looking for well expressed, thoughtful reviews and clear recommendations.
Closing date for entries: 10th March

---

2 Write a short article for a teenage magazine describing a novel you have recently read and enjoyed.

You should:

*   outline the plot
*   say why you enjoyed the novel (e.g. style, setting, development of characters)
*   say why you think other people would enjoy reading it too.

Your article should be about 200 words long.

3 You recently attended a concert or other live performance. Write a review of it for a teenage magazine. You should write about 200 words.

Oral assessment

1 **A film I have enjoyed**

Tell the examiner or your partner about any film or video you have enjoyed recently. Explain what it was about and say why you particularly enjoyed it.

Points to consider are:

*   the influence and importance of the main character(s)
*   the setting and atmosphere
*   why you enjoyed it (special effects, performance of characters)
*   what you learned from watching the film (its 'message').

You are, of course, free to consider any other ideas of your own. You are not allowed to make any written notes.

2 **Live performances**

A CD or audio cassette may be cheaper than paying to hear a concert performance. However, many people think going to a live performance is money well spent. Do you agree? Discuss your ideas with your partner or the examiner.

In your discussion, you could consider such things as:

*   the fact that live performances enable you to see a famous performer 'in person'
*   the unique atmosphere of some live performances
*   the opportunity to see the details of a performance (costumes, setting) etc. exactly as they really are
*   the fact that you can listen to a CD many times but a live performance is a one-off event
*   the fact that some live performances can be disappointing.

You are free to consider any other ideas of your own. You are not allowed to make any written notes.

3 Choose a topic

Choose one of the topics below and talk about it for five minutes. The examiner will ask you a few questions when you have finished. You many take a minute or two to write some brief notes before you begin.

1 'The only real music is classical music.'

2 'Subjects like art, drama and music are the most important subjects on a school's timetable.'

3 'A film or pop star's success depends on good looks and image, not talent.'

EXAMINER'S TIPS

1 Practise your reviewing skills by exchanging views about TV programmes, books and films with your friends. Try to use some of the language you have been learning in this unit and avoid the adjectives 'nice' and 'good'.

2 Read book and film reviews in your own language and English to become more familiar with the language of reviewing.

3 Try to read for pleasure in English. Make time for reading – remember you can do it anywhere! Keep a book in your bag or pocket to fill a few spare minutes profitably. Allow a couple of hours occasionally to really get into a book.

Find authors you enjoy. Book reviews are a useful source of information, and so is exchanging views with friends. Browsing in a library or a bookshop which sells English books can give inspiration too.

4 Look for magazines in English that reflect your own hobbies and interests.

5 Try to enlarge your range of interest. Read about different themes or dip into information books (astronomy, transport, inventions) which you usually pass over. Some libraries carry a wide range of journals and newspapers. Pick up one or two about topics which are new for you.

Try some poetry if you usually ignore it.

6 Watch again a film you have really enjoyed. Analyse why and how it appeals to you. Do this with books too.

EXAM STRATEGY

7 If you write a review for the exam, choose a novel or film you know well and enjoyed. Don't write about books or films you found generally disappointing, as it is more difficult to write in enough detail about something which did not engage your interest in the first place. This doesn't mean the book or film has to be perfect. You can pick out its weak points as well as highlighting what was powerful.

8 Use a broad vocabulary and appropriate structures to express your reactions to a book or film. Give specific details about characters, performance, special effects etc. Avoid writing very generally: it is much better to use specific examples.

9 Don't get too caught up with describing the plot. Plots can be very complicated and it is not necessary to re-tell the story. Just give an idea of what it is about. Describing the beginning can be enough.

10 In the exam, you may have to review a live performance, e.g. a play, dance or music concert. Use the skills you have learned in this unit to:

- describe the costumes, special effects etc. if appropriate
- convey the quality of the performance
- describe your reactions to the performance
- describe the atmosphere in the audience
- say why you would recommend the performance to other people.

Unit focus

In this unit you have learned to present a talk about a film or video and answer questions. This is practice for Papers 5/6.

You have written a **review of a novel and a film/video/ live performance** you have enjoyed. This is practice for Papers 1/2, Part 3.

You have listened to a radio interview and answered short-answer comprehension questions. This is practice for Paper 4, Part 3.

You have answered true/false comprehension questions on a detailed reading text. This is practice for Papers 1/2, Part 1.

Travel and the Outdoor Life

Holiday time

1 Holiday quiz

What do you really like doing on holiday? With a partner, rate the following points on a scale of 1 (unimportant) to 4 (very important). Add anything else you or your partner like doing.

		MYSELF	MY PARTNER
1	Staying in a comfortable, well-equipped hotel/holiday home etc.	4	4
2	Seeing beautiful scenery and new places	3	4
3	Making new friends	2	2
4	Doing outdoor activities, e.g. hiking, climbing, swimming	4	2
5	Learning a new skill, e.g. sailing, fencing, windsurfing	4	3
6	Having an exciting nightlife	3	1
7	Having time for reading and quiet thought	3	3
8	Exploring city attractions, e.g. art galleries, museums	4	4
9	Learning more about local culture and customs	2	3
10	Lazing on a sunny beach with a bottle of suntan lotion	1	1

Share your ideas in your group. What are the most popular things to do on holiday?
What are the least popular?

circle ◯ — opinion
___ — fact

2 Pre-reading discussion

The brochure describes a summer camp aimed at students who want to learn English.

Look carefully at the pictures without reading the text. Who can you see? Where are they? What are they doing? How do you think they are feeling? What is the atmosphere like, do you think?

You join in role-playing exercises, learn from video presentations and take part in debates on topical issues. All materials are supplied by us.

I ♥ English

There is no better place to learn English *opinion* than in England, and no better place in England than at Camp Beaumont. *opinion* Here we offer just the right mix of learning and fun *opinion* with language courses taught *opinion* by dedicated teachers who inspire and give youngsters all the skills needed to speak like a native.

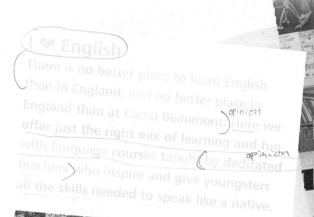

It doesn't matter whether kids are absolute beginners or already quite fluent. In both cases, we help them to make great progress during the holiday, so they return speaking English with *more confidence* than ever.
opinion

opinion
Every minute of the day is filled with fun, excitement and *activities galore*. You never have time to be bored at Camp Beaumont.

Three daily lessons help you to understand and speak the kind of practical English that is used in everyday life.

The programme at Camp Beaumont is a terrific *opinion* opportunity to make new friends and to speak English all day while you swim, sail, go climbing or play tennis.

Camp Beaumont centres *opinion* are also the leading destination for English youngsters on activity and adventure holidays.

The English you learn in class is reinforced, steadily and subconsciously, by taking part in our exciting multi-activity programme alongside youngsters on holiday at the same camp.
fact

activities

fact

Our language courses are taught at three residential centres in the English countryside. Eccles Hall and Beaumont Activity Village are in Norfolk, while Blundell's lies in the southwest, in Devon.

You soon discover that everything you learn adds immensely to the pleasure of your holiday in England.

opinion

WHERE TO GO

factual

Eccles Hall, Norfolk
This centre is most suited to younger students aged 8-12 years who are just starting to study English. For details of the centre see pages 30-31.

Booking dates
Each Saturday, for six weeks, from 13th July to 24th August.

Blundell's, Devon
This centre is most suited to teenage students aged 12-17 years, who have already studied English a little. Full details of the centre are on pages 32-35.

Booking dates
Each Saturday, for six weeks, from 13th July to 24th August.

Beaumont Activity Village, Norfolk
This centre is suited to younger (7-12 years) and older (12-17 years) students of English – both complete beginners and those who have already made good progress. Full details of the centre are on pages 20-24.

Booking dates
Each Saturday, for nine weeks, from 29th June to 1st September.

fact

After you complete the course you will be awarded a Camp Beaumont Diploma. It's a souvenir of the time you spent with us and the friends you made while learning English!

All our centres are at boarding schools with excellent accommodation and good food.

Holiday type	Per week	Extra week
Eccles Hall	£318	£298
Blundell's	£318	£298
Beaumont Activity Village	£318	£298
Super English (Blundell's only)	14 days £950	

To book a place, telephone us at:
+ 44 171 - 724 2233

For further details of Camp Beaumont English courses, travel arrangements and other essential information, please ask for our Camp Beaumont Overseas Guide, available from head office.

We meet students arriving at the airport and escort them to camp. If there is a delay our staff always wait. No youngster is ever left alone.

Fact

BRAINSTORMING

What do you think might be the good points and bad points in general of this kind of holiday? In pairs, jot down any ideas at all that you can think of. Try to add at least another two or three good and bad points.

GOOD POINTS

Trying new skills
Sampling independence away from home

....

....

BAD POINTS

Not enough time to learn a new skill properly
A pressurised schedule which leaves little time for yourself

....

....

When you've finished, share your ideas in your group. Add to your list any new ideas mentioned by your classmates.

3 Reading for gist   8/4/02

Read the brochure quickly for general meaning. Don't worry about understanding every word. As you read, underline anything which is factual about Camp Beaumont and circle anything which is opinion.

factual – based only on facts

4 Comprehension: Scanning the text

Scan the text to find answers to these questions.

1 How many lessons are offered per day?
2 Apart from foreign students, what other group goes to Camp Beaumont?
3 Which is the most suitable camp for children aged ten and thirteen who want to stay at the same camp?
4 You have already paid £318 for a week's course at Blundell's. How much more will you have to pay if you want to have a second week?
5 What is the normal function of Camp Beaumont centres?

5 An eye-catching advert?

A Who are the two MAIN target groups this brochure is aimed at? What persuasive techniques are used to influence the target groups?

Consider:

• opinion language
• the choice of photographs (who is in them and what they are doing)
• the layout.

B What are the factual elements of the brochure? How is the factual information displayed?

6 The best way to learn?

Do you think learning English through the medium of other activities is a good idea? If you are learning a new skill, e.g. scuba diving, what language would you expect to acquire?

Has this advert convinced you that learning English through a summer holiday camp is worth doing? Why/Why not?

7 *Quite*

The brochure says that all levels of English are catered for, whether students are *'absolute beginners or already quite fluent'*.

Quite is a modifier often used before adjectives. It usually means 'moderately' (more than 'a little' but less than 'very'). But it can also mean 'completely', when used with certain adjectives.

Example: *'Don't worry, Mrs Chavez. Your daughter will be quite safe at Camp Beaumont.'*

Which do you think it means in *'quite fluent'*, in the example above?

8 Shifting stress

The pattern of stress in some words alters when they are used as different parts of speech. For example, the words 'progress' and 'escort' found in the text can have different stress depending on whether they are used as nouns or verbs:

You'll make good prógress on the course. (noun)

You can progréss to a higher level. (verb)

An éscort will meet you at the airport. (noun)

We escórt students to the camp. (verb)

MARKING THE STRESS

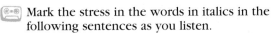 Mark the stress in the words in italics in the following sentences as you listen.

1 The farmers sell their *produce* in the market.
2 The factories *produce* spare parts for cars.
3 Please *record* all accidents in the accident book.
4 His ambition is to break the world *record* for athletics.
5 I *object* to people smoking on public transport.
6 She brought many strange *objects* back from her travels.
7 Black and red make a striking *contrast*.
8 If you *contrast* his early work with his later work, you will see how much it has changed.
9 I can't get a work *permit*.
10 The teacher does not *permit* talking in class.
11 I bought dad a birthday *present* yesterday.
12 The artist will *present* his work at the next exhibition.

Now practise saying the sentences aloud to a partner. Do you both agree about the stress?

Where does the stress fall when the word is a noun and when it is a verb? Can you work out the rule?

Outdoor activities

9 Pairwork

What is your favourite outdoor activity? Work in pairs to ask and answer these questions. If you prefer, one of your group can go to the front of the class to reply to the questions.

What/you like/do/your free time?
Where/you do it?
What/you feel like/when you do it?
What special equipment/you use?
How good/you be/at it?
How/you feel/after/activity?
Why/you recommend it?

10 Reading: Identifying free-time activities

Read the following descriptions. What free-time activities are being described? What key phrases help you to decide? Find at least four in each extract.

Match the photographs with three of the descriptions.

1 I like going to quiet places which are uncrowded. Last week I chose a route where the rough path made it hard to keep the frame straight. I got stuck in a lot of muddy holes which were almost impossible to pedal my way out of. The descent was exhilarating, though. I felt like I was flying. I reached the foot of the mountain in about half an hour. I was exhausted but delighted that I had done it. To enjoy this activity, you need a good, all-round level of fitness before you start. *mountain bike*

2 Each time I set myself a goal, which might be to get to the railway station or all around the park without stopping once. All the equipment you need is a good pair of trainers. While I'm doing it, my mind's blank. I don't think about anything. On the way home, I slow down gradually. I feel satisfied because I've achieved what I set out to do. This is a good activity for someone who enjoys being alone. *running*

3 I practise in a large sports field near my home. I fit an arrow to the bow, pull the bowstring back with all my strength and wait for the 'thunk'! I get another arrow from the quiver without pausing to check the target. My fingers and upper body have become very strong since I started playing. If you don't have the speed for ball games, this could be an ideal sport for you. *Archery*

4 We've got a large outdoor court where you can hire a racquet. I play friendly games with a partner who, like me, is not very competitive. I enjoy concentrating on the ball and I like running, so I usually get to most of the shots. I don't feel I'm very skilled but I can perform the basic strokes adequately. If you want a sociable sport, you would enjoy this. *tennis*

5 I prefer going early in the morning when everything is peaceful. I love listening to the birds and breathing the fresh, clear air. I put on the saddle and bridle and mount by putting my left foot in the stirrup. When I trot, I rise up and down in the stirrups to avoid the 'bumps'. It's an ideal activity if you prefer something non-competitive. *horse horseriding*

6 I've never felt scared or worried doing this. Even at the age of two or three, I loved submerging my face and never used artificial buoyancy aids. I also like floating on my back. I feel as though I'm weightless. It's very soothing and pleasant, and it's cheap. Everyone can enjoy this, however unfit or badly co-ordinated they think they are. *swimming*

11 Writing in a more mature style

Most IGCSE students can write a simple description of an outdoor activity they enjoy. However, writing in a way which engages your listener as well as giving facts demands more skill.

Certain language structures can help you.

The **-ing form (gerund)** is often used when describing how much you like something. Remember that *love, like, enjoy, prefer, hate* etc. are followed by *-ing* forms.
Examples: *I like being in the open air.*
I enjoy testing my own limits.

Clauses (beginning *which, where* etc.) can link two ideas and provide extra information.
Example: *There's a large outdoor court where you can hire racquets.*

Since can be used to indicate the point in time something began.
Example: *I have been skiing since I was tiny.*

Like, as, as though, as if are used to compare one thing to another.
Examples: *After waterskiing my legs feel like jelly.*
I felt as if I was flying.

Using **precise adjectives and adverbs** gives your writing more clarity.
Examples: *I felt scared.*
The descent was exhilarating.
I can perform the basic strokes adequately.

12 Analysing language structures

Study the extracts in exercise 10. Underline any structures or expressions you would like to use in writing about your own favourite outdoor activity.

13 Describing a favourite activity

Write a description of an outdoor activity you enjoy. Aim for a mature style using a wide vocabulary and a range of structures.

You need to mention

- why you like the activity
- the skills and equipment you need (check any technical words)
- when and where you can do it
- any other personal responses to it
- why other people might enjoy it too.

Write at least 100 words.

14 Reading aloud

When you've finished, read out your description to your group. If you like, you can substitute the word *'blank'* instead of naming the activity. Let them guess what you are describing.

15 Pre-listening discussion

A Have you ever been camping? Talk to your partner about what it was like. If you have never been, look at the picture and tell your partner what you think it would be like.

B What qualities do you need to be a good camper? Do you think you have them?

C Camping holidays are good fun but can sometimes be stressful too. What might people find stressful or argue with each other about on a camping trip?

16 Listening for gist   15/4/02

Paul and Marcus have just come back from their first camping holiday with the youth club. What did they find difficult about the holiday? Note three things.
Overall, do you think they enjoyed the trip despite the difficulties?

17 True/false comprehension

Decide whether the following statements about the trip are true or false.

1   Marcus was annoyed with Paul for forgetting the instruction leaflet.
2   The girls had no difficulty putting up their tent.
3   The waterproof boots let in water during the walk.

4   Paul and Marcus wanted to see a war museum rather than go on the walk. T **F**

5   The girls were attracted by the village's unusual name. **T**

6   The boys didn't think the village was more interesting than most other villages. F **T**

7   Paul and Marcus agreed about the group leader's age. F ✓

8   There was no food for breakfast because the girls had forgotten to go shopping. F ✓

9   The girls apologised for the fact that there was no food for breakfast. T **F**

10 Neither of them want to go camping again. T **F**

18 Post-listening discussion   Homework 15/4/02

A Paul and Marcus mention the uncomfortable aspects of camping like stone-cold showers. What do you think they might have enjoyed about their trip which they did not mention? Try to think of three things.

B If you went camping, where would you prefer to go? In your own country or abroad? Try to explain why.

19 Blame

Paul blames himself for forgetting the instruction leaflet. Paul and Marcus blame the girls for some of the things they didn't enjoy on holiday.

Here are some expressions people use to blame each other, admit guilt or absolve each other from blame. Tick the ones the boys use. Which expressions sound most critical? When would it be acceptable to use them? When would it be inappropriate? Think about this carefully – it's easy to give offence!

BLAMING
It's your fault.
You're responsible.
I blame you for it.
It was down to you.

ADMITTING GUILT/RESPONSIBILITY
It's my fault.
I do feel guilty.
I feel bad about it.
I'm responsible.
I should have been more careful.

ABSOLVING SOMEONE FROM BLAME
Don't blame yourself.
It wasn't your fault.
It was just one of those things.
You shouldn't feel bad about it.

20 Comparing cultures

What do you say in your language when you want to blame someone, admit guilt or absolve someone from blame? How does it compare with what is acceptable in English?

21 Functional language: Writing a dialogue

Try to think of a situation where the question of blame might arise. For example, imagine you have gone on a picnic and find that one of you didn't pack the cold drinks. You don't want to cause ill-feeling. What would you say to each other?

Write out this or a similar dialogue. Remember to refer back to exercise 19 for suitable expressions. Practise the dialogue in pairs. Finally, exchange dialogues with another pair in your group.

22 Colloquial expressions: Adjective collocations

On the tape you heard showers described as 'stone cold', bread described as 'rock hard', the night as 'pitch dark' and boots as 'brand new'.

In colloquial language, the meaning of an adjective is often emphasised by the addition of a noun or another adjective before it.
Examples: *stone cold* (noun + adjective),
          icy cold (adjective + adjective)

Combinations like these give extra impact to descriptions.

Complete the gaps in the sentences below with an adjective or noun from the box. You will need to use one word twice.

| bone crystal dirt fast freezing plain |
| sky stiff wafer wide |

1 It was _plain_ stupid of him to leave his bicycle unlocked in a busy street.

2 Wasn't Jeremy's talk fascinating? I'm afraid I don't agree. In fact, I was bored _stiff_.

3 The resort was idyllic – a beautiful sandy beach and _crystal_ clear water.

4 I was scared _stiff_ when the plane began to shake.

5 No wonder it's _freezing_ cold in here. You've left the window _wide_ open.

6 Chantal looked so pretty in her _sky_ blue outfit.

7 I was exhausted after our long trek back to the campsite. As soon as my head hit the pillow, I was _fast_ asleep.

8 Why did you buy so many bananas? I couldn't resist it. They were _dirt_ cheap.

9 These _wafer_ thin sandwiches are no good for hungry hikers.

10 The rain was lashing down, but his feet were _bone_ dry inside his new boots.

23 More colloquial expressions

Homework

Instead of 'getting up very early', you heard Marcus talk about *'Getting up at the crack of dawn'*. Like the collocations, colloquial expressions like this make what you say more emphatic.

Complete the sentences below with these colloquial phrases.

a penny to his name	a speck of dirt
a bite to eat	a stroke of work
in the nick of time	a hair out of place
a drop of rain	hear a pin drop

1 We stopped at a cafe on the way home as we hadn't had ___a bite to eat___ all day.

2 The farmers are very worried about their crops. There hasn't been ___a drop of rain___ for months.

3 The library was so quiet that you could ___hear a pin drop___

4 The hotel kitchen is spotlessly clean. You never see ___a speck of dirt___ anywhere.

5 Her appearance is immaculate. She never has ___a hair out of place___ *clean and unspoilt*

6 We were delayed on the way to the airport and only arrived for our flight ___in the nick of time___ *just in time*

7 Hassan used to be a millionaire but now he doesn't have ___a penny to his___ name *nobody knows him*

8 The workmen they employed didn't do ___a stroke of work___ all day.

Now work in pairs to create some sentences of your own with these expressions. You need to use the whole expression – you can't use just part of it.

24 Word building: Adjective suffixes

Many adjectives are formed by adding suffixes to nouns, etc. Below are some examples from the tape. Notice the way the spelling changes in some words.

waterproof (water + proof)
fortyish (forty + ish)
quaint-sounding (quaint + sounding)
picturesque (pictur\e\ + esque)
historic (histor\y\ + ic)

In groups of two or three, discuss how you could form adjectives from the following words by adding suitable suffixes. In some cases, more than one suffix is possible.

Check your ideas in a dictionary. Then try to create sentences of your own.

1	bullet	4	odd
2	twenty	5	child
3	irony	6	statue

7	Arab	11	Islam
8	boy	12	pleasant
9	panorama	13	scene
10	sound	14	pink

25 Punctuating direct speech

In written English, inverted commas (also called quotation marks) must be put around all the words someone actually says. You open inverted commas at the beginning of the speech and close them at the end.

Study the examples below of the way direct speech is punctuated. Focus in particular on

- the use of capital letters
- the position of other punctuation marks (commas, question marks, etc.)
- the correct way to punctuate quoted words within direct speech.

1 Melissa said, 'I don't have any money, do you?'
2 Gran paused and reached into her bag. 'Do you want to see our holiday photographs? We've just had them developed,' she said.
3 'Have another piece of cake,' urged mum. 'I baked it specially.'
4 John shouted, 'You tell me, "Don't worry about it", but I can't help worrying.'
5 'Look out!' screamed Darren. 'Can't you see that lorry?!'

PRACTICE *18/4/02 Homework in this book*

Complete the punctuation in the following conversation. You need to add inverted commas and commas.

"What was the best part of your holiday in America?" Naomi asked when she saw Kevin again.

"Going along Highway One from Los Angeles to San Francisco" said Kevin without hesitation. I wouldn't have missed it for the world."

"What's so special about Highway One?" Naomi asked wrinkling her nose. Isn't it just another dead straight American highway?

Well replied Kevin. The road runs between a range of mountains on one side and the shores of the Pacific on the other. The views are incredibly beautiful, Seagulls fly over crashing waves. There are great cliffs studded with redwoods. Yes, he paused for a moment it's truly magnificent.

"What was the weather like? Naomi asked thoughtfully. Every time I checked the international weather forecast there was one word hot.

In fact Kevin laughed we had stormy weather but when the sun broke through it created fantastic rainbows. We visited a jade cove where you can hunt for jade. Anything you find is yours and I'd almost given up looking when I found this. He reached into his pocket and pulled out a tiny green fragment. Here, he said it's for you.

Tourism: The pros and cons

26 Brainstorming   *good*   *bad*

By the year 2000, tourism is expected to be the world's biggest single industry.

Work in groups of three or four and jot down anything you can think of under the following headings. Don't worry if it doesn't seem relevant. Pool your ideas with other groups and add any new ones. Keep your notes carefully as you are going to need them later.

A What are some of the pleasures and drawbacks of being a tourist?
PLEASURES
You can see a different way of life.

....

....

DRAWBACKS
Your holiday is too short to get a real understanding of the country.

....

....

B What are the advantages and disadvantages to the host country of a rise in tourism?
ADVANTAGES
It creates jobs.

....

....

DISADVANTAGES
Pollution increases.
Foreign companies take the profits from tourism back to their own countries.

....

....

C How can tourists behave responsibly when they go abroad?
They can buy from local traders.

....

....

Tourism concern is an agency which wants to develop 'sustainable tourism'. This means that tourists try to make sure that tourism benefits the local community. For example, they fly with a local airline and use local accommodation rather than international hotels. What do you think of this idea?

A You are going to read an article about tourism in Sicily and Sardinia, two islands off the Italian coast. First, describe what you can see in the pictures.

B What do you think a holiday on these islands would be like? What do you think you would enjoy? Would you find anything difficult to get used to? Would you like the opportunity to go? Why/Why not?

C What do you think foreign visitors expect your own country to be like? Are their perceptions correct, do you think? How do foreign visitors to your country usually behave? If you get a lot of visitors, does the atmosphere in your area change? How? Try to explain your views.

in this *horgather*

Can you match the following words from the article with their definitions?

1	whiff H	**A**	to shine with a warm, bright light
2	gilded E	**B**	growing thickly and strongly
3	glow incandescently A	**C**	strong
4	pastures F	**D**	to fly high
5	enigmatic J	**E**	covered or decorated with gold
6	soar D	**F**	grassy fields
7	gorges G	**G**	steep, narrow valleys
8	lush B	**H**	a brief smell
9	secluded I	**I**	private, hidden away
10	robust C	**J**	mysterious

Read the article carefully, underlining the descriptive language as you read.

3.

Ami form

Now try to answer the following questions.

1 What, according to the writer, is the main reason that Sicily and Sardina have remained unspoiled? According
2 Why is the writer reminded of North Africa? Give two examples.
3 What has been the result of the combination of Arabic and Italian influences on the architecture? has been produced some of the most beautifully decorated building in this part of the world.
4 What sort of activities is Sardina well suited to? Give two examples.
5 What is a striking feature of the Sardinian landscape? Give one example.

1 According to the writer, is the main reason that Sicily and Sardina have remained unspoiled is the Historically in which local character is preserved and physcial separation from the mainland

2. The writer remined of of North Africa because the Palermo, with its souk-ish Vuccria street and market and couscous cafes, ther with an exciting whiff of North Africa

4. Sardina is well suited to remote valleys and visiting pastures.

5 A striking feature of the Sardinian is Eagles and black vultures soar over the mountains, pink flamingos flash their wings by the coast.

OFFSHORE ITALY

Unspoiled, even wild, the Italian islands of Sicily and Sardinia give an unexpected flavour to holidays in the Mediterranean.

Holidays are often about nostalgia. What most of us want is to visit a 'real' country. We want unspoiled landscapes, markets, traditions, cuisine and distinctive architecture. We want people who are welcoming yet different from us.

Historically there are two ways in which local character is preserved. The first is poverty; the second is physical separation from the mainland – the key reason why Sicily and Sardinia have stayed unspoiled.

SICILY– MOSAICS, RUINS AND GLEAMING CHURCHES

I recently went to Taormina, Sicily's best-known seaside resort. Perching high on Monte Tauro, a funicular ride from its two sweeping bays below, its location is so charming that D H Lawrence made it his home for a while. Now, although the maze of traffic-free medieval streets is crowded in high summer, and pools are stacked up in blue terraces overlooking the sea, nothing has diminished the town's magic. After all, what other major holiday resort has a backdrop that includes a world-class Graeco-Roman amphitheatre, ravishing hills and a 3323-metre volcano, Mount Etna?

Here, in the east of Sicily, there's a link with southern Italy, but move further west and the influence is decidedly more Arab. By the time you enter the Sicilian capital, Palermo, with its souk-ish Vucciria street market and couscous cafés, there's an exciting whiff of North Africa.

In Palermo this fusion of the two traditions has produced some of the most beautifully decorated buildings in this part of the world. There's the Cappella Reale, the chapel which King Roger II built for himself in the 12th century. Entering from the central courtyard, it takes a while for your eyes to adjust to the darkness. But gradually the gilded mosaics which line the walls come alive; while overhead, richly carved ceiling paintings of exotic gardens and hunting scenes glow incandescently against a deep blue sky. The chapel is the undisputed jewel of the city, yet a few kilometres away, on the hilltop at Monreale, is a cathedral which rivals it for the sheer unbroken beauty of its mosaics.

Sicily may not have as much mountain wildness as Sardinia, but it is a lovely broad landscape with rolling plains and corn-coloured hills. Life is taken at a relatively slow pace and sleepy hilltop towns come to life only for a festival or wedding (both astonishingly frequent events). In some of this lovely country, farmers are waking up to the possibilities of *agriturismo*, boosting an income by offering hospitality (converted cottages and, sometimes, country food) to enthusiastic tourists.

Visiting Sicily now, it is easy to forget that for nearly three thousand years it was the most fought-over island in the Mediterranean. The ancient Greeks loved it as one of their richest colonies and left behind a marvellous (and well-preserved) collection of temples to prove it.

SARDINIA – WILD AT HEART, WITH GLAMOROUS RESORTS

Sardinia has some of the most astonishing country in Europe. Much of the population is concentrated in its two main towns, Cagliari in the south and Sassari in the north, so in the centre of the island shepherds still herd sheep and goats to remote valleys, visiting pastures used in Roman times. The land is dotted with enigmatic 'nuraghi', mysterious stone dwellings left behind by the Sardinians' prehistoric ancestors.

Eagles and black vultures soar over the mountains, pink flamingos flash their wings by the coast – everywhere you look is a riot of nature with gorges, caves, wild boar, deer and flowers. All this makes Sardinia a terrific destination for fishing, cycling, walking and riding.

Yet despite extensive areas of wilderness, the island has very sophisticated tourist villages and some of the best resort hotels in all Italy.

One of the most successful of the tourist developments is Forte Village, first opened in 1970. Set in 55 acres of lush garden with a wide range of sports on offer, there are three hotels to choose from, plus a selection of secluded cottages, entertainment and childminding services. It may not be the 'real' Sardinia, but it's hard to find a better quality holiday resort.

32 Post-reading discussion

The writer says that when tourists go on holiday they want to visit a 'real' country. They want *unspoiled landscapes, traditions and people who are welcoming yet different*. However, she also mentions the popularity of specially built 'tourist villages' which offer entertainment and childminding services.

Do you think meeting the needs tourists have for comfort can ever be in conflict with protecting a beautiful landscape and ancient traditions? Do tourists expect too much? What are your views?

33 Adverbs as intensifiers   *22/4/02*

We can use adverbs before adjectives to make the adjective stronger. There are several examples in the text:

beautifully decorated (line 50)
richly carved (line 59)
relatively slow (line 72)
astonishingly frequent (line 75)

Combining adverbs appropriately with adjectives is a matter of practice. There are no hard and fast rules. Choose adverbs from the box to complete the sentences below. After you have finished, compare your answers with a partner's. Sometimes more than one answer is possible.

alarmingly appallingly badly dazzlingly *to make* *unable to see*
faintly fully painstakingly seriously *very much*
strangely strikingly surprisingly utterly *completely*

(handwritten above box: worry shocking infant very bad)

1 I found the standard of service in the hotel *appallingly* bad. ✓

(9/12 in margin)

2 He has *fully* recovered from his accident.

3 The temple is a *strikingly* attractive building. ✓

4 The buildings were *badly* bombed in the war. ✓

5 I was *seriously* ill in hospital. ✓

6 The beggar was *badly* destitute. ✗ *utterly without food*

7 You'll need sunglasses as the midday sun is *dazzlingly* bright. ✓

8 They expected prices to be high on holiday but everything was *utterly* cheap. ✓

9 The ancient relics in the museum had been *painstakingly* restored. ✓

10 Even after washing, the coffee stain on that white tablecloth is still *utterly* visible. *faintly*

11 We held our breath as the coach went *alarmingly* fast around steep mountain bends. ✓

12 The disco, which was usually very noisy, was *surprisingly* quiet. ✓

34 Imagery in descriptions

Striking images convey a lot of information in a few words.

The writer describes Sicily as *'a lovely, broad landscape with rolling plains and corn-coloured hills'*.

Does she describe everything about the Sicilian countryside or select a few key features? What kind of image does the phrase 'rolling plains and corn-coloured hills' convey? *select a few key features*

What kind of images of Sardinia come to your mind when you read that *'shepherds still herd sheep and goats to remote valleys, visiting pastures used in Roman times'* *(quiet)*
or
'Eagles and black vultures soar over the mountains, pink flamingos flash their wings by the coast'? *(huge birds, fly)*

Study the examples carefully and underline key adjectives or images that suggest the area is still wild and untouched by modern life.

35 Adjectives: Quality not quantity

Using numerous adjectives before a noun is unsophisticated. It's far better to be selective.

How many adjectives have been used before the nouns in the following examples? How successfully do they evoke a particular atmosphere?

traffic-free medieval streets (lines 28-29)
exotic gardens (line 60)
sleepy hilltop towns (line 73)

Choose an example of descriptive writing from the text which you think contains pleasing images. Comment on it in the same way.

36 Comparing two styles

Compare the following two descriptions of the same place. In which extract is the style more mature? What techniques have been used to create a more sophisticated effect?

STYLE ONE

The village is very, very nice. Tourists like going there but there is not a lot of new development, crowds or traffic or things like that. There are stone houses near the harbour. The buildings are not painted in dark colours. They are painted white or cream. The buildings have blue, grey or brown shutters. There are hills around the village. There are many pine trees on the hills. The view from the top of the hills is very good. You can see the whole area.

STYLE TWO

The village is strikingly pretty and unspoilt. The houses, rising up from the harbour, are pale-coloured with painted shutters and made of stone. The village is surrounded by pine-clad hills which provide panoramic views of the area.

37 Developing a mature style

There are a number of ways you can make your writing more mature:

- Choose your adjectives with care and use them **precisely**. You don't need a great many – just a few fresh or powerful ones.

- Remember that you can create adjectives by adding **suffixes** to nouns or adjectives, e.g. *panoramic, colourful*. (See exercise 24.)

- You can make adjectives more emphatic by using adverbs as **intensifiers**, e.g. *staggeringly, exceptionally*. (See exercise 33.)

- Adjective **collocations,** such as *crystal clear*, are another way of adding impact to your descriptions. (See exercise 22.)

- Use **clauses** to link ideas beginning with *which, where, when* etc., and **phrases** beginning with *made of, with* etc.

- Use **comparisons**: *like, as, as though, as if.*

- All the above techniques will help you to write more **concisely** – using fewer words to greater effect.

PRACTICE   *Read, and how to improve yet*

Now rewrite this description in a more mature style.

The town developed around a marketplace. The marketplace is very, very old. It is in the shape of a rectangle. In the town, the people live in the way that they used to live hundreds of years ago. They like visitors, they do not commit crimes. They will always help you. You do not need to be afraid of them. They wear clothes that are very simple. They wear long, loose, white cotton robes. The town has many very, very old buildings. The buildings were built in the 13th century. It also has many restaurants. There are many different kinds of restaurants. You can eat nice food. The food is from different cultures.

[handwritten annotations: small; busy; has reisted for a long time; the same; are; drn't; fear; casual; nice; delicous; are]

38 Writing your own description *in ex book*

Think about your last holiday or day out. Try to recall what was distinctive about the experience. Was it the people's way of life? The landscape? The food? The places of interest? Where you stayed? Or a combination of all of these?

What particular images come to your mind? When you are ready, jot them down. Don't worry about trying to write neatly or accurately. Just let the words flow out onto the page.

Re-read what you have written and select the most outstanding images. Concentrate on those that convey the flavour of the experience. Don't try to describe everything.

Now try to write a sophisticated description. Remember, your writing will be more mature if you use the techniques you have learned in the unit so far. Write about 100 words.

INTERNATIONAL OVERVIEW

The bar chart shows how important the income from tourism is for a number of central and southern African countries. Which country receives about half of what South Africa gets from tourism?

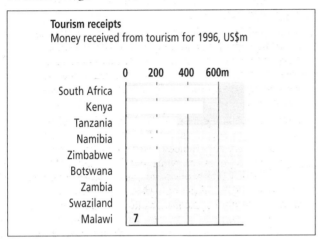

Can you find out how much your country receives from tourism?

'More tourists = more economic and social benefits'

Prepare a talk about five minutes on the above topic for your group.

PLANNING THE TALK

Remember to plan your talk first, before you begin. Use the notes you made earlier to help you produce a list of key points under main headings.

Give your talk depth by adding examples of your own. Try to think of specific ways tourism affects your country. What have you noticed yourself about the behaviour of tourists, the effect they have on the environment/the local atmosphere etc?

If you have travelled, you could compare tourism in your country with tourism abroad. What was your own experience of being a tourist in a foreign country like? How were you treated? What did you learn from that about the treatment of tourists in your own country?

PRESENTATION

Use your notes to jog your memory, but don't read from a 'script'. It is artificial and boring. Try to interest your listeners. Make eye contact with them, speak clearly and be prepared to answer questions.

BEING A GOOD LISTENER

Remember, it's kind and courteous to show an interest in the speaker. Listen attentively and have at least one question or comment ready to put to the speaker at the end.

ex book

Words from names

The island of Sardinia gave its name to *sardines*. Many words in English are derived from the names of people or places.

Try to match these names to the people in the sentences below. Check the meaning of any unfamiliar words.

**Morse   Volta   Cardigan   Fahrenheit   Marx
Pasteur   Diesel   Sandwich**

1   Lord <u>sandwich</u> didn't have time for a proper meal so he <u>devised</u> a way of eating meat between two slices of bread.

2   Lord <u>Cardigan</u> was the first person to wear a long sleeved jacket made of wool.

3   Louis <u>Pasteur</u> invented a method of making milk safe to drink.

4   Gabriel <u>Fahrenheit</u> developed a thermometer which showed boiling and freezing points.

5   Samuel <u>Morse</u> invented a secret code to be used for sending messages.

6   Alessandro <u>Volta</u> invented the electric battery.

7   Karl <u>Marx</u> developed the idea of communism.

8   Rudolf <u>Diesel</u> devised a special type of oil-burning engine.

Can suffixes be added to any of the names? Which ones?

Are any words in your own language derived from these names? Compare ideas with your classmates.

More homophones

homework in text bk

Problems with homophones are the root of many spelling errors. Remember that homophones have the same sound but different spellings. They have to be memorised as there is no rule. (Look back at exercises 19 and 20 in Unit 1.)

Work with a partner to try to find a homophone for each of these words. The words have come from the texts you have read in the unit so far.

1	real	rail	7	scene	seen
2	boar	bored	8	flower	
3	sea	see	9	right	write
4	soar	saw	10	blue	
5	two	to	11	sail	
6	herd	hurt	12	deer	dear

Finally, put each homophone into a sentence.

Personal challenges

42 Reading a model letter

Read the letter which describes an activity holiday.
How good a description do you think it is?

43 Comprehension

1 Where did Rosie go on holiday? *Wales*
2 How did she feel before she went? Were her feelings justified? *(correct)* *scared, yes*
3 What was her favourite activity? Why? *Canoeing session*
4 Why does she think Lucia would like the same type of holiday?
5 How does she feel overall about the trip?

44 Analysing the letter

1 What is the main topic of each paragraph?

2 Analyse the language Rosie uses to describe:
   • the place
   • the activities
   • the instructor
   • her feelings.

3 How does she close the letter? Consider the last sentence of the final paragraph, and the closing phrase.

45 Vocabulary: The weather

The weather, particularly on holiday, is a popular topic of conversation among English people. Decide whether the following statements about the weather are likely to be true or false.

1 I was pleased to find a lot of slush when I went skiing.
2 The blizzard made driving home easy.
3 Early in the morning the grass is wet with dew.
4 People usually switch on the lights at dusk.
5 I put on my sunglasses because the sky was overcast.
6 The weather was so mild that we did not need coats.
7 It's not worth hanging out the washing as it has begun to drizzle.
8 The gale blew several trees over.
9 Constant low temperatures and hard frosts meant there was no chance of a thaw.
10 Farmers are very happy about the recent drought.

46 Spelling revision

Some adjectives are formed from nouns by adding **-y**. You need to remember the rules for adding suffixes.

A final **-e** in a word is usually dropped when adding **-y**: *ice icy*

The rule for one-syllable words is that we double the final consonant if the word ends in **one** vowel and **one** consonant:

sun sunny BUT *cloud cloudy*

Dear Lucia,

Just a quick letter to let you know about my activity holiday in Wales. As you know, I was a bit scared about going away by myself, but I loved every minute of it. The group leaders were caring and thoughtful and I never felt alone.

We stayed in a strikingly scenic area in a converted boarding school. I shared my room with two other girls and we are now firm friends. I had heard the weather in that area is rather unpredictable but we were lucky. It was mostly fine, with only one heavy downpour.

Each day we chose an activity from an incredibly varied programme. I liked the canoeing sessions best. We had a very experienced instructor who made us laugh and forget our nervousness. First he taught us safety drills, which were quite easy to learn. Then we practised our technique on a placid river which stretched through a pleasant valley. It's amazing what you can accomplish in a week. I now feel quite confident. I was thrilled because I didn't capsize the canoe once!

I think you would really enjoy this kind of holiday too, Lucia. It's stimulating, you feel independent and you get the chance to learn new skills in a safe and friendly environment. As for me, I only wish it could begin again!

Write soon.

Love,

Rosie

47 Writing about the weather

Choose an appropriate noun from the box and change it into an adjective to fill each gap in the postcard. Take care with your spelling.

storm	muddy *smoke*	hazey	frosty	misty *cloudy air*
rain	chilly	fog		

Dear All, *cold* *freezing* *very* *thick mist* *ice*

We're having a good time here but the weather isn't great. Every day starts ___frosty___ or even ___chilly___. This clears up by midday and we get a little ___mist___ sunshine. We had a ___rainy___ day yesterday and the ground was too ___muddy___ for walking. It's generally ___chilly___ and I'm glad we brought warm clothes. Our boat trip was cancelled because it was ___stormy___. We're hoping for calmer weather tomorrow.

Love,

Ashwin

48 Discussion: Voluntary work abroad

Spending a year in a developing country as a volunteer in a school, hospital or a charity project is very popular with young people. However, it is sometimes claimed that young, inexperienced students from affluent nations have little to offer the world's poorer countries. They enter a difficult situation with little training or worldly knowledge. They might have ideas which are inappropriate for the country. In addition, they might be very homesick – almost an extra burden on the charity.

How far do you agree with these ideas? Is there any way problems like these could be overcome? Discuss your views with your partner.

49 Building a letter from notes

This letter was written by a student to her old school friends. She is working as a voluntary teacher in Cameroon. Use the notes to build up a complete letter.

Dear Everyone,

The first month/I be/very lonely/but now/I begin/enjoy/myself here. The climate be/warm/sunny/except for/last night/there be/big storm/which turn/paths/into rivers.

The family/I stay with/be/very kind. The house be/three bedroomed/and be quite comfortable. I be/very close/my 'sisters' who/tell me off/if I do anything wrong! Each morning I wake up/sound/exotic birds/dart/among trees.

Yesterday I take/bus/through breathtaking countryside/to local city. I go/bustling market. Everywhere/people sell things/but I be not sure/who buy!

I help/teach/young children/junior school. The children be/delightful/and be/very polite. The work be/demanding but rewarding.

I miss everyone/home/but I feel/grow up quickly/and I be/more confident now.

Love to you all,

Elaine

50 Look, say, cover, write, check

The following words are especially problematic. Most of them come from various exercises in the unit. Use the 'look, say, cover, write check' method to help you learn them.

1	Mediterranean	6	exhilarating
2	restaurant	7	jewel
3	separate	8	jewellery
4	separation	9	confidence
5	glamour	10	accommodation

51 Discussion: Working as a tour guide

A Talk to your partner about what you can see in the photograph on page 113.

B Study these comments made by tour guides working in the tourist industry. Discuss each of them with your partner and decide if this work attracts either of you.

1 It's essential that you like travel and, above all, have a lot of patience with people.

2 Although the clients are on holiday, you've got to remember *you're* not on holiday and always be prepared to be responsible.

3 Touring a country with a group makes it hard to keep up friendships at home.

4 You have to be able to live for two weeks out of a suitcase or rucksack.

5 You're with the group 24 hours a day on a tour. There's not much privacy.

6 You've got to be well organised and methodical at all times. The arrangements you are in charge of can be very complicated.

52 Reordering a magazine article

The following article was printed in a school magazine. Reorder the sentences logically and divide the article into three paragraphs. Underline the words and phrases which help you to link the text.

LIFE AS A RESORT REP IN RHODES *by a former pupil*

a Initially, they relied a lot on me to explain about the banks and shops and to recommend local restaurants and the best sightseeing trips.

b Finally, I hope this has given you some idea of what life as a resort rep is all about.

c The work itself is very varied and I have the opportunity to meet new people and see interesting places.

d I have groups of all ages.

e In addition, there are many stunning, unspoilt beaches and peaceful villages.

f It is the first time they have been abroad.

g Although it gives you the chance to have lots of fun, it's not all glamour.

h Now, however, they are much more relaxed.

i However, if any of you are keen to get involved, I would definitely recommend it!

j It's got an impressive old town and a new town with graceful, modern buildings.

k In fact, they are more independent than many much younger tourists.

l First of all, let me give you an idea of what Rhodes is like.

m Next, I'd like to tell you a bit about my job.

n At the moment, for example, I'm looking after a group of elderly people.

Exam-format questions

Writing

1 You have just returned from a week's activity holiday. Write an account of the holiday for your school newsletter. In the article you should:

- describe the place
- say what the weather was like
- say what the instructors were like
- say what activity/activities you enjoyed doing on holiday
- explain why you think other people would enjoy such a holiday.

The pictures may give you some ideas, but you are free to write about any activity holiday of your choice. Write about 200 words.

homework

2 Form-filling

Lin Ho and a group of school friends recently spent a fascinating week visiting Mulu National Park in Sarawak, Malaysia.

Lin stayed in a basic but adequate longhouse by the river on the outskirts of the park. She reached the park by boat from Miri. She walked along nature trails, explored limestone caves and observed birds and wildlife. She particularly enjoyed seeing a cloud of bats flying out at dusk from the Deer Cave. She nearly got hurt when she disturbed a poisonous snake whilst out walking but managed to get away safely.

The guide provided was extremely helpful and told Lin and her friends all about the ecosystem of the park, and what they were and were not allowed to do whilst there.

Lin is 17 years old. She lives at 12 Legaspi Towers, 200 Roxas Road, Metro, Manilla, Philippines.

After the holiday, Lin filled in a holiday evaluation form for the tour operator, giving her opinion of the trip to Mulu National Park. Please complete the form.

GOING PLACES HOLIDAY EVALUATION FORM

Please use block capitals for your name and address.

Name: Lin   Ho

Address: 12 Legaspi Towers, 200 Roxas Road, Metro, Manilla, Philipiness

Please circle your age group:

(16–19)   20–25   Over 25

For the following questions, please tick the boxes or write in the spaces as indicated.

Length of stay:

Less than a week ☐   Seven days ☑   Two weeks ☐

Longer (please specify) _____

How did you reach the Park?

By boat ☑   By air ☐

By another means (please specify) ____Miri____

Accommodation:

Riverside accommodation ☑   Hotel ☐   Campsite ☐

Other (please specify) _____

The standard of accommodation was:

luxurious ☐   comfortable ☐   average ☑   poor ☐

What activities did you participate in?

Visiting caves ☑ Mountain trekking ☐ Nature trails ☑ Birdwatching ☑ River boat sailing ☐

The guide was:

generally helpful and well informed ☑   not as well-informed as I would have liked ☐   unhelpful ☐

Did you encounter any dangers on the trip?   **If *yes*, did the encounter require First Aid?**

Yes ☑   No ☐   Yes ☑   No ☐

What was the highlight of the trip, in your opinion?

Thank you for filling in this evaluation form!

3 A travel company 'Explore Worldwide' awarded you first prize in a recent competition. You were given the chance to travel to any of the destinations mentioned below. You have just arrived home from your holiday. Write a letter to a friend about the holiday.

In your letter you should:

- explain why you chose that particular holiday
- say what you did on holiday
- tell your friend about special places of interest you visited
- say why you would recommend this place to other people.

Write about 200 words.

EXPLORE Travel to new and unusual destinations!

Adventure Tours Worldwide

Many of our trips have a strong cultural feeling. The focus might be the local culture, ancient classical sites, native markets or other special places. Short walks of 2-4 hours to visit unusual sites are often an integral part of a trip. Perhaps exploring the glittering Islamic architecture of cities like Isfahan in Iran, wandering through the bustling street markets of Vietnam or discovering the ancient Mayan temples of Guatemala.

Wilderness Experience

Discovering a remote wilderness area is a rewarding and memorable experience. Such places have a strong fascination for the intrepid traveller. Discover the haunting beauty of the living rainforest in Borneo or Costa Rica, and experience the powerful mystique of deserts like the Namib, Gobi or Sahara.

Wildlife and Natural History

We visit many of the world's greatest game parks – tracking rare mountain gorillas in Uganda, bush walking with guides in Kenya, or paddling a canoe on Zimbabwe's Zambezi river. Throughout the world, whether it's photographing ring-tail lemurs in Madagascar's rainforests, searching for tiger on elephant-back in India or whale watching off Newfoundland, our wildlife safaris offer a thrilling encounter with animals in their natural environment.

Major Treks

Some tours offer major treks for strong mountain walkers. These can involve walking for between 6 to 8 hours per day, sometimes at elevations over 10,000 feet. Such trips usually involve support vehicles, porters or pack animals. This allows access to some of the world's great mountain ranges like the Himalayas or Andes.
You could hike the ancient Inca trail to the Lost City of Machu Picchu in Peru, trek through the jungles to Mt Kinabalu in Borneo, follow the famous Mont Blanc circuit in the Alps ... .

Raft and River Journeys

River journeys can last from a few hours to several days, and range from 2-person inflatables on the Dordogne River in France to the excitement of an Amazon riverboat in Brazil. Or all the fun and thrills of whitewater rafting along the wild Trisuli River in Nepal. No previous experience is necessary and the appropriate safety skills are quickly learned.

4 A friend has written to you complaining that he/she is bored and asking you to recommend a new spare time activity.

Write a letter to your friend suggesting a spare time activity you think he or she would enjoy. In your letter you should:

- describe the activity
- explain when and where it can be done
- say if special equipment or training is required
- explain why you think he/she would enjoy it.

Write about 200 words.

Oral assessment

Tourism

Imagine that an area near where you live is going to be developed for tourism. Discuss with the examiner or your partner the advantages and disadvantages this development might bring. What suggestions would you like to make to ensure that the development is controlled properly? How could local people benefit from the development?

You are not allowed to make any written notes.

EXAMINER'S TIPS

1 Students often say they have difficulty concentrating on a topic for very long. We become skilled at taking in condensed information from different sources (TV, radio, computers etc.) but find sustaining attention on a topic for a longer time quite hard.

Try to strengthen your powers of concentration. Time your ability to concentrate on a topic without getting distracted or having a break. Gradually try to extend the length of time you can do this. If distracting thoughts come, try to bring your mind back to what you are doing. Slowly, you will build up the length of time you can concentrate. This will empower you, not only for exams, but for the rest of your life.

EXAM STRATEGY

2 Read the composition question carefully and underline what you have to do. If you are given a detailed stimulus, such as a printed text from a magazine, be extra careful. Make sure you only write what is expected of you.

3 Make a very brief plan before you begin. Students sometimes panic at the thought of planning because they think it will use up valuable time. However, it is essential if you are to have a clear structure for your writing. If there is no time to write a complete essay, a clear plan will gain some marks.

4 Try to draw on personal experience in developing ideas for a description. This will make writing come more easily and convey more individuality to the examiner.

Aim to produce a mature style by using some of the techniques you've developed in this unit. Avoid lots of bald, short sentences with the words 'nice' or 'good'. Use clauses, comparisons, unusual adjectives and images to make your descriptions interesting and distinctive.

5 Description alone is not enough. You will have to explain your reasons for liking something. You usually have to say why you think other people would enjoy whatever it is too. Try to give clear, interesting reasons that relate sensibly to your topic.

6 As always, check through your work for mistakes in spelling, grammar and punctuation.

Make sure you have written in paragraphs. If you did not, indicating where they should be is the next best thing. Aim to leave enough time to do this.

7 In the exam you will be required to scan read an advert, notice or page from a brochure for factual detail. Look for clues to meaning from pictures, headings etc. first. Then read the information quickly to get the sense before you try to answer the questions. Usually it's possible to 'spot' the information in the text.

Sometimes information is given about prices, total amounts etc. Careful reading is required, not adding or subtracting skills.

Unit focus

In this unit you have developed skills for **describing places and activities**. This is practice for Papers 1/2, Part 3.

You have read an **advertising brochure** and answered questions on **factual detail**. This is practice for Papers 1/2, Part 1.

You have read and answered comprehension questions on a detailed travel article. This is also practice for Papers 1/2, Part 1.

You have listened to a conversation about a camping holiday and answered true/false questions. This is practice for Paper 3, Part 3 and Paper 4, Part 2.

You have presented a short talk on a topical issue. This is practice for Papers 5/6.

Student Life

29/4/02

Challenges of student life

MARCH

19 MONDAY
10.30 Anatomy lecture
(Pasteur Building)
3.00 Biology lecture
8.00 Drama Society?

20 TUESDAY
11.00 Biology practical
-1.00 (Main lab)
3.00 Tennis lesson
5.30 Coffee with Andy?

21 WEDNESDAY
10.00-12.00 Chemistry practical
(lab B)
4.00 Tutorial, Prof Wilkin
(Deadline for psychology essay)

1 Completing a checklist

In Britain and some other countries it is traditional for students to leave home and attend a college or university in another town. This is usually an exciting and challenging time. If you were to leave home to study, what do you think you would look forward to? What do you think you might find difficult?

Work by yourself. To help focus your thoughts, complete the checklist on the next page. Mark the ideas like this:

✓✓ *I'd really look forward to this.*
✓ *I wouldn't mind this.*
? *I'm not sure how I'd feel about this.*
✗ *This would definitely worry me. I don't know how I'd cope.*

☑ Having my own place

☑ Shopping for food and other essentials

☑ Making sure I eat regularly and sensibly

☑ Cooking for myself

☐ Finding new friends

☑ Organising myself and working alone

☑ Managing on a budget

☑ Being more responsible for my own studies

☑ Deciding how to spend my free time

☑ Doing my own laundry

☑ Keeping where I live clean and tidy

☑ Being more responsible for my own health

☑ Keeping in touch with my family and friends

If you have already left home to study, mark the checklist according to what you know about your ability to cope from your actual experience:

✓✓   *I've really enjoyed this.*
✓   *This has been demanding but I've managed.*
?   *I'm still learning to cope with this.*
✗   *This is a problem for me.*

30/4/02

2 Before you listen: Interactive skills

You are going to analyse the way two teenagers talking about starting university interact with each other.

Before you listen, answer these questions:

that you have a lot to answer.

*   What do you think makes a good listener?
*   What makes a conversation lively and interesting?
*   What makes it dull or boring?
*   A good conversation may be likened to a ping pong game. Why?

IMPROVING COMMUNICATION

Here are some strategies people use to improve communication. Can you extend the list?

Using good body language
Looking and sounding interested. Making eye contact. Smiling and nodding.

Asking open questions
How/What do you feel/think about ....?
Why ....?
Where ....?
Is there anything else ....?

Spoken encouragement
That's interesting. Tell me more.
That surprises me. I've always thought you were a capable student/a confident cook, etc.

Paraphrasing
You mean ....?
What you're trying to say is ....?
In other words you feel ....?

Asking for more information/clarification
Why do you feel like that? Can you explain a bit more?
I'm not sure I follow you. Can you give me an example?

Reflecting the speaker's feelings/state of mind
I can see you're excited/anxious/at the thought of starting university/your new independence/developing a new social life.

Making suggestions/offering advice
Maybe you could .....
If I were you I'd .....
Your best idea would be to .....
Have you considered .....?
Why don't you .....?

2/5/02

3 Reading and listening at the same time

Now follow the conversation. As you listen, underline examples of interactive techniques.

Alison: I'm really looking forward to having my own room when I start college.

Peter: Why do you feel like that?

Alison: Well, I've always had to share with my younger sister and she keeps bursting in when I'm trying to have a few moments to myself. She's got another annoying habit too. She's always borrowing my clothes without asking.

Peter: I can see you'll be glad to get some privacy. But won't it be a bore keeping your own place clean and tidy?

Alison: No, because I like to keep things in order. How do *you* feel about going to college?

Peter: Actually, I'm a bit nervous about leaving home and coping alone.

Alison: That surprises me. You always seem so confident.

Peter: People think I am, but I don't think I'll be very good at looking after myself. To be honest, I've never even made myself beans on toast. Mum always does the washing and ironing so I've no experience of that either.

Alison: So what you're really saying is that it's the chores that are bothering you rather than your social life?

Peter: Yes, you could say that.

Alison: Well, how about learning now? Get your Mum to teach you a few easy recipes. You could even have a go at ironing a shirt! Why not do it while you've still got someone around to show you?

Peter: Now, that's a good idea. Perhaps I will. Is there anything else about leaving home that you're worried about?

Alison: Yes. I'm really hoping to have a good social life. I think I'm good at making friends, and I like parties and going to clubs. But I'm sure money will be a big issue.

Peter: I'm not sure I follow you. What do you mean?

Alison: I mean I'll have to be careful that I don't spend all my money at once. I'm really impulsive in shops. I don't know what I'm going to do about it.

Peter: Maybe you could work out a budget, so you know how much you'll need each week for things like rent and food. It's the opposite for me. My family can't afford to give me a lot of money, so I'll need a part-time job to get through college. There's no way I want to get into debt.

Alison: I've heard they need helpers in the college social centre. It might be a good idea to contact them. There are usually some part-time jobs in the restaurant or the office. You get paid and you can get into all the events for nothing. What do you think?

Peter: Thanks for the tip. I'll think it over.

4 Conversation study

Do you feel the conversation between Peter and Alison sounds friendly? With a partner, try to work out the tone of the conversation. To help you do this, circle an example in the dialogue which illustrates each of these points.

a The speaker shows a desire to understand.
b The speaker offers advice in an understated way.
c The speaker feels warm and positive towards the other person.
d The speaker is using a chatty, informal register.

5 Developing your own conversation

Look back at the list you marked in exercise 1 about the challenges of going to college. Think about the reasons you had for your answers. When you're ready, work in pairs to develop a conversation like the one above.

You can base the conversation on starting college or any other situation you find challenging, such as going away to stay with friends, starting a new school, or going on a group holiday without your family.

Remember:

* Explain your ideas clearly. Give reasons and examples.
* Say things which are true about yourself.
* Be good listeners to each other – interact well.
* Try to offer appropriate advice.
* Don't forget your body language.

6 Taping your conversation

Why not tape your conversation and listen to it carefully? How well did you interact? Does it sound friendly and supportive? Have you helped each other explain your ideas?

7 Comparing languages

You might like to tape an informal discussion in your first language and compare the similarities and differences in interactive patterns with those of English. How do these affect the tone of the conversation?

8 Reading and discussing a problem letter

Read this extract from a letter written by Sheryl, a young university student, to a friend. What does she enjoy about university? What is she finding difficult? Did you note any of these points yourself in your own discussion?

Dear Kate,

I can't believe I'm already in my sixth week of university. I'm thrilled that I've got a grant* rather than being dependent on Mum and Dad.

I meant to write earlier but there just seems to be so much going on all the time – lectures to go to, interesting people to meet, societies to join – that I seem to be in a state of permanent confusion! I know organisation has always been my weak point but things are getting ridiculous. I keep forgetting or losing things, or being late for lectures and tutorials. I'm behind with my assignments as well. Sometimes I think I'll never learn to cope with it all!

Is there any way I can get my act together? What do you think? Looking forward to hearing from you.

Love,

Sheryl

* *grant*: money given to students for tuition and living expenses

What advice would you give in reply? Share your ideas with your partner. Use suitable advice phrases, such as:

She should ...
She could consider ...
If I were her I'd ...

9 Reading a model letter of reply

With a partner, read Kate's letter of reply. What do you think of the advice offered? How does it compare with your own ideas? Underline the advice phrases as you read.

Dear Sheryl,

It was great to hear from you. We miss you here – you're such a special person. I saw your Mum and Dad last week and they showed me the photos of the university – what an impressive building! And right by the sea. You lucky thing!

I'm not surprised you feel chaotic and a bit overwhelmed. After all, only a few weeks ago you were bound not only by your parents' routine and expectations but by a strict school timetable as well. Suddenly you're expected to be completely responsible for yourself. When I started university I remember finding things a bit scary, but I found planning ahead was the key to getting organised. *advice*

A little tip I'd like to pass on is to make a list each morning of things you have to do that day. Try to include everything on your list, from attending a lecture to returning your books to the library. Keeping on top of the assignments is challenging too, but all you really have to do is draw up your own study timetable and stick to it. I know you're a 'morning' person, so why not schedule demanding intellectual tasks then? When you've got a minute during the day, don't forget to tick off things that have been completed.

The university social scene sounds brilliant. You seem to be really living it up*. I remember how popular and outgoing you were at school, so it must be tempting to say 'yes' to every social invitation. It's not a good idea to go out every night, though! You won't forget to pace yourself and save some time for recharging your batteries*, will you?

I'll definitely be able to make the weekend of the 22nd. I'm really looking forward to seeing the college and meeting some of your new friends. I'm sure by the time we meet you'll be super organised and my advice will be irrelevant! *useless*

Love,

Kate

* *living it up:* enjoying a very good social life
* *recharging your batteries:* resting after effort

10 Analysing the model letter

A How does Kate achieve an appropriate tone in the opening of the letter? Which details are included to develop the opening more fully?

B Paragraph 2 shows that the writer understands why Sheryl feels confused. How does she define the problem for Sheryl? What link does she make with her own experience? How does this affect the tone?

C Paragraph 3 offers Sheryl advice on being organised. Kate doesn't sound bossy or superior - how does she achieve this? How is the advice linked to the writer's knowledge of Sheryl? How does this affect the tone of the letter?

D Paragraph 4 shows Kate's attitude to Sheryl's social life. Her recognition of Sheryl's enthusiasm for parties is balanced by a note of caution. How is this expressed? Do you think Sheryl is going to be annoyed when she reads this, or is she likely to accept the advice?

E The last paragraph confirms an invitation. How? Does Kate manage to round off the letter appropriately? Why?

F Circle the words and phrases in the letter which create a warm and informal tone and register.

11 Advice phrases

Here are some typical advice phrases. Which phrases are stronger (S)? Which are more low key (LK)? Tick the phrases which appeal to you.

You need to ...
You'd better ...
You really should ...
If I were you I'd ...
Why not ...?
Remember ...
You could always ...
You could consider ...
Maybe you could ...
All you have to do is ...
Try to ...
You may like to try ...

How about ...?
You really ought to ...
You absolutely must ...
Have you ever thought of ...?
Perhaps you need to ...
You know best, but perhaps you could ...
It's a good idea/not a good idea to ...
A little tip I'd like to pass on is ...

12 Expressing problems

The way people express their problems or ask for advice in English varies according to the seriousness of the situation and the formality of the context. Discuss the following statements and questions with a partner and suggest a context in which you might use each one.

a *I'm at my wits' end.*
b *I hope an acceptable solution can be found.*
c *I'm not sure what to do.*
d *I don't know where to turn.*
e *What do you think would be best?*
f *I'd like some advice about this, please.*
g *I'm out of my mind with worry.*
h *What on earth should I do?*
i *I would be grateful for any suggestions you can make.*
j *Do you have any ideas about this?*

COMPARING LANGUAGES AND CULTURES

How do you express problems in your own language and culture? Do you use dramatic or low key language?

13 Tone and register in students' letters

A   Oliver has just moved to a new town and started going to college. Working in groups of three or four, select one of you to read aloud this extract from a letter he wrote to a friend at his old school.

The tutors are very helpful at my new college but it's hard to make friends. I spend all my spare time watching TV. How can I meet some friendly people?

If you were in Oliver's shoes, how would you be feeling? What would you hope to hear in a letter of reply? Share your ideas in the group.

B   The following are openings to letters that students wrote in reply. Take turns in your group in reading them aloud. Decide whether the tone and register sound right or not, and why.

1   I received your letter of December 1st explaining that you are not satisfied with your new life. If people don't like you, you must face the situation and solve it. There are many suitable activities you should take up which would help you overcome this feeling.

2   It was great to hear from you – knowing you had problems really made my day. The way I see it is that you are glued to the TV. All I can say is you should join a sports club and get some of your weight off as well. It will be useful for your health and good exercise for your legs.

3   You might want to know why I haven't written. I have been working in my grandfather's shop. I get paid even though I'm working for my family. I meet lots of new people and the work is interesting too. What is your ideal career?

4   I hope you are now happy since writing me that awful letter. Why do you feel lonely? Don't you have friends there? You said how boring you are at your new college. I think there are many places of entertainment obtaining in that area which you have not looked for. Don't always be sorry for yourself. You ought to adapt yourself to your new world.

5   I was sorry to hear that you are not enjoying your new college as much as you deserve to. I know how you must be feeling because we had to move a lot with Dad's job. However, have you considered joining the college drama club? You used to give some brilliant performances in the school theatre society. With your acting talent and sociable personality, I'm sure it won't be long before you are striking up new friendships.

14 Rewriting a paragraph

Choose one of the paragraphs you didn't like and rewrite it. When you are ready, read out your new version to the group, explaining the reasons for any alterations you have made.

The pressure of exams

15 Pre-reading task

Studying for exams can be a stressful time. You are going to read interviews with three students, their mothers and an education expert, about exam tension.

Here are some of the problems students say they have with exams. Read them through in twos or threes. Can you or your partner(s) suggest any solutions? Finally, share your ideas with other groups.

C My parents still expect me to help in the house even though I've got to study.

D I'm worried about turning up late for exams or getting the day wrong.

G I don't like sitting alone in my room with my books.

E I hate having to give up sport and seeing my friends.

A Getting bad marks in the mocks* makes me nervous about the real exams.

F I've fallen behind with my coursework* and I haven't got time to catch up.

H I hate listening to other students comparing answers after a test.

B I don't have time to watch my favourite TV programmes.

mocks: tests which are set by teachers in preparation for the real exams

coursework: work such as projects, assignments and classwork done during the school year. Coursework is marked by the teacher but the grades go towards the final exam mark.

16 Reading for gist

Skim read the magazine article. Does the advice given include any of the ideas you thought of? Try to work out the meaning of any unfamiliar words from the context.

EXAM TENSION: WHAT CAN YOU DO?

Sam Parry, 16 is taking nine GCSEs.

Pupils of equal ability can end up with vastly differing grades. To find out why, Linda Gray talked to three teenagers, and asked behaviour specialist Juliet Neill-Hall how parents can help.

What homework did you do last night?
'English and Geography coursework, though it should have been in three days ago. I was tired at first but I worked until 2 a.m., mostly on the computer. I can't work in my bedroom. I like to be with others, so I work in the dining room or on the floor.'

What do you give up during exams?
'I've been working in a newsagent's every day after school and on Saturdays, and going out every night. Now I've cut back on the work and I only see my friends at weekends and on Tuesdays, when I babysit.'

Are exams stressful?
'Yes! There's so much pressure to get coursework done and then there are exam nerves. It's stressful hearing other people saying what they've done when you haven't learnt it.'

What's the most helpful/irritating thing your parents do?
'Mum says, "I must have the brainiest daughter in the school, because she never needs to do her homework." And it can be noisy because Dad goes out to work at nights. The most helpful thing is they don't moan about the paper all over the house.'

Is there anything you'd do differently?
'Although I didn't work for my mocks, I did all right. For GCSEs, I'll make a revision timetable and really stick to it.'

Ann Parry says: 'I've tried nagging and I've tried not. I warn her that unless she gets on with it, she's going to panic. I've put my foot down about her going out during the week – I'm not popular! But she has only one chance and if she doesn't get the right grades, she can't go to sixth-form college.'

Expert advice: 'It does sound as though Sam is trying to do too much. While her newsagent's job is bringing in money short-term, her long-term prospects for earning are more important. GCSEs require three to four hours' homework daily, and three nights out a week seems quite enough without a job after school (the best time for getting down to study). Rather than laying down the law, Ann should try to get Sam to see this for herself and take more responsibility for her own work patterns. Where Sam does need support and encouragement is in planning what needs to be done by when, and plenty of praise for 'getting on' and completing tasks. I felt that wanting to work in the middle of the family, rather than working in her bedroom, was Sam's way of asking for this kind of constructive daily input.'

Khalid Helal, 17, has seven B- and C-grade GCSEs. He is taking Photography GCSE this summer and Photography, Design and Theatre Studies at A level next year.

What homework did you do last night?
'None – but I did loads the night before, finishing a design assignment. It took till 1 o'clock in the morning.'

What do you give up during exams?
'I gave up going out at weekends and stopped my sport – mountain-biking, circuit-training and rowing – so I put on weight. I did go to a concert the day before my Geography exam – a big mistake! I didn't get back until early next morning.'

Are exams stressful?
'There's pressure from other students as well as the school. If they say they've finished revising, and you haven't started, you don't show you're worried about it, but you are. Music helps – our teachers say it's okay to have it on while you work as long as it's not too loud.'

What's the most helpful/irritating thing your parents do?
'Maths was a problem. I'd got a really bad mark in the mocks, so my Mum gave me extra work and marked it – she's a science graduate. She bought me loads of revision books too.'

Is there anything you'd do differently?
'I should have revised more. My Mum didn't push me because she was worried about my Dad. He was very ill in hospital the term before the exams and she moved to London to be with him.'

Krysia Helal says:
'I had so much on my mind, the exam period just went by, but I did help with his maths. He gets exam nerves, which is a worry, and always panics afterwards when they compare answers.'

Expert advice: 'Khalid did remarkably well in his GCSEs considering the emotional pressure he must have been under with his father so ill. Krysia did an excellent job of supporting him with his maths by taking a positive interest and being prepared to be involved. She needs to encourage Khalid to keep up with his sport – sport is an excellent way to calm nerves, and a balance of work, exercise and fun is essential. Khalid should be encouraged not to compare himself with other people – he's obviously trying to do his best.'

Matthew Ryan, 15, is taking nine GCSEs. He passed Italian with a starred A last year.

What homework did you do last night?
'None. I don't do much unless I'm interested in it, like Technology, which I do at lunchtime.'

What do you give up during exams?
'I'm out at weekends, either working in a hotel, or at football or enjoying myself. Mum and Dad want me to give up my job and they say they'll make up the money.'

Are exams stressful?
'The coursework is worrying me. It should be in by now, but I've got lots to do. Exams aren't so bad. I didn't revise for my mocks, but I got good grades. Listening to music and working out help.'

What's the most helpful/irritating thing your parents do?
'I hate it when they compare me with my brother or discuss me with friends.'

Is there anything you'd do differently?
'I'd look at the exam timetable! I missed one of my mocks and had to do it later.'

Barbara Ryan says:
'Until recently Matt was okay, now I have to nag. I don't like him going to the gym so often – he's too tired to work.'

Expert advice:
'Matthew is a bright boy but he has lost his motivation. The job and the exercise have become ways of distracting himself. His parents need to sit down with Matthew and his teachers to find out exactly where he is up to with his coursework. Rather than comparing him with others, they should address his particular worries. Their offer of making up his money is generous but must be linked to Matthew using his time more constructively. As he loves music, maybe Barbara could offer him a reward of a CD for every completed set of subject coursework.'

Comprehension check

1 Tick any statements which are true for Sam.
  a She works best in her bedroom.
  b She leaves the work she is doing for her exams in different rooms.
  c Her mother has tried different approaches to encourage her to study.
  d The expert thinks Sam has found the right balance between studies, her part-time job and her social life.

2 Tick any statements which are true for Khalid.
  a He doesn't get anxious about exams.
  b He likes listening to music while studying.
  c His mother gave him practical help with his maths.
  d The expert thinks it is wrong for Khalid to give up sport and a social life during his exams.

3 Tick any statements which are true for Matthew.

    a He finds it hard to do homework unless he is very interested in the subject.

    b He was disappointed with his grades for his mocks.

    c His mother was happy with his progress until a short time ago.

    d The expert thinks Matthew needs to be much more motivated, and to use his parents' help to plan his study programme.

18 Post-reading discussion

1 Who do you think is the most hard-working of the students? Try to say why.

2 Do you sympathise with Sam, Khalid and Matthew in any way? Try to explain why or why not.

3 Do you agree with the expert's advice for each student? Do you think the expert was generally helpful or rather too critical?

4 What do you think, in general, of the attitudes of the mothers?

5 Are there any other ways Sam, Khalid and Matthew could help themselves? What do you think?

6 What are the methods you feel work best for you when you are studying for exams? Share your thoughts in your group.

7 Sam says she is going to make a revision timetable. How useful are timetables? Some people claim 'time budgets' are better because they are more flexible. What do you think?

19 Vocabulary: Colloquial words and phrases

A The following colloquial words and phrases were used in the text. Use them to replace the words in italics in the sentences below. There is one more than you need.

> exam nerves   moan   stick to
>
> put your foot down about it
>
> loads   working out   nagging

1 You *complain* about your daughter coming in late. It's time you *insisted it stopped*.

2 Luckily, we don't suffer from *worry and tension about exams*.

3 I have a study timetable and I am determined to *persevere with* it.

4 He enjoys *taking exercise in a gym*.

5 She does *a great deal* of work for her favourite charity.

B Do you know any other meanings of *moan, loads, working out* and *stick to?* Try to think of some examples.

20 Word building

BUILDING NOUNS FROM VERBS

Sam's mother was advised to give her 'support and *encouragement*'. The suffix *-ment* can be added to some verbs to make nouns.

Add *-ment* to each of the following verbs to make a noun. Then use each one in a sentence to show its meaning.

appoint	advertise
astonish	improve
arrange	manage
entertain	disagree

BUILDING ADJECTIVES FROM NOUNS

Khalid was described as having been 'under *emotional* pressure'. The suffix *-al* can be added to some nouns to make adjectives.

Add *-al* to each of the following nouns to make an adjective. Then use each one in a sentence to show its meaning. Be careful, as the spelling sometimes changes too.

magic	culture
music	function
classic	mathematics
person	nature

21 Language study: Giving advice

Here are some expressions the expert used in the text to give advice.

a *Khalid should be encouraged not to compare himself with other people.*

b *Khalid's mother needs to encourage him to keep up with his sport.*

c *Matthew's parents' offer of making up his money is generous but must be linked to Matthew using his time more constructively.*

d *His parents need to sit down with Matthew and his teachers to find exactly where he is up to with his coursework.*

1 Which advice sounds most direct? Which least direct?

2 Which advice verb is followed by the infinitive with 'to'? Which are followed by the infinitive without 'to'?

3 How would you change statements **a**, **b** and **d** into questions?

4 How would you make **b**, **c** and **d** into negative statements?

5 Can you replace *should, need(s) to* and *must* with any other expressions of similar meaning? What are they?

....

....

22 Should/shouldn't have

Should/Shouldn't + *have* + past participle have a different meaning from giving advice. With a partner try to work out the meaning from these examples.

1   You shouldn't have bought her a box of chocolates when you knew she was trying to lose weight.
2   He should have checked the exam timetable before he took the day off to play football.
3   I shouldn't have lost my temper about something so unimportant.
4   You should have telephoned to cancel your appointment if you couldn't come.

Write down your ideas with your partner.

PRACTICE

Join each pair of sentences to make one sentence containing *should have* or *shouldn't have* and a suitable linking word.

1   Joseph took a part-time job. He had exams coming up.
2   Trudi went to the concert. She had an exam the next day.
3   He didn't check his bank balance. He spent a lot of money.
4   I shouted at my brother. He was trying to be helpful.
5   I borrowed my sister's jacket. I didn't ask her first.
6   Why didn't you buy some extra bread? You knew we needed to make sandwiches.

23 Using a more informal tone

Rewrite these sentences to make them sound more informal. Use the verbs *should, ought, need, must* or *had better*.

1   It isn't necessary for me to cook. Damian's taking us out for a meal.
2   It is necessary to do your homework at a regular time each evening.
3   It was unwise to make a promise you can't keep.
4   It was wrong to leave all my revision to the last minute.
5   It's vital that Abdul gets more rest or he will fail his exams.
6   I regret not having listened to her advice.
7   It was wrong of him to play computer games instead of revising for the exam.

24 Spelling and pronunciation: Silent letters

Many English words contain silent letters. They can be at the beginning of words as in:

wrinkle   **k**nitting
psychology   **h**onour

in the middle, as in:

sal**m**on   foreig**n**er
cup**b**oard   liste**n**er

or at the end, as in :

com**b**   autum**n**

Sometimes a pair of letters is silent, as in:

ri**gh**t   dau**gh**ter

Practise saying the words above with a partner. Check each other's pronunciation.

25 Crossing out silent letters

These words, taken from the text 'Exam Tension', contain silent letters. Work with a partner to cross out the letters which are not pronounced.

1   design   7   should
2   answers   8   calm
3   what   9   circuit
4   law   10   assignment
5   night   11   weight
6   science   12   hours

Now practise saying the words correctly with your partner. Do you both agree your pronunciation is correct.

26 Adding silent letters

Complete these sentences with the missing silent letters. Choose from the letters in the box.

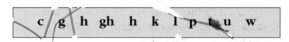

c   g   h   gh   h   k   l   p   t   u   w

1   The drou**gh**t has ruined the crops.
2   Please ta**l**k to them about it.
3   Wo**u**ld you like a bisc**u**it with your coffee?
4   W**h**erabouts do you live?
5   Do you want a ha**l**f or a **w**hole bag of sweets?
6   Can you **w**rite your ans**w**ers here?
7   We turn on the li**gh**ts when it gets dark.
8   He hurt his **w**rist and his **k**nee when he fell over.
9   Snow is always w**h**ite.
10   **H**onesty is the best policy.
11   These flowers have a lovely s**c**ent.
12   The referee blows the w**h**is**t**le if something is **w**rong.
13   She **w**rote under a **p**seudonym as she wanted to keep her identity secret.
14   Queen Victoria rei**g**ned for over sixty years.
15   She is **p**sychic and can tell the future.

27 Detecting patterns

A Can you see a regular pattern for any of the silent letters? Discuss your ideas with a partner and note any patterns you can detect.

B Are there any silent letters in your own language? Share some examples in your group.

28 Idiomatic expressions

Can you work out the meaning of these idiomatic expressions from the context? (They each contain silent letters.)

1 I don't like the country and prefer the *hustle and bustle* of city life.
2 I thought the suitcase would be heavy, but when I picked it up it was *as light as a feather.*
3 He *risked life and limb* to save the baby from the burning car.

29 Look, say, cover, write, check

Silent letters often cause spelling mistakes. Students say they sometimes forget to include them in a word. Here is a list of words with silent letters which cause common spelling problems. First check the meaning and then try to identify the silent letter(s) in each word. Finally, use the 'look, say, cover, write, check' method to learn each word correctly.

solemn	yolk
sign	honour
yacht	doubt
scene	psychiatrist
rhyme	calf
rhythm	wreath
handkerchief	knock
lightning	daughter
height	drought
listener	government

Studying effectively

30 Punctuation reminders

Correct punctuation is important because it helps make meaning clear.

FULL STOPS AND CAPITAL LETTERS

Remember, full stops are used to end a sentence. Capital letters are needed after a full stop. Capital letters are also used for proper names (*Mary, Pepe*), place names (*Cairo, the Amazon*) and acronyms (*BBC, DNA*).

Here is a description of how one student does homework. Punctuate it correctly. Remember to read it first to get the sense correct.

I need a few quiet moments to myself when I get in from school I have a drink and relax for a while then I get out my homework I work at a desk in the corner of the living room it is peaceful but not silent I like french and maths homework the best .

APOSTROPHES

Remember, apostrophes are used to indicate possession (*Toby's pen, the girls' coats*) and to show that a letter is missing. (*It's hot.*)

Continue to punctuate the description.

Ive got a few reference books which i keep on a shelf above my desk i borrow my brothers paints for artwork and i use my mums computer for gcse coursework ive used my dads tools for some technology projects too they dont mind me borrowing their things as long as i take care of them

COMMAS

Commas are used

a to separate things in a list:
I need pens, pencils, rulers and a rubber.

b to separate a non-defining clause or an extra phrase from the main sentence:

Mr Rivers, our geography teacher, comes from Nigeria.

c To separate a participle phrase from the main clause:

Having run all the way to the station, we were disappointed to find the train had just left.

d After certain linking words and phrases:
On the other hand, Nevertheless, However,

These are just some of the uses of commas. Remember: we generally put commas where we would pause in speech.

Now punctuate the rest of the extract correctly.

our school cardiff high has a homework hotline this means that you can telephone the school to check the homework youve been set it also stops teachers setting too many subjects for homework at once about two years ago i had english history german physics biology maths and technology homework on the same night it was a nightmare the homework hotline prevents these problems however it also means teachers refuse to accept silly excuses for not handing in homework

Ex 25, 26 Pg 125 in the text book
rewrite the letter

Rewriting a letter

rewrite - paper

Read this letter which was written to a student who is not able to join his friends on holiday as he needs to retake an examination.

First read it carefully to get the sense. Then discuss it with a partner and rewrite it as necessary. Expect to make at least two drafts.

You should consider:

a the paragraphing
Remember – a new paragraph is usually needed for a change of topic.

b the tone and register
Are they right for this situation? If not, think of alternative expressions you could use.

Dear Harry,

I was overcome with sorrow at your terrible news that you're dropping out of the trip because you have to resit the exam. Don't you feel full of guilt and remorse? After all, it was your own fault you failed. Well, Harry, I urge you to stop being bone idle and to start revising in good time before the resit. Did you know Toby failed too? Why not study with him, as you are both slow learners? You ought to do what I did if you want to become a big success like me. I got the syllabus and underlined the sections I needed to revise. You must look at past papers as well and identify typical questions. You've got to practise answering the questions quickly, too. I want to be overwhelmed with happiness when I hear your results because I don't want to be let down again. We will all miss you a lot on holiday and will be thinking of you while we enjoy ourselves. Just remember to stop wasting your time.

Lots of love,

Oscar

Read your new version to your group. Do you all agree you have achieved a sympathetic letter which sounds 'balanced'?

More idiomatic expressions

The idioms in italics in the following sentences express feelings and attitudes. Discuss each with a partner and choose the definition you feel is correct.

1 At the party the other students *gave her the cold shoulder.*
   a They ignored her.
   b They offered her cold meat.
   c They told her they disliked her.
   d They made her promise to keep a secret.

2 When I read the exam paper *I couldn't make head or tail of it.*
   a I realised I could not finish in the time.
   b I could not understand any of the questions.
   c I found the second part of the paper very difficult.
   d I could do only half the total number of questions.

3 The tutor's warning that her work was below standard was *like water off a duck's back.*
   a She was worried that she was going to fail.
   b She made up her mind to do better.
   c The advice made no difference to her attitude.
   d She decided to leave the college.

4 He's *set his heart on* becoming a doctor.
   a He's sure he'll be a successful doctor.
   b He's very emotional about becoming a doctor.
   c He's very realistic about his prospects.
   d He really wants to qualify as a doctor.

5 I've never failed an exam, *touch wood.*
   a It's due to my careful preparation.
   b I really hope my good luck continues.
   c I always expect to do well in exams.
   d I believe I shall fail the next one.

6 When I told her she'd won the scholarship, she thought I was *pulling her leg.*
   a She didn't like the way I explained it.
   b She was convinced I was joking.
   c She thought I wanted something from her.
   d She was angry and walked away.

7 I thought this training programme would be right for me, but now I feel that I'm *out of my depth.*
   a The programme is generally too difficult for me.
   b The programme is working out more expensive than I expected.
   c The other trainees dominate the discussions.
   d The instructors misrepresented the course to me.

34 Increasing your stock of idioms

Select the idiomatic expressions you would like to remember from exercise 33. Use each in a sentence of your own to show their meaning.

35 Sentence correction

The following sentences from students' letters contain mistakes of grammar and vocabulary. Try to rewrite them correctly.

1 *If you be wisdom one you follow your professor advice.*
2 *You should build up a correct concept of mind to your work.*
3 *The qualities of good friend is invisible but uncountable.*
4 *You should never take the drugs they give much trouble more than they bring the pleasure.*
5 *Your letter talking ideas many people thinking too.*

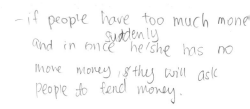

INTERNATIONAL OVERVIEW

Researchers have found that pupils in Singapore are among the most hard-working in the world in terms of the amount of time spent doing homework in maths and science or studying.

98% of Singapore's 9-year-olds did maths homework once a week, compared with only 47% of English pupils.

13-year-olds in Singapore devote much more time to homework than children in many other countries. They do 4.6 hours per day.

However, children in Singapore watched about the same amount of TV as children in other countries (3-4 hours a day).

What do you think is the right number of hours homework per day for a student of your age?

A range of advice

36 Pre-listening tasks

A More and more people are now said to be turning to professional counsellors if they have problems. The following points are sometimes made in favour of counsellors. In groups of three or four, discuss how far you agree with them.
1 Counselling is a real skill and the counsellors are properly trained and qualified.
2 Their advice is objective.
3 It's not embarrassing to see them because you won't have to deal with them in any other role, e.g. employer, friend.

B Can you see any disadvantages in going to a counsellor? Would you consult one. Why/Why not?

C You are going to listen to a college counsellor talking about her job. Her talk will cover the following topics:

- students' problems
- approaches to counselling
- her feelings about being a counsellor.

What would you like to find out about each of these? Write a question of your own on each topic. Compare your questions with those of a partner.

37 Listening for gist: A college counsellor

16/5/02

 Listen to the interview. Which of the questions that you wrote are answered?

38 Detailed listening

 Now listen for detail and try to find answers to these questions.

1 The counsellor can offer help to students who are worried about money. What does she suggest students might do? Give two examples.
2 What does the counsellor look for when students complain of tension before exams?
3 How might she approach resolving the difficulties of a student who was not getting on with her parents?
4 Under what circumstances would the counsellor consider breaching confidentiality?
5 Explain why she feels counselling is different from advice-giving.
6 Describe the attitude she takes to the emotional demands of her work.

Remember, your answers do not have to be in complete sentences.

39 Rewriting a letter of advice

A You know that a friend of yours, Roberto, has difficulty getting on with his younger brother. He says that his brother scribbles on his posters, damages his CDs and starts arguments with him. What kind of advice would you give? Note your ideas.

B Tone and register
Now read the letter of advice that was written to Roberto by a fellow student. Do you think the tone and register sound right for the situation? Try to work out why or why not.

Dear Roberto,

I was devastated to hear of this tragic problem. It seems as if your brother has ruined your life. I know that you have always been untidy and careless. The result of this behaviour is that your little brother can find your things and spoil them. It seems as if you are bad-tempered and impatient with him too. Of course he will not like you if you are unkind to him. You must learn to put away your things and control your moods. I also have a younger brother so I am very careful to put my things away in a place where he cannot reach them. My younger brother and I have a close relationship. We play football together and I help him with his homework. We no longer quarrel because I am not selfish and have tried to understand him. We discussed the problem calmly with my parents. I did not shout or get angry which, as I see it, would be your reaction. It is a pity you cannot do the same.

Please write to me telling me that you have resolved your horrible problem. I hope to hear that you have achieved a pleasant atmosphere in your home.

All the best,

Crispin

Rewrite the letter, making any changes you think are appropriate.

15/5/02

40 Building a letter from a list of points

'I'm having serious trouble getting down to my homework. Any ideas?'

A friend has asked you for your help with this problem. Discuss it with a partner and jot down your thoughts about what could help him/her.

Now read the list of helpful homework tips below.

1   Get into a regular routine.
2   Don't leave it too late in the evening to start.
3   Make sure you understand what homework you have to do before you leave school.
4   Work in a quiet place.
5   Keep the equipment you need for your homework (pens, reference books) where you can find it at home.
6   Bring home the papers etc. from school that you need to help you do your homework.
7   Plan your time: short, concentrated sessions are better than one long session.
8   Use a clear surface to work on.
9   Give yourself something enjoyable to look forward to after finishing your homework in the evening.
10 Keep a homework diary to help you keep a check on the homework you have done.

Add any ideas of your own to the list.

WRITING

Write a letter of reply to your friend. Offer him or her some advice about doing homework. Choose ideas from the list above. Develop the points into three coherent, interesting paragraphs. Use a friendly tone and register. Remember to add an opening and closing sentence.

15/5/02

41 Pre-writing discussion

Do you think bullying is a common problem? Why do you think some people become bullies? Why do some people become the victims of bullies, but others don't?

A younger friend of yours writes to you saying:

A boy in my class is bullying me. When I arrive at school he calls me names, and he threatens to push me off my bike and take it for himself. He says he will hurt me if I report him to a teacher.

What advice would you give to help your friend? Jot down a few ideas.

42 Letter completion

hw

Now try to complete this letter of advice about bullying.

3-4 points

Dear Gerald,

Thanks for your letter which I got this morning. It's always good to hear from you.

I was really upset to hear that you are going through a hard time at your new school. That boy sounds like a complete thug! However, you mustn't let it get you down too much. There are a number of things you could do to improve the situation ......

Exam-format questions

Writing

1   You have a pen friend who was hoping to learn your language fluently and eventually to study it at university. However, in his last letter he sounded discouraged about his progress and is thinking of giving up his ambitions.

Write him a letter which will cheer him up and suggest some techniques which might help him learn more effectively. You should draw on your own experience of language learning and describe techniques which have worked for you.

The sentences below may give you some ideas, but you are free to choose your own.

"A good teacher who involves you in the lesson is the best aid."

"Videos, audio tapes and computers make learning fun."

"Radio and TV have interesting, helpful programmes."

"15 minutes a day is more constructive than three hours once a week."

"An opportunity to visit the country and speak the language is invaluable."

Your letter should be about 200 words long.

2   You have a friend who, although a competent student, becomes very nervous before exams and doesn't always do well in them. You know she has some important exams coming up and you would like to see her be successful.

Select an appropriate tone and register and write her a letter suggesting some ways in which she could control her nervousness and improve her examination results.

You may wish to write about:

- the importance of positive thinking
- the need for pacing yourself
- the benefits of relaxation, proper sleep and enough exercise
- the usefulness of a study timetable
- techniques to improve memory
- revising effectively
- studying with a friend
- the importance of following the examination rubric.

Your letter should be about 200 words long.

3   Your grandparents, who are both quite elderly, live in another town and would like to visit you at your school or college. They are not well off and would like to stay in a modestly-priced hotel or guest house. They can stay for only three days and are anxious to see as much as possible in the time they have. Your grandfather has some difficulty walking long distances and uses a stick.

Write them a letter welcoming them and offering advice and suggestions about ways to make the most of their trip.

You may like to write about:

- aspects of the school or college itself which are worth a visit
- suitable accommodation
- interesting places to see locally
- good local restaurants and cafés
- places of entertainment
- arrangements for meeting up with them.

Your letter should be about 200 words long.

Oral assessment

Living more independently

Many young people look forward to the day when they can leave their parents' home and live a more independent life. What problems and challenges might leaving home bring? Discuss your ideas with the examiner or your partner.

You could consider such things as:

- finding a place to live
- balancing a budget

- cooking, cleaning and generally looking after yourself
- coping with lonely feelings
- learning to be responsible for your own health
- coping with the possible dangers that you might meet.

You are free to consider any other ideas of your own. You are not allowed to make any written notes.

EXAMINER'S TIPS

1 Listening to English radio, watching TV and reading magazines, newspapers and books can help you understand more about the way people adapt their language to different occasions and for different target groups. For example, a magazine article for adults about ways of studying will be written in a different tone and register from an article on the same topic for 12-year-olds.

2 Speaking or writing on the same topic in a variety of tones and registers will also develop your ability.

3 Students often say they would like to improve their grammar. Here are some suggestions:

   - Study the errors you frequently make. Use your knowledge of regular grammar patterns and the exceptions to try to work out the differences between your version and the correct version.

   - Use a good grammar book to check explanations of points you usually make mistakes with. You need a book which gives lots of examples, not just the rules and their exceptions.

   - Work with a friend who speaks your first language. Work together to analyse your mistakes. As always, investigate the grammar pattern and think about exceptions too. See if you can work out a rule for that particular grammar point before looking it up in your grammar book.

   - Apply your new knowledge of grammar in different situations. This will help you remember the point, and help you understand when it is correct and when grammar has to change to fit new situations.

   - Exploring meaningful patterns and their exceptions will help your spelling and vocabulary work too. In fact, you can detect patterns in all the subjects you're learning (maths, science, art, etc.) if you look for them.

EXAM STRATEGY: ORAL ASSESSMENT

4 The first part of your Oral Assessment is the warm up phase. The examiner will ask you a few questions about yourself. Remember that this phase is not marked.

5 In the assessment, marks are given to candidates who make the most of their ability with spoken English. Try to answer questions as fully as possible. Avoid 'Yes/No' replies or 'I don't know'. Don't be afraid to take a little extra time to think of replies which will be helpful in keeping an interesting conversation going between you and the examiner.

   Remember, communicating effectively in a natural and lively way is much more important than having perfect grammar or pronunciation. If you are in a small group, show interest in what the other candidates say as well as putting forward your own ideas.

6 Ask for clarification if necessary with questions such as 'Do you mean ...?', 'Could you repeat that? I didn't quite understand.'

7 The highest marks go to candidates who can show they are capable of abstract thought. Try to think around a topic from many different angles. Be prepared for a wide range of questions.

Unit focus

In this unit you have studied tone and register and learned to write a **letter of advice**. This is practice for Papers 1/2, Part 3.

You have learned to become more aware of conversational techniques. This will help improve your classroom talk and provide more understanding and practice for Papers 5/6.

You have read a detailed magazine article and answered comprehension questions. This is practice for Papers 1/2, Part 1.

You have listened to an informal discussion and answered short-answer comprehension questions. This practises the skills you need for Paper 4, Part 3.

Happy Endings

The call of the sea

1 Visualisation

Close your eyes and think of the sea. What sights and sounds come to your mind? What do you feel when you think about the sea? Now open your eyes and spend a few minutes writing down whatever came into your mind, in your own language or English.

2 Discussion

From the days of pirates and 'running away to sea', to modern-day beach holidays and scuba diving, the sea has drawn people like a magnet. Why do you think this is?

Discuss these remarks about the sea with a partner. Grade them as

A *I identify strongly with this idea.*
B *This idea is interesting but I don't identify closely with it.*
C *I don't identify in any way with this idea.*

1 'The sea is a place of great adventure. When you set sail in a boat, you never know what you are going to find.'

2 'I love swimming. Being in water, especially the sea, brings great pleasure.'

3 'I live by the sea and love its changing atmospheres. On hot days the atmosphere is cool and restful. On bleak winter days, great storms bring drama and excitement.'

4 'When I go out in my boat, I feel free. All my worries are left behind on the shore.'

5 'Below its surface, the sea is full of life. I'd love to explore its depths and see the underwater world for myself.'

6 'I think the sea is mysterious. Animals, people, huge ships, even cities have disappeared in it, never to be found again.'

7 'I live in a dry area far away from the sea. My dream is to see the magnificence of the ocean and hear its wonderful sounds.'

8 'I admire anyone whose employment is connected with the sea. No other work requires such presence of mind.'

9 'Sailing presents a great spiritual challenge. In a storm or crisis, I discover unknown aspects of myself. After each trip I think I become a slightly different, more developed, person.'

133

3 Sea vocabulary: Odd word out

In pairs or small groups, circle the word which does not belong in each of the following groups. Use a dictionary to help you. You'll need many of the words later in the unit, so make a note in your vocabulary book of any that are unfamiliar.

SEA ASSOCIATIONS

Which word is not associated with the sea?

spray tides waves ocean cliffs bay shore rocks hive current port horizon channel shipwreck voyage cargo dock jetty surf

ON THE BEACH

Which item would you not expect to find on the beach?

shingle pebbles shells rocks starfish sand spanner sand dunes flotsam and jetsam seaweed driftwood turtle

SEA CREATURES

Which creature is not associated with the sea?

porpoise turtle lobster whale shark seal dolphin puffin penguin crab squirrel

WORDS FOR BOATS

Which of the following is not a word for a kind of boat?

yacht dinghy raft tram tug speedboat liner vessel canoe barge car ferry catamaran oil tanker galleon trawler

OCCUPATIONS CONNECTED WITH THE SEA

Which is the odd one out in this group of occupations?

captain coastguard helmsman solicitor sailor pirate fisherman skipper purser lighthouse keeper mariner smuggler

WATERSPORTS

Which of these sports is not connected with water?

scuba diving surfing rowing canoeing swimming diving sailing windsurfing jet-skiing abseiling snorkelling

4 Sea vocabulary: Onomatopoeic words

A Certain words are called *onomatopoeic* because the sound of the word is like its meaning.

Example:
*I love hearing the birds **twitter** on a sunny morning.*

Twitter is an onomatopoeic word because it sounds like the sound birds actually make.

Sea vocabulary is often onomatopoeic. Match these sounds to the things which make them. Some sounds can be linked to more than one thing.

lapping   slapping
screeching   hooting
roaring   squelching
howling   splashing
crashing

boats waves seagulls wind mud

B What other onomatopoeic words do you know? Make a list with your partner.

C What onomatopaeic words do you know in your own language? Share them with your group.

5 Writing a descriptive paragraph

Yesterday you made a trip to the coast. Write a paragraph describing what you saw, the sounds you heard and the way you felt.

Write about 75 words.

6 Reading aloud

In small groups, read your paragraphs aloud to each other. Be good listeners and make comments on what you hear.

7 Pre-reading discussion

A Britain is sometimes called the 'kingdom by the sea'. The sea has been a means of defence in war, a source of riches from trade, and a way of maintaining separation from the rest of Europe. It is an important part of Britain's identity. What part, if any, has the sea played in the history of your country?

B There are many, many stories which centre around the excitement and drama of the sea. Do you have any favourites?

C Daniel Defoe's novel *Robinson Crusoe* is one of the most famous of these stories. What, if anything, do you know of it?

8 Reading and sequencing

Read the version below of the story of Robinson Crusoe. Try to guess the meaning of unfamiliar words.

As you read, number these events in the order in which they happened.

a Crusoe is shipwrecked. *4*
b He meets Friday. *8*
c He is made a slave. *2*
d He returns to England. *11*
e He manages a plantation. *3*
f He sees an English ship on the horizon. *9*
g He rescues the ship's captain. *10*
h He builds a home on the island. *6*
i He runs away to sea. *1*
j He accepts his life on the island. *7*
k He salvages things from the shipwreck. *5*

1 Never have any adventurer's misfortunes, I believe, begun earlier or continued longer than mine. I am Robinson Crusoe and this is my story .....

2 I was born in the year 1632 in the city of York. I had always wanted to go to sea but my father wanted me to enter the law. Against the wishes of my parents I joined a big trading ship when it was in dock at Hull. I knew I was breaking my father's heart but the call of the sea was too strong.

3 At first I was terribly seasick but I gradually learned to adapt and weather the great storms which blew up. On one occasion, to my misfortune, I was taken as a slave but I escaped. For some time I even ran a plantation in Brazil but I could not resist returning to the sea. This time, however, the ship was wrecked and I was the only survivor.

4 The sea had washed me up onto a deserted tropical island. 'Am I all alone?' I called, and my despair knew no depths as I realised I was condemned to live in a silent world, forever an outcast in this horrid place.

5 I knew I had to swim back to the ship before it sank completely and salvage everything of value. The task was urgent as my survival depended on it. On the boat I found the ship's dog and two cats. These creatures, with a parrot I taught to speak, and a goat, were for many years my only companions on the island.

6 For a home, I built a strong shelter close to fresh water. I explored the island and found fruit trees and a herd of goats. I sowed barley I had taken from the ship, and made a calendar to mark the passing of the days. I resolved to look on the bright side rather than the dark side of my condition. The doings of the greedy, material world and my own past wickedness became more and more remote. I spent many hours in hard labour, improvising baskets, pots, a boat and other necessities, but I always made time for spiritual contemplation.

7 Each year the crops increased, my 'family' was contented and I learned to love the beauty of the island. Yet I longed to see a human face and hear a human voice.

8 My solitude ended when, walking towards my boat, I stopped, thunderstruck, at the sight of a strange footprint in the sand. This incident marked the beginning of my friendship with a man who lived on a distant island. He was escaping the anger of his countrymen and I gave him refuge. 'Friday', as I called him, wanted to learn English and gradually we learned to understand one another and appreciate each other's way of life.

9 My luck changed when an English ship appeared on the horizon. Friday and I observed a rowing boat coming ashore. My guess was right. The crew of the ship had mutinied and the captain and some of his loyal followers had been taken prisoner. Friday and I worked out a way to capture the mutineers and set the captain free.

10 The captain of the ship offered to take me back to England. Friday, who I had found as true and good a friend as a man could ever wish for, was going to accompany me.

11 So, on December 19th 1686, after 28 years on the island, one of the strangest stories ever told ended as I, Robinson Crusoe, sailed away from the island, never to return.

9 Comprehension check

homework

1 What future did Crusoe's father want for his son? *Crusoe's father wanted his son to study law*

2 Even before the shipwreck, Crusoe had many adventures. What were they? *slave / seasick*

3 How did Crusoe feel when he realised he was all alone on the island? *He felt isolated and lonely*

4 What did he manage to do before the wrecked ship sank?

5 Describe Crusoe's way of life on the island. *He plan his crops*

6 What was the first sign that another human being had visited the island?

7 How did Crusoe finally manage to escape from the island? *The captain set him free*

8 Explain the meaning of the word *mutineer.* *mutineer taking control from another person*

10 Language study: Narrative tenses

To help the reader follow a story and understand how the events are connected, we use narrative tenses. Useful narrative tenses are the past simple, the past continuous, the past perfect and the 'future in the past'. *(I swam, I was swimming, I had swum, I was going to swim/would swim.)*

Study the tenses in the story of Robinson Crusoe with a partner. Underline each verb and decide which tense it is. Notice how the tense is formed. Add * if the verb is in the passive.

Ask each other why each tense is used.

With your partner, make notes for each narrative tense, like this:

THE PAST SIMPLE

Typical examples in text ....

Formed by ....

Used in text because ....

Finally, check your notes with a grammar book.

11 Beginnings and endings

Beginnings and endings are important in a story. How is our interest aroused at the beginning of the story of Robinson Crusoe? How satisfying did you find the ending?

What tenses are used at the beginning and end of the story? Why?

12 Discussion: Heroism

Someone who help with another person

A What do we mean when we say someone is a 'hero' or 'heroine'? In what way do you think Robinson Crusoe could be described as a heroic figure? *He survided in the island the cat and the dog.*

B Can ordinary people living uneventful lives ever be called 'heroic'? Why/Why not? *yes because ordinary people help other people / anyone*

C Who are your personal heroes or heroines? Share your ideas in your group.

D Crusoe changes a negative experience, being shipwrecked, into a positive one. What can we learn from our own negative experiences? How can the struggles and annoyances of daily life build our character and develop our understanding of ourselves and other people's problems? Do suffering and hardship ennoble the spirit or make people bitter and angry? *learn to repeat the mistakes*

E Crusoe says he learned a lot from Friday, who came from a completely different, much simpler society. Give some examples of what he might have learned. Think both about survival skills and human values.

13 Continuing a story creatively

Try to imagine you are Robinson Crusoe, on your way back to England. Use these questions to help you continue his story.

- What will you most miss about your island life?
- What did you choose to take with you?
- What have you learned from your experiences? Do you feel the hardships of the island have made you a better and more understanding person?
- Who will remember you at home? Who will you want to see?
- How will you make your living?
- What might be the difficulties of fitting into a normal life again?

Share your ideas with your classmates.

14 Writing from notes

Hw

Most narratives use a variety of past tenses. The following paragraph describes Crusoe's return to England. Write the paragraph in full using the past simple, past continuous, past perfect, future in the past and past perfect continuous tenses.

We be/stand/deck/ship/when/captain say/English coast be/sight. I feel/very strange. Be I/really go/see England again? After so many years/solitude/noise bustle/crowds/ dock/almost overwhelm me. I be/walk/towards town/when I hear/voice/call my name. I turn/and see/sister. She embrace me/ warmly. I know/from tears/her eyes/she forgive me/for hurt/our parents. She tell me/she wait/me/ since day/I leave. She almost give up hope/when she get/message/I be alive.

15 Comparing cultures

What stories in your culture have a sea theme? Think carefully about a story you know well and like. Then retell it to your group.

16 Showing surprise: Stress and intonation

Listen to the intonation patterns in these *wh-* questions and answers. When does the intonation rise? When does it fall?

1 Who arrived on the island in a rowing boat?
Some mutineers.
Who arrived?

2 What did Crusoe use to make a calendar?
A wooden post.
What did he use?

3 How long was he on the island?
Twenty-eight years.
How long was he there?

4 Why did Crusoe call the man 'Friday'?
Because that was the day he saved his life.
Why did he call him Friday?

Listen again and repeat the pattern.

PRACTICE

Work in pairs. Ask each question with the falling tune. Then repeat the question showing surprise.

Try to continue with some questions and answers of your own.

Adrift on the Pacific

19/6/02

17 Pre-listening tasks

You are going to hear the true story of a couple, Maurice and Vita, who were attempting to sail across the world when their boat sank. They survived on a life raft for four months before they were rescued.

Hw

VOCABULARY CHECK

Match these words which you are going to hear with their definitions

F 1 emigrate ✓   A extremely thin
B 2 adrift B ✓ E   B floating without purpose
E 3 counter-current   C to make something using whatever materials are available
C 4 improvise   D unaware of, not noticing
A 5 emaciated   E a sea current running in the opposite direction
G 6 malnourished   F to go to another country to live there permanently
D 7 oblivious to   G unwell from lack of food

NARRATIVE QUESTIONS

A narrative should answer these questions:

Who.....?	Why .....?
What .....?	How .....?
Where .....?	When .....?

who rescued you?
what was the weather like?
where did the boat sink?
why did the wood sink
How to you did you survived?
when did the boat sink?

Write a question about the story beginning with each word.
Example: *Where did the boat sink?*

Try to make your questions grammatically correct.

18 Detailed listening

Listen to the interview with the couple who survived. Try to note down answers to the questions you wrote.

19 Checking your answers

Did you find answers to your questions? Why/Why not?

20 Listening and note taking

Listen again and complete the notes.

a   Reason for the trip ...emigrate......................
....

b   Where and why the boat sank ....
....

c   Immediate reaction to the accident ....
....

d   Rowing towards the Galapagos Islands was a mistake because ...used up more of the...... energy...

e   Conditions on the raft ...4 foot 6 inches............ small

f   What they ate ...turtles, birds, fish....................

g   Length of time adrift ...to 119 days....................
....

h   How they attracted the attention of their rescuers ...P wait..................................
....

i   Length of time to recover ...14 moths........ months

j   How they coped emotionally during their experience ...Hour by hour, day by day... They took it one day at a time

21 Discussion: Motivation and adventure

A   What makes people want to become involved in risky projects such as sailing across the world in a very small boat?

•   Is it fame and money? Or a desire for risk and adventure? Or the competitive spirit?

•   Is it a need to discover their potential and find out what they are capable of in the most testing circumstances – a kind of 'spiritual quest'?

Do you think people who undertake this kind of thing have greater 'inner strength' than others?

B   Is it right that each year large sums are spent rescuing people whose expeditions have gone wrong?

Could the urge for adventure be channelled more constructively into doing voluntary work on projects such as helping refugees? Or is this too 'tame' and over-organised?

When conditions on a dangerous expedition become very difficult, is it braver to accept defeat than to risk everything for success?

22 Ordering events   19/6/02

Put these statements about the couple on the life raft into the correct order by numbering them. Then link them using time expressions and conjunctions where appropriate. Choose from:

first, then, when, eventually, finally, before, until, next, after that, after many days

and conjunctions like *and, but* etc.

☐ The Sandpiper was damaged by a sperm whale. 2 wh

☐ They rowed towards the Galapagos islands. 5 First

☐ They attempted to get to the Central American coast. 6 next

☐ The boat sank. before 4

☐ A hostile current dragged them back out to sea. 7 but

☐ They tried to attract the attention of passing ships. 8 but

☐ They were rescued by South Korean fishermen. 10 eventual

☐ They returned to Britain. eventually 11

☐ They sailed by unaware of the couple's situation. 9

☐ They escaped onto a life raft. 3

☐ They left England for New Zealand. 1

Check whether the order of events is correct by listening to the recording again.

23 Expressing emotions end

In the interview Vita says '*We continued towards that coast for three weeks. Then, to our horror, a hostile current dragged us out to the middle of the ocean.*

'*To our horror*' expresses the drama and emotion of the situation. Look at these similar expressions:

to our amazement 4	to our (great) relief
to my astonishment	to their joy 1
to his annoyance 3	to her disappointment 5
to their alarm	to her concern
to our sorrow	to our delight 2

These expressions highlight the responses of the people involved in the events.

Study the following situations. Choose a suitable emotional phrase to add to each description.

Example:
We were waiting outside the operating theatre when, to our great relief, the surgeon came out and told us the difficult operation had been a success.

1 I was looking through the TV guide when I realised I had missed my favourite programme.

2 We feared the worst when our son disappeared driving in the desert but yesterday he telephoned to say he was safe.

3 The racing driver was driving at top speed when he noticed his brakes were not working.

4 I was just going to have dinner when the telephone rang and I learned I had won £1million in the lottery. *amazement*

5 We drove quickly when we heard Grandad had had a heart attack, but when we arrived at the hospital we heard that he had just died. *to our sorrow*

6 I was looking forward to eating my favourite cake at the café when I found that the previous customer had ordered the last one. 5

TENSES

Examine the uses of tenses in the sentences. What tenses are used and why? Some sentences use more than one tense. Why, do you think?

24 Dictionary work: Prefixes *Textbook*

THE PREFIX *MAL-*

Maurice says that during their ordeal on the raft they became *malnourished*. The prefix **mal-** means 'badly' or 'wrongly'.

Replace the word(s) in italics in the sentences below with one of these words beginning with *mal-*. Work with a partner and use a good dictionary to help you.

malfunctioning malignant malicious malevolent a malingerer malnutrition malpractice   *harm/strong*   *the rash*

1 The aid programme should save thousands of refugees from dying of *lack of food*. malnutrition ✓

2 The surgeon said the growth would have to be removed as it was *cancerous*. malignant ✓

3 To his horror the pilot realised that one of the engines was *not working properly*. malpractice / malfunctioning ✓

4 The doctor was taken to court for *failing to care properly for his patients*. malfunctioning / malpractice ✓

5 Children's fairy stories often contain a character who is *very evil*. malevolent ✓

6 This little boy is *deliberately hurtful* towards other children. malicious ✓

7 She's not really ill, you know. In my opinion she's *staying away from work for no good reason*. a malingerer ✓

THE PREFIX *COUNTER-*

In the interview you heard that Vita and Maurice had hoped to get to the equatorial *counter-current*. The prefix *counter-* means 'opposite', 'contrary' or 'reverse'.

Complete each sentence below with one of these words beginning with *counter -*. Continue using your dictionary if you need to.

counterbalance counteract counterproductive counterpart counterargument counterattack

1 Weights of the same size on this machine should be used to counterproductive each other.

2 If our aim is to make the workers do a good job, paying them less would surely be counterargument .

3 In spite of heavy casualties, the rebel soldiers launched a determined counteract against the government forces.

4 The doctor gave the child some medicine to counterattack the poison she had swallowed.

5 The Danish Prime Minister met his Swedish counterpart in Stockholm today for urgent talks on the fishing crisis.

6 James came up with good reasons for continuing the journey on foot, but Celine put forward equally strong counterbalance s.

25 Revision of reported speech *Read*

When we are telling a story, we may want to change someone's actual words to reported speech.

For example, Maurice might have said to Vita: 'It's absolutely silent here. You can't have heard the engine of a boat. No one is coming to rescue us. You must be going mad.'

If this speech were reported it would change to:

Maurice told Vita it was absolutely silent there and she couldn't have heard the engine of a boat. No one was coming to rescue them. She must be going mad.

Study the example carefully.

What has happened to the verbs? What is the rule for **tenses** when direct speech is reported?

What has happened to *must*? Do other **modals** (*would, could, should, might, need, had better* and *ought to*) stay the same when speech is reported?

How have the **pronouns** changed? What usually happens to pronouns in reported speech?

What has happened to the **infinitive**? Do infinitives in direct speech change when the speech is reported?

26 Reporting verbs

Verbs such as *admit, promise, declare, invite, ask, explain, reflect, remind, mention, suggest, insist, refuse* are often used when we change direct speech into reported speech. Using them is a good idea because it brings breadth and variety into your writing.

Example:
'Remember to send your aunt a good luck message,' said their mother.
Their mother reminded them to send their aunt a good luck message.

What other reporting verbs do you know?

PRACTICE

The following comments were made by a young woman, Silvia, who is planning to sail around the world single-handedly.

Change her actual words to reported speech, using suitable reporting verbs from the list. Some of the verbs are similar in meaning, so decide which you prefer.

acknowledge add admit confess declare explain insist mention reveal say

Example:
'I'm a yachtswoman and a loner. I would rather go hill climbing alone than in a group.'
She declared (that) she was a yachtswoman and a loner. She insisted (that) she would rather go hill climbing alone than in a group.

1 'I'm attempting to break the world record for sailing non-stop east to west the 'wrong way' around the world.'
2 'I suppose my worst fear is personal failure. But I'm not trying to prove myself by sailing alone around the world. I've always been involved in challenging projects.'
3 'Yes, I'm doing it because I'm hoping to beat the present world record of 161 days.'

4 'I'm taking food and drink to last me up to 200 days.'
5 'The food includes 500 dried meals, 150 apples, 144 bars of chocolate, 36 jars of jam and marmalade and 14 tubs of dried fruit and nuts.'
6 'When I'm thousands of miles from shore, and if I'm injured, then I'll be scared.'
7 'I've been taught to stitch my own flesh in an emergency.'
8 'If there's a crisis, as long as danger is not imminent, I think the answer is not instant action, but to make a cup of tea and think about it.'
9 'I know I can handle the boat and I'll find out whether I have the strength to beat the world record.'
10 'I'm being sponsored on the trip by security firms and credit agencies.'

27 Writing a report of an interview

Imagine that you are a journalist. You have been asked to interview the yachtswoman. Write a report of the interview for your newspaper. Invent extra details to make your report convincing. Aim for a balance between reported and direct speech.

INTERNATIONAL OVERVIEW

Vita and Maurice had a disastrous experience at sea. However, they had placed themselves at risk through their actions. For many people, disasters such as earthquakes, tornadoes and floods happen in the middle of everyday life and can have terrible consequences.

In Peru alone, for example, approximately 2,900 people die every year from natural disasters. Worldwide, between 1981 and 1990, tsunamis (unusually strong ocean waves) killed at least 1,600 people, tropical cyclones killed 38,700, floods killed 61,000, earthquakes killed 120,000 and drought and famine killed more than 560,000 people.

Study these bar charts.

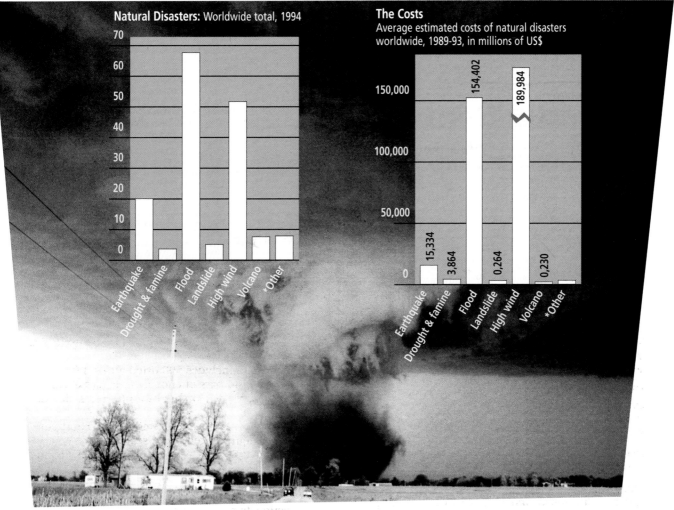

Natural Disasters: Worldwide total, 1994

The Costs
Average estimated costs of natural disasters worldwide, 1989-93, in millions of US$

*Other includes: avalanche, cold wave, heat wave, insect infestation, tsunami

1 What were the two commonest natural disasters worldwide in 1994?
2 Which two kinds of natural disaster were least costly in terms of money between 1989-93?

Japan, New Zealand and California are often shaken by earthquakes, and rules for building houses take the possibilities of earthquakes into account. Is your country vulnerable to any particular kind of natural disaster? Are any precautions taken to limit its effects?

Back from the dead

28 Pre-reading tasks

Have you ever lost anything that was important to you? In pairs, ask each other:

Where/be you?
Be you/alone?

What/be you/do/when you realise/it be lost?
What/you do/when you realise/what happen?
How/you react?
How/other people react?
What/happen/in the end?

PREDICTING

You are going to read a newspaper article about a seaside holiday which went wrong. Look carefully at the headlines and picture. What do they tell you about the story you are going to read?

Do you think the story will have a happy ending? Why/Why not?

LANGUAGE AND AUDIENCE

Do you expect the language to be chatty and colloquial? Or formal and serious? Why?

Who do you think would enjoy reading this story?

29 Reading for gist

Read the newspaper article carefully, trying to guess any unknown words from the context. Most of the story is told using past tenses. As you read, underline examples of the past simple, past continuous and past perfect tenses.

DOG SURVIVED ON WATER FOR TWO WEEKS, STRANDED AT THE FOOT OF A CLIFF

Back from the dead
Owner is reunited with pet he thought he'd never see again after 100 ft plunge.

BY LUKE HARDING

WHEN Judy the mongrel spotted her first sheep, she did what comes naturally.

The 4-year-old set off in pursuit across several fields and, being a pampered city animal, lost both her quarry and her sense of direction.

Then she rounded the edge of a cliff and plummeted 100 ft, bouncing off a rock into the sea and, everyone thought, oblivion.

Her owner Mike Holden called the coastguard. Six volunteers abseiled down the cliff but gave up all hope of finding her alive after a 90-minute search.

Three days later, a hurricane pounded the coast near St Just in Cornwall and a distraught Mr Holden returned home from his holiday convinced his pet was dead.

For the next two weeks, the Holden household at Halesowen, West Midlands, was heartbroken. Then, on Monday, the phone rang and a man asked if he would like his dog back.

A birdwatcher, armed with a telescope, had spotted the pet two days earlier sitting forlornly on a rock. While he raised the alarm, a student from Leeds, Chris Hague, climbed down the cliff between Morvah and Gunnard's Head north of St Just to collect Judy.

The black and white bitch had initially been knocked unconscious but survived by drinking water from a fresh stream at the base of the cliff. She may have fed on the body of a sheep which had also tumbled over the edge.

It was, as Mr Holden admitted yesterday, 'a minor miracle'.

He recalled yesterday how he had left his rented cottage at St Just with five friends and set off on a coast walk. 'Judy was running in a field. Then she spotted a sheep and went chasing after it. She ran for about a quarter of a mile and tumbled head first down the cliffs and bounced off jagged rocks into the sea.

'We just stood there in stunned silence. I was distraught. We couldn't get down the cliffs because they were so sheer. I ran back to St Just to get help. I went into the Star pub and they phoned the coastguard. He turned up in seconds and a rescue party abseiled down the cliff.

'This was on the second day of the holiday. It ruined it. I gave her up for lost and went home very depressed.

'I consoled myself with the thought she had died in the most beautiful part of the country. The trauma has been very stressful.'

Before her adventure: Judy in the arms of her owner's daughter, Rosie Holden, 12

Mr Holden, a 38-year-old electronics engineer, was on his way to Cornwall last night to be reunited with Judy.

Steve Tregear, who was in charge of the rescue, said the dog was emaciated, a bit scratched and bruised but otherwise healthy.

He said: 'It was a very lucky dog. I think it must have been crossed with a cat somewhere along the line!'

St Just vet Stephen Sawyer, who was looking after Judy yesterday, said she had survived because of a plentiful supply of fresh water.

'She was also a very pampered dog before and it was probably those few extra pounds that saved her,' he added. 'She is very thin and hungry. But considering she had been there two weeks her condition is very good.'

30 Vocabulary check   19/8/02

Find words in the article and headlines to match these definitions. To help you, the definitions are in the same order as the words.

1 unable to get back *naturally strengthed*
2 a sudden fall *plummeted / plunge*
3 noticed *convinced / spotted*
4 too well cared for *plump*
5 an animal being chased *quarry*
6 fell quickly and suddenly *tumbled*
7 extremely upset *depressed / heartbroken*
8 looking lost and sad *forlornly*
9 a female dog *bitch*
10 fell *sheer*
11 sharp *jagged*
12 very steep, almost vertical *cliff / abseil*

31 True/false comprehension

Decide whether the following statements about the story are true or false.

1 Judy was used to the countryside. *F*
2 She followed a sheep over a cliff. *F*
3 She lost consciousness when she fell. *T*
4 Her owner climbed down the cliff to find her. *F*
5 The rescue party arrived very quickly. *F T*
6 Her owner continued his holiday without her. *F*
7 Judy was identified by a student. *T F*
8 She was a little overweight before her fall. *T*
9 She was in poor health when she was rescued. *T*
10 She had survived because of access to fresh water. *T*

32 Narrative structure

Like many newspaper accounts, the story is not reported in chronological order. It begins by explaining how Judy got lost and the failed rescue attempt. We are then told that a second rescue attempt was successful. Halfway through the report the events of her fall and safe return are repeated, with more detail.

Why do you think the story is told like this? Consider the following:

• to provide a dramatic opening which is not slowed down by too much detail
• to enable us to hear actual spoken comments from the people who were involved
• to make the narrative as varied, moving and personal as possible.

33 Writing a summary from notes 19/6/02

Write a summary of the story describing how the dog got lost, what the owner did and felt, and how they were reunited. Use these notes to help you.

Mike Holden be/holiday/Cornwall. On second day/he go out/walk/with dog/Judy. Judy start/chasing sheep. Unfortunately she be/not used to/countryside/and she fall over/cliff/towards/sea. Her owner contact/coastguard/and rescue team/abseiled down/cliff. However, Judy can not/found/and owner

return/his home/feel/very distressed. Two weeks later/man/ring. He say/birdwatcher/notice Judy/on rock. Student/rescue her. She be thin/but well. Yet say/Judy probably survive/by drink/fresh water/and feed on/dead sheep.

34 Vocabulary: Adjectives

Judy is described as a *pampered* dog who becomes *emaciated*. Her owner is *heartbroken* when he loses her.

The following adjectives describe emotion, appearance and the way a person or animal is treated. With a partner, try to rank them in order. Use a dictionary as necessary.

EMOTION

heartbroken indifferent distraught happy irritated pleased satisfied ecstatic miserable

APPEARANCE

slim emaciated skinny plump scrawny fat obese overweight

TREATMENT

pampered neglected well cared-for ignored worshipped abused

35 Homonyms

Homonyms are words which have the same sound and spelling but different meanings. There are a number of examples in the article 'Back from the dead'.

1 'The 4-year-old lost both her *quarry* and her sense of direction.'

   Quarry in this sentence means 'prey'. *Quarry* can also refer to a place where minerals such as limestone, marble etc are extracted.

2 'A birdwatcher, armed with a telescope, had *spotted* the pet two days earlier.'

   Spotted in this sentence is a verb which means 'noticed'.

   What does *spotted* mean in the following sentence? What part of speech is it?

   'He had a green and white *spotted* scarf around his neck.'

3 'We couldn't get down the cliffs because they were so *sheer*.'

   In this sentence *sheer* means 'extremely steep'.

   What does *sheer* mean in the following sentence? What part of speech is it?

   'Driving fast on a motorway without a seatbelt is *sheer* madness.'

PRACTICE

Work with a partner to check the meanings of the following homonyms. Use a dictionary if you need to. Then write example sentences to show the different meanings each word can have. Indicate whether the word is being used as a noun, verb, adjective etc.

1 mine   5 file
2 sound   6 book
3 stamp   7 light
4 dash   8 match

What other homonyms do you know? Share your ideas in your group.

36 Revision of defining relative clauses

Study this sentence from the text:
'She may have fed on the body of a sheep *which had also tumbled over the edge.*'

The clause in italics is important to the meaning of the sentence. It is called a defining clause, because it defines or makes clear which person or thing is being talked about. Here are some more examples:

1 *The vet who treated Judy was very efficient.*
2 *They interviewed the man whose dog had been rescued.*
3 *Have you read the leaflet which/that explains what to do if you have an accident?*
4 *He told me what was in the suitcase.*

A defining clause is essential to the meaning of the sentence. If it is left out, the sentence does not make complete sense or the meaning changes. No commas are needed before defining clauses. Relative pronouns are **who** and **whose**, referring to people, and **that** or **which** referring to things.

PRACTICE

Complete these sentences with suitable defining clauses.

1 They prefer stories _which have an_ endings.

2 The man _whose_ dog on holiday has gone home without her.

3 The student _who had_ received an award for bravery.

4 The watersport _that I went_ on holiday has become my hobby.

5 The owner of the dog _who fall –_ cliff was distraught.

6 The man _who looked the_ cliff was convinced his pet was dead.

37 Revision of non-defining relative clauses

Non-defining relative clauses give extra information about something. They can be in the middle or at the end of a sentence. Commas are used to separate them from the rest of the sentence.

Study these examples:

1 *Steve Tregear, who was in charge of the rescue, said the dog was emaciated.*
2 *Pablo, whose father is an ambulance driver, is learning what to do in an emergency.*
3 *Forecasting the eruptions of volcanoes, which can let off steam lightly for years, is very difficult.*
4 *He gave the dog some water, which she obviously needed.*

Who, **whose** and **which** are used in non-defining clauses. **That** is never used.

Non-defining clauses 'round out' your sentences. Try to use them, as they make your writing more interesting and complex.

PRACTICE

Add suitable non-defining clauses to these sentences. You should use *whose* in at least one of the clauses.

1 Rahmia Altat, _who is there_ (who gave up), now does voluntary work.

2 We heard about the heroic acts of the rescue workers, _who did a great job_

3 Nurse Thompson, _who is in the hospital_ demonstrated the life-saving techniques.

4 Drowning, _that happened recent_, can usually be prevented.

5 Smoke alarms, _which prevent fire_, should be fitted in every home.

6 My cousin Gina, _who parents are died_, is being brought up by her grandparents.

Try to expand these simple sentences into more complex ones, using non-defining clauses to add extra information.

7 Mrs Nazir _who for a lucky draw has_ won a trip to the Caribbean.

8 Edward Smith left his fortune to the dogs' home. _who was away for days_

9 Our sailing teacher took us to an island. _which was beaut_

Write some sentences of your own using non-defining clauses.

38 Functions quiz: Consoling and commiserating   2/6/02

Working in pairs, decide which is the most appropriate way to respond to the following statements giving bad news. Tick as many of the answers as you think are suitable.

1 I've just failed my driving test.

   a What a shame.
   b How horrific!
   c That's sheer tragedy.
   d You should have done better.
   e Better luck next time.

2 My grandma died recently.

    a Oh, I am sorry. Is there anything I can do to help?
    b You must be really fed up.
    c How sad. Was it sudden?
    d Don't get too worried about it.
    e What bad luck!

3 I forgot my door key and had to wait outside for two hours until my father got back from work.

    a How annoying!
    b That was forgetful of you.
    c My heart goes out to you.
    d I'd just like to say how sad I am for you.
    e You must remember to put it in your bag in future.

4 I thought I'd videoed the last episode of 'Jewel in the Crown'. When I put the cassette in I found I'd taped the wrong programme.

    a Never mind. I can let you have the video I made.
    b I bet you were furious.
    c I'd have been really annoyed.
    d You've got all my sympathy for what you're going through.
    e Remember to follow the instructions next time.

Study the following comments. Write down some appropriate responses and then try them out on your partner.

5 I didn't get the job I applied for.

try to look up the newspaper for more jobs

6 I'm really disappointed with my new hair cut.

so, don't go to the salon again

7 My dog fell over a cliff and is seriously hurt.

How is your dog now?

39 Spelling and pronunciation: The suffix -tion or -ion

The suffix *-tion* or *-ion* is quite common in English. Examples in the text were *direction* and *condition*. How is the final syllable pronounced in these words?

Other examples are:

1	revision	7	qualification
2	fashion	8	definition
3	occupation	9	recognition
4	demonstration	10	ignition
5	passion	11	exhibition
6	invention	12	promotion

Listen carefully and try to mark the main stress in each of the words. Then practise saying them.

Question, *opinion* and *oblivion* are exceptions to the rule. How are they pronounced?

Now match ten of the words from the list to these definitions.

    a Will improve your chances of getting a job.
    b Another word for work.
    c A machine or gadget that is original.
    d Strong emotion.
    e A display of books or pictures.
    f The dictionary will give you this information about a word.
    g A better job with more money.
    h If this is turned off, the car will not start.
    i Artists can work for twenty years without getting this.
    j The latest styles in clothes and shoes.

40 Language study: Adverbs

Adverbs have a large number of different uses.

They can tell us more about a verb.
Example: *She walked slowly.*

They can be used before an adjective.
Example: *It was fairly difficult.*

They can be used before another adverb.
Example: *He drove terribly slowly.*

They can tell us when or how often something happens.
Examples: *occasionally, regularly, never*

They can give information about how certain we are of something.
Examples: *definitely, probably, perhaps*

They can connect ideas.
Examples: *firstly, however, lastly*

FORMATION OF ADVERBS

Many adverbs are formed by adding *-ly* to adjectives. *Naturally, forlornly* and *initially* are examples from the text 'Back from the Dead'.

Other examples are: *quick ~ quickly, cheap ~ cheaply.*

If the adjective ends in *-y*, you change the *-y* to *-i* before adding *-ly*.
Example: *angry ~ angrily*

If the adjective ends in *-ic*, you add *-ally*.
Example: *heroic ~ heroically*

If the adjective ends in *-le*, you drop the *-e* and add *-y*.
Example: *reasonable ~ reasonably*

Remember that some adjectives look like adverbs.
Examples: *lovely, elderly, friendly*

Notice also: *early ~ early, fast ~ fast, good ~ well*

PRACTICE

Correct this report on jobs at sea from a careers magazine for young people. Change the words in italics to adverbs. Ask your partner to mark it when you have finished to check that your spelling is correct.

Photograph courtesy of the Royal Fleet Auxiliary.

CAREERS AT SEA

Working at sea sounds romantic but it can also be *surprising* hard work! Voyages last at least a week and *possible* much longer. As you will see, it is *definite* not for the *lazy* inclined.

Here are some of the main jobs at sea.

The Captain

The captain is in overall control of the vessel. He or she (modern captains are not *necessary* male) is *direct* responsible for the vessel, crew, cargo and passengers. It is essential that the captain can think *quick* in an emergency. The captain *normally* takes the vessel in and out of port.

Engineering Officer

Engineering officers are responsible for the ship's engines and all the equipment which is *electronic* operated. The equipment is checked *day* and any faults must be corrected *immediate*. Officers are *able* assisted by ratings – workers who maintain equipment in the engine room and elsewhere.

The Purser

The purser is responsible for buying and storing food and making sure it is prepared and served *hygienic*. Pursers must make sure that all those on the vessel are fed *healthy* and *economic*. They are also in charge of the cooks and stewards, who are *usual full* trained chefs and waiters.

Navigating Officer

The navigating officers are responsible for navigating the ship *proper* and for making sure the loading and unloading of cargo is *total* safe. They respond *appropriate* to any changes in weather (in some areas the climate can change *dramatic* in seconds) and adjust the ship's speed *according*. In difficult conditions, when it's snowing very *heavy* for example, they may take over *temporary* from the helmsman.

Skills and qualities needed for work at sea

You must be:
- *technical* minded (for most jobs)
- *suitable* qualified, *preferable* GCSE standard or higher
- able to work *capable* and *efficient* for long periods
- able to get on *happy* with others as part of a team
- able to react *responsible* in times of crisis
- able to stay calm even when *frantic* busy.

41 Look, say, cover, write, check

In the text 'Back from the Dead' you saw the word *distraught*. The letters *aught* are a common combination in many words. The phonetic spelling is /ɔːt/.

Use the 'look, say, cover, write, check' method to learn these words. Make sure you understand the meaning of each one.

1	distraught	**4**	naughty
2	fraught	**5**	haughty
3	caught	**6**	taught

'*Ought*' is also pronounced /ɔːt/. Use the same method to learn to spell these words correctly.

7	thought	**10**	fought
8	nought	**11**	sought
9	bought	**12**	brought

Reacting to the unexpected

42 Pre-reading task: Making notes

Read about these unexpected events that happened to various people.

A

I was on my way home when a passer-by collapsed in the street.

B

I wasn't interested, but the other party guests insisted I tried the disco-dancing competition and I won first prize!

C

I'd just got out my homework when water started pouring down the walls of the kitchen.

D

We had just gone to bed when the smoke alarms went off.

E

My neighbour knocked on the door. She was sure her little girl had swallowed some poisonous berries.

Have you ever had to cope with something, pleasant or unpleasant, that was completely unexpected? Think carefully about the event and then make notes under these headings.

The background to the event

Where were you? ....
....

What were you doing? ....
....

Who was with you and what were they doing? ....
....

The event itself

What happened? ....

....

How did you react? ....

....

What did other people do? ....

....

What happened then? ....

....

The outcome

What happened in the end? ....

....

What do you feel you have learned from the experience? ....

....

How has the experience affected other people? ....

....

Has the event had any other permanent effects? ....

....

Compare your notes with your partner. Look after them as you'll need
them later.

43 Reading a model narrative

Read this narrative written for a school newsletter. Do you think you
would react in the same way as the writer?

As you read, underline the tenses and the examples of non-defining
relative clauses.

THE BIGGEST EVENT OF MY SUMMER

by Naila Khan Afza

It seemed like another ordinary day. My family and I had decided to spend the day on the beach. I sat in the sun watching the children throwing pebbles or paddling. I was just going to have a swim when I noticed a strange object bobbing about in the sea. To my horror, I realised the 'object' was a child drowning. Without stopping to think, I plunged into the water and grabbed the child. With my free arm I swam back to the shore. The child, who was a boy of about five, was like a dead weight but I felt powered by a superhuman strength.

I laid the boy, who appeared to be unconscious, gently on the ground and gave him mouth to mouth resuscitation which revived him immediately. I was dimly aware that a large crowd had gathered and someone was telling me an ambulance was on its way. By the time the ambulance arrived, to my great relief, the boy was sitting up and talking.

Dale's parents were delighted with his quick recovery. They telephoned me later to thank me and we had a long discussion about the dangers of playing near water. They have arranged for him to have swimming lessons, which I think is a very good idea. I would definitely recommend that all the students in the school learn to swim. I'd also like to remind everyone to take care near the sea, rivers or swimming pools. You can drown much more easily than you think!

COMPREHENSION CHECK

1 What was Naila doing when the incident happened?
2 Did she have time to tell anyone else what was happening?
3 What helped the boy regain consciousness?
4 How did the boy's parents express their thanks?
5 What does Naila suggest everyone should do?

44 Analysing the narrative

A Openings are important in narratives. Does the story interest you immediately? Why/Why not?

B In the first paragraph, a number of different tenses are used. What are they, how are they formed and what are their functions?

C *To my horror*, *Without stopping to think* and *To my great relief* are used for effect. What other phrases could be used?

D Endings are important in a narrative. The reader should not feel there are unanswered questions. Do you think the story is brought to a satisfactory conclusion? Why/Why not?

E Remember, a narrative should answer these questions:

Who .....?   Why .....?
What .....?   How .....?
Where .....?   When .....?

How does Naila's narrative do this?

45 Dramatic expressions

My hair stood on end ...
My heart missed a beat ...

Your sentences can be made more dramatic by starting them with this kind of expression. Make complete sentences by matching the following openings 1–6 with the endings A–F. More than one option may be possible, so decide which you prefer.

1 With my heart in my mouth ...
2 A piercing scream cut through the air ...
3 I froze to the spot ...
4 Panic mounted ...
5 With trembling fingers ...
6 Sweat poured from us ...

A ... as we fought to rescue the children trapped by the earthquake.
B ... when flames appeared at the side of the plane.
C ... as the hijacker produced a gun!
D ...when the ghostly figure appeared in the graveyard.
E ... I tiptoed past the sleeping kidnappers.
F ... he struggled to open his parachute.

Now write four sentences of your own using dramatic expressions.

46 Pre-writing discussion

1 What does windsurfing involve? it involved stregth fitness
2 What do you think is exciting about this sport? it is challeging
3 Could it ever be dangerous? Why/Why not? Yes, the person may laugh
4 Does this hobby appeal to you? Why/Why not? no, because I never play this before

47 Ways of developing an outline

The following list of sentences is an outline of a story. It describes how a windsurfer was swept out to sea and what happened in the end. Read the sentences carefully. Make sure you understand all the points clearly.

I Fought To Stay Alive

I was sailing off the coast of Devon.
It was a calm sunny day.
I'm a very experienced windsurfer.
Everything was going well.
The wind turned, forcing me off-shore.
I tried for an hour to get back to the shore.
I began to feel weaker.
The wind started coming in gusts.
The sea was rough.
I clung hard to the board.
A helicopter flew over.
I thought it was coming to rescue me.
I waved and shouted.
It flew over me to the other side of the bay.
I was wearing a dark wetsuit on a blue and white board.
I was part of the sea and no one could see me.
When night fell, I lay down on the board, wrapped in my sail.
I was in my own little world.
Then I heard a helicopter.
I waved.
They saw me.
They rescued me.

25/6/02

Obviously, a list of events does not make a complete narrative. In fact, the pleasure of reading a good story often lies not in the plot, but in the details.

What details could you add to the outline above to produce an exciting, well-written story? With your partner, tick off the points which could make your story come alive.

a ✓ Beginning the story with some interesting details which set the scene. E.g. *It was a beautiful, sunny day and I was doing what I like best – windsurfing.*

b Describing the weather and the sea in a vivid way. E.g. *The wind was howling/The waves were crashing.*

c Using dramatic expressions. E.g. *My heart sank as the sailboard was carried far out to sea.*

d Using emotional expressions to add drama. E.g. *to my horror/to my intense relief.* (See exercise 23.)

e Writing a clear conclusion to the story which expresses the feelings of the writer about the experience. E.g. *I am so grateful to the people who rescued me. I was not ready to die at sea!*

※ DON'T FORGET!

Time expressions make the sequence of events clear, E.g. *Many hours passed, some time later, until, when, then, while, next, finally.*

Conjunctions connect clauses or show connections between sentences. E.g. *however, although.*

Non-defining relative clauses round out sentences and make them more interesting to read.

48 Building a story from a dialogue

In pairs, read this conversation about what happened during a school outing to the seaside.

Sophie: Where did you go for your school trip this year?

Anne: We went to the coast. It was so hot that we all wanted to get out of the city.

Sophie: How did it go?

Anne: Well, we had a great day, apart from one incident.

Sophie: Oh, what was that?

Anne: Well, we all got to the beach without any trouble. We'd finished putting on suntan cream and were just going for a swim when Mrs Jordan noticed that her purse, which had all our return train tickets in it, was missing.

Sophie: Oh no!

Anne: Yes, she was dreadfully upset. She decided that the purse must have dropped out of her bag on the walk to the beach from the station. You see, Thomas had offered to carry the bag for her and she thought maybe it had fallen out then – but she wasn't really sure.

Sophie: So did you all go back to look for it or what?

Anne: Well, I offered to go with her, but in the end she said she'd retrace her steps with Thomas and see if they could see any sign of it.

Sophie: Poor Thomas. He must have felt awful.

Anne: I think he did. I mean, he was just going to have a swim when he had to put his clothes back on and go back to the station with Mrs Jordan.

Sophie: And did they find it?

Anne: Well, they walked right back to the station without seeing it. At the station they asked at the information desk but it hadn't been handed in.

Sophie: Oh dear.

Anne: On the way back to the beach they stopped at a café for a drink. They were talking about the purse and wondering what to do next when the owner came over. He asked if they'd lost anything. They mentioned her purse and the man produced it from under the counter. A passer-by had spotted it on the pavement outside and had handed it in at the café.

Sophie: Well that was lucky! And was everything still inside?

Anne: Yes, it was, thank goodness.

WRITING THE STORY *Read.*

You are Thomas. Write an account of the incident for the class newsletter. Before you begin writing, plan what you will say. Use these notes to help you.

* Give the story a clear **shape**: background details, main events and the outcome should be clear.

* **Tenses** and **pronouns** should be appropriate.

* Try to write **vividly**, using a range of vocabulary and expressions.

* Use clearly defined **paragraphs**.

Exam-format questions

Writing

1 You were walking on the beach with some friends when you discovered a valuable object. You decide to write an account of the incident for your school magazine.

In the account you should describe:

- how you found the object
- how you felt
- how other people reacted
- what you did about the object
- what happened in the end.

The pictures may give you some ideas, but you are free to write about any object of your choice.

Your account should be about 200 words long.

2 You and your family were on a ship when a storm blew up. Fortunately, you were able to return to the coast unhurt. Write a letter of about 200 words to a close relative, describing what happened.

In your letter you should:

- explain what you were doing when the storm blew up
- describe how people reacted
- say what the captain of the ship decided to do
- explain how you felt afterwards.

3 You were on a school outing when one of the younger children got lost. You helped your teacher find him or her. Write an account of the incident for the school newsletter. In the account you should:

- explain how the child got lost
- describe how the other members of the party reacted
- explain how you managed to find him/her
- say what you learned from the incident.

Your account should be about 200 words long.

Oral assessment

A happy ending

Tell the examiner or your partner about an incident which was worrying or frightening when it happened but which had a good outcome. Try to explain what you, and other people involved, learned from the incident.

You are not allowed to make any written notes.

EXAMINER'S TIPS

1   When asked to write a **narrative**, students sometimes say they don't know what to write about. The ingredients for stories are all around us: in the incidents that happen in everyday life; in the stories your friends tell you about things that have happened to them; in newspaper articles; in the letters read out on radio talk shows and so on. With a little ingenuity you can rework intriguing ideas into your own writing.

2   The plot isn't everything. Many wonderful stories do not have particularly original plots. The main interest in a story often lies in the beauty of the writing. Giving **attention to details** in your writing is as important as having an original plot.

3   **Planning** your composition before you start composing will help you structure it. Narratives usually start with background information. The story then develops and you explain what happened. Finally there should be a definite rounding off so the reader isn't left wondering what happened in the end.

4   Aim to **make your writing interesting** so the reader really wants to read on and find out what happened next. Here are some ways you can do this:

- Use a mixture of short sentences and longer, more complex sentences.
- Use vivid language and a range of emotional and dramatic expressions.

- Try to set the scene at the beginning in a powerful, unusual way if you can.
- Endings are important too. Try to make the ending satisfying and logical.

5   If you enjoy reading and have any favourite authors, try to work out what you particularly like about their books. Study their style. What techniques do they use to help you 'picture' the story in your mind? Could you adopt any of these techniques in your own work?

Remember, regular readers do much better in exams than those who don't read very often.

EXAM STRATEGY

6   Try to get into the habit of punctuating as you go along, by 'hearing' the prose in your mind.

7   In Part 2 of Papers 3/4 (Listening) you will probably have to **complete a set of notes**. Sometimes you can use the words exactly as you heard them, but at other times you will need to change the word order or use words and phrases of your own to complete the gaps.

You will hear each exercise twice. Use the second listening to check your answers for complete sense.

Unit focus

In this unit you have learned to write a **narrative composition**. You have studied narrative tenses, and how to write strong openings and endings. You have learned to add interest to your writing by using relative clauses, and emotional and dramatic expressions. This is practice for Papers 1/2, Part 3.

You have read a detailed newspaper text and answered true/false questions. This is practice for Papers 1/2, Part 1.

You have listened to an interview and taken notes. This is practice for Papers 3/4, Part 2.

The Animal World

A fresh look at zoos

1 Animal vocabulary

Working with a partner, match seven of these words with the pictures.
Make sure you know the meaning of all of them. Then decide whether
each creature is a *mammal*, *reptile*, *fish* or *bird*.

shark	kangaroo	goat
rhino	eagle	frog
monkey	lizard	lion
gorilla	parrot	dolphin
camel	crocodile	salmon
owl	leopard	bear
penguin	elephant	wolf

A

B

C

D

F

E

G

2 Definitions

Choose the correct word or phrase to match these definitions.
Work with a partner and consult a dictionary if necessary.

1 A person in a zoo who looks after animals is known as
   a a carer.   **c** a warder.
   b a keeper.   **d** a poacher.

2 The natural surroundings of an animal are called its
   a habitat.   **c** home.
   b location.   **d** enclosure.

3 Animals which hunt and kill other animals for food are known as
   a scavengers.   **c** predators.
   b beasts.   **d** prey.

4 Animals which may die out altogether are known as
   a an endangered species.   **c** indigenous wildlife.
   b animals in captivity.   **d** migrating herds.

5 Animals which once lived but have now died out are known as
   a domesticated.   **c** fossils.
   b extinct.   **d** amphibians.

3 Pre-reading discussion

A   How do you feel about zoos? Talk to your partner about a zoo you have visited. Which aspects did you find particularly interesting?

Think about
* the range of animals and birds
* the conditions under which they were kept
* whether they seemed contented
* the atmosphere of the zoo in general.

B   Was there anything about the zoo that you did not enjoy?

C   If you have never been to a zoo, would you like to visit one? Why?

Keep a record of your views to use later in the unit.

4 Reading a model school magazine article

Hammerton High School paid a visit to a zoo. After the visit, Michael wrote about the trip for his school magazine. Read his article below. How does his impression of the zoo compare with your own experiences?

As you read, underline the opinion words and phrases he uses.

CAN ZOOS EVER BE ANIMAL-FRIENDLY?

The theme of our last class discussion was 'How can zoos provide animals with a decent life?' Everyone except me (I just wasn't sure) believed it was impossible for zoos to give animals a decent environment. Mr Hennessy suggested that, now the exams are over, actually visiting a modern zoo might give us a wider perspective.

I went to the zoo with an open mind and I was pleasantly surprised by what I found. In our debate, many people said that zoos are full of smelly cages containing animals with miserable, hunted-looking expressions. Metro Park Zoo, however, was set in an attractive, open environment. Trees and bushes had been planted around the enclosures, and small ponds had been dug out so the animals had access to water. In my opinion, the animals, rather than seeming depressed or frustrated, were peaceful and contented.

As we entered, we were given information packs about the origins and habits of the animals. The zoo takes a lot of trouble to keep the animals' diet, living quarters and social groupings as natural as possible. Expert veterinary attention is on hand if they become ill.

At school, some people accused zoos of exploiting animals for profit but at Metro Park, as I see it, nothing could be further from the truth. Most of the profits are ploughed back to improve conditions at the zoo or donated to charities for endangered species.

Before I visited Metro Park Zoo, I wasn't sure about the rights and wrongs of zoos. It was difficult to say how a zoo could really compensate animals for their loss of freedom. On balance I feel that, although zoos can't provide the stimulation and freedom of the wild, they can be animal-friendly by giving animals a safe, secure and caring environment where they are well fed and protected from predators. As long as they do this well, to my mind they make a positive contribution to animal welfare. They also play an important part in educating us about wildlife. I think lots of my friends changed their minds, too.

On the bus back to school we all agreed that what we liked most was the zoo's atmosphere and we would definitely recommend it for next year's group.

5 Comprehension check

1   Why did Michael's class visit the zoo?
2   What was his first impression of the zoo?
3   What did he find out from the zoo's publicity?
4   What kind of role does he think zoos have in modern society?
5   What do you think are the bad points about zoos which Michael has not mentioned?

6 Analysing the article

A Does the first paragraph form a good opening to the article? Do you feel you want to read on? Why/Why not? How is it obviously intended for an audience of school pupils?

B Paragraph 2 questions the attitudes many people have to zoos by contrasting their opinion with the reality (as Michael sees it) of Metro Park Zoo. Find the words and phrases which do this.

C Paragraphs 3 and 4 continue the theme of disagreeing with other people's opinions about zoos. Underline the phrase which expresses disagreement.

D Paragraph 5 sums up Michael's view of zoos. Which phrase tells us that he has thought about both sides of the argument before coming to a decision? Which connector is used to develop his argument and link his ideas together?

E Does the final paragraph round off the article effectively? How do we know that the writer is aware of his audience?

7 Typical opinion language

In paragraph 2, Michael introduces an opinion with *In my opinion*. What other opinion words and phrases does he use? Make a list.

....

....

What other opinion words and phrases do you know? Add them to your list.

DISAGREEING WITH OTHER PEOPLE'S VIEWS

In explaining his views, Michael thinks about and rejects the ideas other people have about zoos. Study the list and tick off the phrases Michael used. Can you add any phrases?

A common misconception is that ...
Contrary to popular belief, ...
It is believed that ... , yet ...
People think ... but ...
Some people accuse them of ... but nothing could be further from the truth.
Many people say that ... However, ...
It's unfair for people to say that ...
People make the absurd/ridiculous claim that ...
Despite claims that ... ,

8 Making your mind up

Here are ways you can show that you have thought carefully about a variety of opinions before making up your mind. Can you recognise the phrase Michael used? Which do you prefer?

Now that I have considered both sides, I feel ...
After weighing up the pros and cons, I would say that ...
On balance I feel that ...
There are points in favour of each argument but overall I believe ...
I tend to come down on the side of ...

9 Writing a paragraph

Choose one of the following topics and write a short paragraph giving your own opinions on the subject. Don't forget that you need clear reasons to back up your views. Try to select appropriate phrases from exercise 7 to help frame your views.

Animals – healthy and happy in the wild, bored and fed-up in the zoo?

Pets – treasured companions or dirty nuisances?

Eating meat: vital for health or unnecessary and unfair to animals?

10 Reading aloud

When you are ready, take turns reading your paragraphs aloud. This will give you a chance to get an overview of your classmates' opinions. Does hearing other students' paragraphs make a difference to your own views? If so, you may like to choose a 'making your mind up' phrase to express your feelings.

11 Expressions of contrasting meaning

In his article, Michael says people think of zoos as full of 'smelly cages' but in fact the animals were kept in 'an attractive, open environment' – the opposite, you could say, of what was expected.

For each idea below, try to develop an expression which conveys a contrasting meaning.

Example: *a bare, cramped room*
a comfortably furnished, spacious room

Work in pairs or small groups, and take time to check words in a dictionary when you need to.

1. a dull, uninformative lesson
2. a scuffed, down-at-heel pair of shoes
3. a whining, sickly child
4. an overcooked, tasteless meal
5. an awkward, clumsy dance
6. an untidy, neglected garden
7. ugly, illegible handwriting
8. a rusty, battered bicycle
9. a loud, aggressive person
10. a hard, lumpy bed

When you have finished, compare your answers with the other groups. Which expressions do you think were most effective?

12 Before you listen

You are going to listen to a radio talk about the concept of an electronic zoo. Modern technology is used to portray the animals in natural settings.

Write down three things you would like to find out about this type of zoo.

13 Vocabulary check

Make sure you know the meaning of these words and phrases.

- audio-visual
- filmed on location
- live exhibits
- natural history

14 Listening for gist

 Now listen to the radio talk. Does the speaker answer your questions about electronic zoos?

15 True/false comprehension ???

Decide whether the following statements about the electronic zoo are true or false.

1 Visitors to the electronic zoo will gain a greater insight into animal behaviour.
2 The large animals will be allowed to wander freely, watched by cameras.
3 The technology at the zoo will help people feel they are watching a particularly good film show.
4 95% of the world's species will be represented.
5 The pre-recorded film of live exhibits will be produced by staff at the electronic zoo itself.
6 Visitors will be disappointed if animals at the electronic zoo are asleep.

16 Post-listening discussion

A If you could choose between a visit to a 'real zoo' and an electronic zoo, which would you prefer? Try to explain your reasons.

B Do you think the electronic zoo will become popular with the public? Would it appeal more to one target group rather than another? Discuss your views in groups.

17 Functions Read

Have you ever been to a circus? Tell your partner what you thought of it.

Now listen to the dialogue on the tape. Silvia is expressing disappointment. Does her voice go up or down?

Malik: What did you think of the circus?
Silvia: Well, to be honest, I was just a bit disappointed.
Malik: Why was that?
Silvia: The trapeze artists weren't very exciting and I didn't like seeing large animals performing tricks.
Malik: Surely the jugglers were good fun to watch?
Silvia: As a matter of fact, they weren't as skilful as I thought they'd be.

Malik: But wasn't seeing a real live fire-eater amazing?
Silvia: To be frank, I've seen better things on television.
Malik: Sounds like a waste of money, then.
Silvia: It was! In fact, we left before the end.

EXPRESSING DISAPPOINTMENT

I was just a little bit disappointed.
It didn't come up to my expectations.
It wasn't as interesting/enjoyable/well done/polished/as I thought it would be.
I've seen better things on television.
It was a let down.

EXPRESSING DISAGREEMENT INFORMALLY

Surely the clowns/costumes/performances/songs were amusing/intriguing/absorbing/spectacular?
But wasn't a real live fire-eater/film star/pop singer/famous athlete amazing/superb/unforgettable to watch?
Wasn't it wonderful to see the real thing?

INTRODUCING PERSONAL OPINION

As a matter of fact,/In fact,
To be honest,/If you want my honest opinion,
To be frank/Frankly,
Actually,

COMMENTING

It sounds like a waste of money, then.
It sounds as if it wasn't worth going to.
It sounds as if you'd have been better off at home.

18 Practice dialogues Read

Try to make a complete dialogue from the prompts. Make sure the person expressing disappointment SOUNDS disappointed!

A: What/you think/electronic zoo?
B: Frank/just bit/disappointed.
A: Why/that?
B: Most exhibits/asleep/interactive video/not work.
A: Surely/sounds/elephants/African waterhole/fascinating?
B: Actually/not be/realistic/thought/it be.
A: But/not be/Magic Windows/fantastic?
B: Matter/fact/be/let down.
A: You/be/better off/home.
B: That's right! And saved my money, too.

Try to create similar dialogues around the following situations.

- A disappointing visit to an animal sanctuary where injured animals are cared for before being returned to the wild.
- A disappointing visit to a theatre or concert to see well-known performers.
- Some other disappointing event you have personally experienced.

Animal experimentation

19 Pre-reading discussion

Experiments on animals play a large part in medical research. Scientists say they hope to find cures for many human diseases by finding out how animals react to being given drugs or having operations.

Animals are living beings. Experimenting on them raises ethical questions. Ethical questions ask if something is right or wrong.

ETHICAL QUESTIONS

Here are some ethical questions to discuss with your partner. Use a dictionary to check unfamiliar language.

Try to back up your answers with reasons and opinions.

1 Is it ethical to experiment on animals without painkillers or anaesthetics?
2 Is it acceptable to give a laboratory animal a human ear or heart?
3 Minor illnesses like colds and sore throats usually get better by themselves. Should animals be subjected to experiments to find cures for unimportant illnesses like these?

4 Genetic engineering can mean that laboratory animals are given genes which cause birth defects. When they reproduce, their young will be born with genetic problems. How justifiable is this?
5 Some serious illnesses are caused by overeating or smoking. Should animals suffer because of our bad habits?
6 Laboratory animals are used for non-medical experiments too. Is it fair to use animals to test the safety of luxury products such as perfume and after-shave?

Overall, what is your view of animal experimentation?

- *It doesn't trouble me at all.*
- *It's cruel and unjustifiable. I am totally opposed to it.*
- *It's a necessary evil – all right so long as animals are not exposed to unnecessary suffering.*

It has been said that the average pet has more stress from living with its owner than the laboratory animal ever suffers.

Do you think that's a reasonable view? Why/Why not?

20 Predicting content

You are going to read an article written by a doctor who is a campaigner for medical experiments on animals. Would you expect the opinions expressed in the article to be:

a balanced?
b a bit extreme?
c undecided?

21 Vocabulary check

Make sure you understand the meanings of

- an *emotive* issue
- a *controversial* issue.

22 Reading for detail

Read the article carefully and try to find answers to these questions. The questions reflect the opinions of the writer and not everyone would agree with them.

1　What does finding a cure for cystic fibrosis depend upon, according to the writer?

2　List the advances in medical understanding which have come as a result of animal research.

3　Why are particular diseases given to laboratory animals?

4　What dilemma is faced by researchers?

5　How might medical experiments on animals help animals?

Each year, around one million animals are used in laboratory experiments. Can their suffering be justified? Dr Mark Matfield, Director of the Research Defence Society, defends testing.

The use of animals for research is an emotive, controversial issue – many people oppose their use on the grounds that the experiments are cruel and unnecessary.

Twelve-year-old Laura thinks differently. Although she appears healthy, she has to take 30 different drugs each day and is expected to live for only another ten, maybe twelve, years. Every year, hundreds of children are born, like her, with cystic fibrosis. There is no cure – at least not yet.

Laura may, just may, be one of the first cystic fibrosis children to be saved. A few years ago, scientists developed a new mouse – the cystic fibrosis mouse – with the identical genetic defect as Laura. This made it much easier to develop new treatments. Within ten years, there will probably be ways of curing Laura, as long as that research, using those animals, continues.

There are plenty of emotional arguments both for and against animal testing, but let's start with the most obvious facts. If you examine the history of medicine, you find that experiments on animals have been an important part of almost every major medical advance. Many cornerstones of medical science – the discovery that blood circulates through our veins, understanding the way lungs work, the discovery of vitamins and hormones – were made this way.

Most of the main advances in medicine itself also depended on animal experiments. In the Fifties, between 2,000 and 4,000 people each year in the UK were paralysed or killed by polio but, thanks to the polio vaccine, this number has now dropped to just one or two cases a year. Modern surgery would be impossible without today's anaesthetics. The list goes on: organ transplants, heart surgery, hip replacements, drugs for cancer and asthma – animals played an important part in these medical advances.

Animal experimentation wasn't the only type of research crucial to the medical advances that save human lives. Studies on human volunteers were also essential, and test-tube experiments were vital in many cases. But the history of medicine tells us that animal experiments are essential if we want to tackle the diseases and illnesses that afflict people.

If we are going to carry out research into serious diseases such as cancer or Aids, at some point in the process we are going to have to give those diseases to animals so we can study them.

This is the dilemma we face. We want to prevent suffering. The crucial issue is *how* we use animals in research. Modern science has developed humane experimental techniques. It is possible to do animal experiments using methods that the animals don't even notice. The worst these animals have to put up with is living in a cage with regular food and water, with animal handlers and vets looking after them.

The golden rule of laboratory animal welfare is to minimise any distress involved using the principle of the three Rs. First you reduce the number of animals used in each experiment to the minimum that will give a scientifically valid result. Then, whenever possible, you replace animal experiments with alternatives – experiments that don't use animals but will give equally valid results. Finally, you refine the animal experiments that you do, so they cause the least possible harm to the animals. If an experiment involves surgery on the animal, give it an anaesthetic. When it comes round, give it painkillers and antibiotics to combat infection.

The principle of the three Rs has been the basis for animal experimentation in many countries for the past ten years or more. It has been written into the law and is enforced by strict codes of practice, government guidelines and inspections. As a result, the number of animal experiments in the UK was reduced from more than 5.2 million in 1978 to 2.8 million in 1993.

People who experiment on animals are just the same as the rest of us – they know it's wrong to cause suffering if it can be avoided. But just because we like animals, we can't avoid the difficult decisions that have to be made in medicine and science. Sometimes, however, those decisions actually benefit animals. Distemper used to kill 500,000 puppies every year. Scientists believed they could find a vaccine but to succeed they would have to experiment on several hundred dogs, killing almost all of them. Not an easy decision. It took years to produce a vaccine that worked but now, every single year, 500,000 dogs are saved as a result.

23 Vocabulary

Try to match these words and phrases from the text with their definitions.

1	cornerstones (*line 34*)	A	worthwhile in terms of science
2	crucial (*line 57*)	B	reduce to the smallest amount
3	humane (*line 77*)	C	showing kindness
4	minimise (*line 87*)	D	improve
5	scientifically valid (*line 92*)	E	extremely important, vital
6	refine (*line 97*)	F	fundamental elements

24 Post-reading discussion

How sympathetic do you feel to the writer's view that medical experiments on animals are humane and necessary? Try to explain your views to your classmates.

25 Note-taking

Make notes from the text of the reasons for carrying out medical experiments on animals, the achievements that have come about through animal research and the steps that are taken to make medical experimentation as humane as possible. Try to find at least six points.

- ....
- ....
- ....
- ....
- ....
- ....

26 How the writer achieves his effects

A The writer achieves a calm, objective-sounding tone and style. He tries not to sound biased.

How do you think he achieves this? Write down your ideas.

....

....

Compare your ideas in your groups.

B The following list shows techniques the writer uses to help him achieve the impression of being fair. How do the points compare with your list?

One of these points is incorrect. Try to find it and cross it out.

- He says the animals are well cared for.
- He uses a lot of statistics.
- He gives a lot of facts.
- He says researchers care about animals.
- He makes us laugh at people who campaign against animal experiments.
- He seems to try to understand the point of view of his opponents.

Try to find examples of these points in the text and circle them.

Compare your findings with the other groups. Is there anything you disagree about?

27 The angle of the argument

The writer suggests that the real issue is not whether you should be for or against animal experiments but HOW animal research can be as kind as possible to animals. This is an important change in the angle of the usual argument. Why, do you think?

28 Understanding bias in an argument

A Not everyone would agree that the writer is completely fair or unbiased. What points against animal experiments did the writer, as you see it, choose not to include? Write down some ideas.

....

....

B Study these opinions, which view animal experiments from a different perspective. Make sure you understand each one. Compare them with your own ideas and tick off any points which appeared on your list. Are there any ideas which you did not note but which you think are important points to consider? Tick them off too.

1 "Animals are physically different from people so they react differently to drugs and medical experiments. You can't always extrapolate* from animals to people. As a result, many animal experiments are a waste of time."

2 "Many members of the public think of medical research scientists as torturers and murderers."

3 "Not all laboratories are wonderful. An American laboratory was taken to court recently for its disgraceful treatment of animals."

4 "It's difficult for the public to see behind the closed doors of a laboratory. So scientists have a lot of freedom in the way they work and what they say they do."

5 "Great improvements in health and life expectancy have come since the development of clean water systems and sanitation. This had nothing to do with laboratory animals."

6 "Health education has helped people avoid disease. People have learned about a good diet, not smoking, being hygienic and taking exercise. Laboratory animals are irrelevant."

7 "Research studies using human volunteers have been responsible for major advances in medical understanding. For example, the link between cancer and smoking came from studying people's behaviour and their reactions."

8 "Advanced technology such as lasers and ultrasound is improving our understanding of the causes of disease. We could make more use of advanced technology and less use of living creatures in research."

* *extrapolate:* to make predictions based on what you know

29 Writing an article for the school newsletter

'Is animal experimentation really worth it?'

Your school debating club has been discussing the rights and wrongs of animal experimentation. You feel that medical experiments on animals are useful and necessary but it is important to consider alternative techniques too.

Write an article for your school newsletter explaining

- how animal experimentation has contributed to medical understanding
- why animal experiments do not always give useful results
- the alternatives to medical experiments on animals.

THE ANGLE OF THE ARGUMENT

Get the angle clear. You are not writing a composition which is totally against animal experimentation, because you accept the need for it. Your aim is to show that medical experiments on animals, while sometimes helpful, do not always produce useful results. You want to explain how our health can be improved using alternative methods.

PLANNING THE CONTENT

What points do you want to include? Can you give any explanations or examples to develop your points? How can you relate your content to the interests of the readers of the newsletter?

STRUCTURE AND LANGUAGE

Use a strong opening for your article: get the reader's attention and keep it. Use a closing paragraph which clearly rounds off what you write. Don't let your composition 'tail off' so that the reader wonders what you really believe.

Structure your composition so the argument you are presenting is clear and easy to follow. Using opinion language and linking words will help you do this. Some of the expressions in exercise 7 will be helpful.

30 Prepositions after verbs

There are many examples of prepositions following verbs in the article about animal experiments.

Examples:
Hundreds of children are *born with* cystic fibrosis.
Let's *start with* the most obvious facts.
Blood *circulates through* our veins.
Between 2,000 and 4,000 people each year were *killed by* polio.
You *replace* animal experiments *with* alternatives.
People who *experiment on* animals are just the same as the rest of us.

PRACTICE

Try to fill the gaps in the following sentences. Choose from these prepositions.

about   at   from   of   on   to   with

1   Is it right to experiment _____ animals?
2   Why bother _____ animal suffering when children are dying _____ incurable diseases?
3   I am surprised _____ you.
4   I object _____ all this animal rights propaganda.
5   Alan decided to contribute _____ an animal charity.
6   I won't quarrel _____ them.

7 Elephants depend _____ their keepers.

8 He died _____ a broken heart, so they say.

9 Can you provide him _____ an information pack?

10 Baby rhinos respond well _____ human contact.

What other verbs do you know followed by these prepositions? Discuss with a partner and try to make a list.

31 Spelling and pronunciation: Regular plurals

Most regular plurals in English simply add **-s**.

Look at this list of regular plurals. Check the meaning of each word and write a translation if necessary.

1	cats	9	horses
2	hens	10	goats
3	insects	11	birds
4	cages	12	cows
5	wasps	13	houses
6	dogs	14	monkeys
7	spiders	15	bees
8	faces	16	roses

The **s** at the end of the noun plural can be pronounced /s/ or /z/ or /ɪz/. Listen to the list of words and write each word in the correct box, according to the sound of its ending.

```
/s/
cats



```

```
/z/
hens



```

```
/ɪz/
faces



```

Now say the words aloud to your partner. Does he/she agree the sound of each ending is clear?

32 Spelling and pronunciation: Irregular plurals

The following rules show how irregular plurals are formed. Say the examples aloud clearly, checking your pronunciation with a partner.

1 Nouns which end in -ch, -s, -sh, -ss or -x add **-es** to form the plural. The -es ending is pronounced /ɪz/.
Examples: _bench - benches   bus - buses_
rash - rashes   pass - passes   box - boxes

2 Nouns ending in -f or -fe replace the ending by **-ves** to form the plural. The -s is pronounced /z/.
Examples: _calf - calves   leaf - leaves_
wife - wives

3 Some nouns form the plural simply by changing the vowel. The pronunciation changes too.
Examples: _goose - geese   mouse - mice_
tooth - teeth   man - men

4 Nouns which end in -o usually form the plural by adding **-es**, which is pronounced /z/.
Examples: _tomato - tomatoes_
Common exceptions: _photos   pianos   rhinos_

5 Nouns ending in a consonant and -y form the plural by changing the -y to **-ies**, which is pronounced /z/.
Examples: _fly - flies   lady - ladies_

Nouns ending in a vowel and -y just add **-s**, which is pronounced /z/.
Example: _donkey - donkeys_

6 Some nouns are always plural.
Examples: _trousers   scissors   spectacles_

7 Some nouns are the same in the singular and the plural.
Examples: _sheep   deer   fish   salmon   bison_

33 Vocabulary

Work with a partner to fill the gaps with the plural forms of the nouns in brackets. Make sure you understand the meaning of each sentence. Check your pronunciation too!

1 The _____ have just given birth to several _____. _(sheep, lamb)_

2 Watch out for _____, _____ and _____ if you go camping in the wild. _(bear, wolf, wildcat)_

3 If you're lucky you'll be able to see _____, _____ and _____ in the park. _(deer, goose, fox)_

4 A pet mouse needs a friend. The problem is you might soon have lots of baby _____. _(mouse)_

5 _____ and _____ have the most amazing _____. _(crocodile, rhino, tooth)_

6 Tropical _____ need special care but make interesting pets. _(fish)_

7 It's strange to think that ugly _____ can turn into lovely _____. _(caterpillar, butterfly)_

34 Look, say, cover, write, check

Are you confident you know the meaning of the words below? You have already met some in the unit; you will come across others in later exercises.

Check any meanings you are unsure of in a dictionary. Then use the 'look, say, cover, write, check' method to memorise the words.

potato	anaesthetic
potatoes	elephant
clothes	leopard
calf	laboratory
calves	innocent
leaf	benefit
leaves	terrible
vaccine	veterinary
scissors	rhino

Finally, why not ask your partner to test you?

Animals in sport

35 Discussion

A   Horse racing, dog racing and polo are popular ways of using animals in sport. Do you feel it's fair to animals to involve them in human pursuits in this way?

B   How are animals used for sport in your country?

C   Sports in which animals are hunted are called *fieldsports*. Are these sports popular in your country? Have you ever seen or taken part in this form of sport? How did you feel about it?

36 Fieldsports: People's opinions

Here are some reasons why people say they like fieldsports. Discuss them with your partner and give them a ✓ or ✗ depending on whether they reflect your own views.

'What makes me sick is hearing animal rights groups moaning about cruelty to foxes. The people who object most to foxes are farmers because foxes are a real nuisance to farm animals. I do think foxhunting is misunderstood. The fox doesn't suffer because it's killed quickly and humanely.'

'What I most enjoy is watching a good bullfight. It's thrilling because the matador needs total concentration – without it he'll be dead or maimed.'

'Shooting birds, rabbits or pigeons demands a steady aim and perfect eye-hand coordination. The places where I prefer to shoot are the woods and fields near my house. What makes me cross is people who criticise people who shoot animals for sport but think nothing of eating meat.'

The opponents of fieldsports prefer, however, to dwell on the horrific aspects of the sports. They describe them as *bloodsports*.

37 Letter completion: My views on foxhunting

The following text is a letter written by a student giving the reasons why she is against foxhunting. The blanks need to be filled with words and phrases which link her ideas and show her opinions and attitudes.

Working in pairs or groups of three, choose the most appropriate suggestions from the ones given. Then compare your answers to those of other groups.

Dear Mrs Ross,

I read in our local paper that you are planning a foxhunting day on Saturday. I am writing to say that 1)_____ foxhunting is a very 2)_____ practice and I want to see a complete ban on it.

What makes me really angry is the way your organisation 3)_____ that foxhunting is a traditional sport with a long history. 4)_____ I can't see how this justifies inflicting a terrible death on 5)_____ animal. 6)_____, the fox does not have a clean death. It suffers agonies.

7)_____, I think that a sport which depends for thrills and excitement on killing is feeding the worst side of human nature. 8)_____, sport should uplift the human spirit not debase it.

At my school, I am starting a campaign to increase young people's awareness of foxhunting. I know we shall not be in time to stop the event on Saturday, 9)_____ we shall do all we can to mount public pressure against this 10)_____ activity.

Yours sincerely,

Rosie Greenwood

1 **a** for instance **b** naturally **c** I think
   d personally

2 **a** unhealthy **b** cruel **c** absorbing
   d misunderstood

3 **a** claims **b** denies **c** appeals **d** expects

4 **a** Definitely **b** Frankly **c** Of course
   d Therefore

5 **a** a delightful **b** an endangered
   c a domesticated **d** an innocent

6 **a** Contrary to popular belief **b** On balance
   c In other words **d** Surely

7 **a** However **b** On the other hand
   c Furthermore **d** But

8 **a** It's all very well **b** As I see it
   c Nevertheless **d** Even

9 **a** to be honest **b** therefore **c** so **d** but

10 **a** disgusting **b** intriguing **c** harmless
   d unkind

When you have filled the gaps correctly, re-read the letter to get a sense of the flow of the argument.

Do you agree that the opening is clear and gets straight to the point? In your opinion, is the ending of the letter a firm way to round it off?

38 Vocabulary: Words for feelings

Rosie expresses her feelings and attitudes in a forceful, impassioned way. The following exercise shows how adjectives of similar meaning can be used to describe feelings and attitudes. Can you complete each group of synonyms with an appropriate word chosen from the box?

1 I am disgusted / appalled / horrified / _____ by your actions.

2 He is worried / uneasy / fretful / _____ about the dog's illness.

3 It is wicked / immoral / depraved / _____ to use animals in medical experiments.

4 We are delighted / enraptured / enchanted / _____ with our new puppy.

5 He is remorseful / apologetic / regretful / _____ about the harm he has done.

6 It is absurd / ridiculous / ludicrous / _____ to say animals are as important as people.

7 They are soft-hearted / tender / caring _____ towards injured animals.

8 I feel emotional / distressed / upset / _____ when I hear about cruelty to children.

thrilled   tearful   preposterous
compassionate   contemptible   sickened
anxious   penitent

163

39 Language study: Adding extra emphasis

WHAT ... CLAUSES

We can use a clause beginning with *what* to give extra emphasis. For example, Rosie says:
What makes me really angry is the claim that foxhunting is a traditional sport.

Another way of saying this is:
The claim that foxhunting is a traditional sport makes me really angry.

Restructuring the sentence using *what* makes Rosie sound more emphatic.

Contrast the structure of these pairs of sentences. Which one is more emphatic? Why? How has the structure been changed to achieve this?

She hates the pretence that the zoo doesn't make a profit.
***What** she hates is the pretence that the zoo doesn't make a profit.*

We doubted that the animals were happy.
***What** we doubted was that the animals were happy.*

I respect organisations that campaign on behalf of endangered species.
***What** I respect are organisations that campaign on behalf of endangered species.*

THE PERSON WHO ... , THE PLACE WHERE ...

Consider these two similar constructions for adding emphasis.

The keeper understands the animals best.
***The person who** understands the animals best is the keeper.*

Polar bears thrive best in their natural habitat.
***The place where** polar bears thrive best is (in) their natural habitat.*

SO + ADJECTIVE

Consider the use of *so* before an adjective.

Their attitudes were caring.
*Their attitudes were **so** caring.*

He was thoughtful.
*He was **so** thoughtful.*

DO + MAIN VERB

Consider the use of *do* before a main verb. Are any other changes necessary?

I like your project work.
*I **do** like your project work.*

We're late. Hurry up!
*We're late. **Do** hurry up!*

Take a seat.
***Do** take a seat.*

He enjoys his work with orphaned elephants.
*He **does** enjoy his work with orphaned elephants.*

Look back at the comments in exercise 36 and underline any examples of emphatic forms. Why are they effective in that context?

40 Practice

Rewrite these sentences beginning with the words in brackets, to make them more emphatic.

1. She admires attempts to alleviate animal suffering. *(What ...)*
2. We need better fences to stop animals wandering onto the road. *(What ...)*
3. The safari park wardens worry about animals escaping. *(What ...)*
4. You can see owls, eagles and hawks in a falconry centre. *(The place where ...)*
5. We didn't understand that animals are adapted to live in certain habitats. *(What ...)*
6. I didn't realise how animals depend on each other. *(What ...)*
7. Hunters are responsible for the reduction in rhino numbers. *(The people who ...)*
8. The golden eagle prefers to nest in treeless, mountainous country. *(The place where ...)*
9. Endangered species in our own country ought to concern us. *(What ...)*
10. I want the right to object to things I think are wrong. *(What ...)*

41 More practice

Add *so* or *do* to these sentences for greater emphasis. Make any changes to the sentences that you need to.

1. Having a pet has made her happy.
2. We all shouted, 'Tell us more about your adventures.'
3. Take lots of photos when you visit the wildlife park.
4. I never realised that baby rhinos were affectionate.
5. Raising orphaned wildlife is worthwhile.
6. Your cat enjoys his milk, doesn't he?
7. You look tired today.
8. Caged animals are miserable.
9. Gordon felt sorry for the animals he saw at the circus.
10. I worry about you, you know.
11. Help yourself to some more cake.
12. Come in, Sophie. I'm pleased to see you.

42 Comparing languages

How do you add emphasis in your own language? Share words or structures you use with your group.

43 Writing sentences

Make up some sentences of your own using emphatic forms.

Animals at work

44 Thinking about working animals

A   In what way do animals 'work' in your country?

For example:

☐   on farms producing milk

☐   being raised for meat

☐   being raised to provide skins, leather, wool etc.

☐   as guard dogs or police dogs

☐   as rescue dogs

☐   being used for transport

Are animals used for work in any other way?

....

B   People who keep animals have a responsibility to feed them. What other responsibilities do they have?

....

....

....

45 Discussing ethical issues

A   Generally speaking, do you feel working animals in your country get a decent life? Try to explain your opinions to your friends.

B   In Britain, people who are cruel to their animals may be fined or even prevented from keeping animals in the future. Are these controls right, do you think? What is your view?

46 Building a letter from prompts

Using the prompts below, try to build up a complete letter to the editor of a national newspaper.

Why it is wrong to accuse shepherds of cruelty

Dear Sir,

I write/response/recent articles/say/people/keep/animals for profit/be 'cruel and heartless'. My family make/living from/keep/sheep. In my view/our life/be harder/the animals'!

In lambing time/example/there be/no day off/no rest. My father get up/as soon as it/be light/and hurry out/to first task/of day/without even bothering/to have/drink. He work/for several hours/without break. He check/lambs that/be born/in night/or attend/ewes that have difficulty/give birth. He bring/sickly lambs indoors/be bottle-fed.

He try/get round the flock/four or five times/day/often in driving snow/cruel winds. If there be/specific problem/he have to/go out several times/night/ with flash light. Although/expensive/vet/always call/when he be needed.

It be/true that every ewe or lamb that/die/be a financial loss/us/so it be/in own interest/care for/sheep. Sheep/eventually be sold/at market. How/we can live/any other way? But we be/certainly not/'ruthless exploiters'/of your article. In fact, nothing be/further from truth.

Yours faithfully,

Gillian O'Connor

47 Assessing the argument

When you have written the complete letter, re-read it to get a better sense of the argument. Has Gillian convinced you that her family provide a high standard of care for animals?

48 The closing paragraph

Study the closing paragraph of the letter carefully. Closing paragraphs of opinion arguments should draw the argument to a clear end; the reader should be sure what you think. The language you use to end the letter depends on what you said before.

Do you think Gillian's final paragraph is effective?

49 Vocabulary: Collective nouns

Decide which of the words in the box can follow these collective nouns. Sometimes more than one answer is possible.

bees dogs fish cows elephants wolves sheep locusts ants goats deer

1 A herd of _____

2 A flock of_____

3 A shoal of _____

4 A pack of _____

5 A swarm of _____

50 Discussion: Intensive farming

Consider these issues related to food production.

Many farmers are using modern technology to rear their animals intensively. Some kinds of animals and birds (calves and hens, for example) can be reared inside, in very small spaces. Feeding can be provided artificially and controlled very carefully. Some animals are given hormones to increase their growth. This is sometimes called 'factory farming'.

Pesticides are widely used by farmers to keep crops free of disease.

WHY PEOPLE OBJECT

Some people object to modern farming methods because they think they are cruel to animals. Also, they are increasingly worried about the effect of hormones and pesticides in the food chain.

Because intensive farming relies on machines, not people, this has resulted in fewer jobs for agricultural workers.

WHAT THE FARMERS THINK

Farmers using intensive systems argue that they are an efficient method of producing food cheaply.

Some farmers are reluctant to change to 'organic' farming because they have invested a lot in new technology. Also, they feel organic methods will be less reliable, will involve higher labour costs, and might lead to higher food prices for the consumer.

Finally, in some countries farmers receive a subsidy (a payment from the government) for using intensive farming methods.

What are your views? How do you think food should be produced? Work in groups and note down your ideas.

51 Punctuation

Read the following letter for meaning. When you feel you have understood it, rewrite it with punctuation and paragraphs so that the sense is clear.

Remember to use a comma after an introductory linking word or phrase such as *Nevertheless, ..., In fact, ... Despite claims to the contrary, ...*

Fair methods of food production

dear sir like many of your readers i want to buy healthy food which is produced in a way which is fair to farm workers and animals furthermore i don't believe food production should damage the environment many farmers in our area say that it is cheaper to rear animals under intensive conditions than it is to give them a decent life however if farmers were given subsidies they would be able to afford more space and comfort for animals farmers get subsidies for intensive methods so why not pay them for a kinder approach similarly many of the farms around here use harmful pesticides which can get into the food chain farmers say it is less expensive to use pesticides than to use more natural or 'organic' methods which require a bigger labour force and so would be more expensive what is more expensive in the end subsidies to the farmers for organic farming or a damaged environment in my view we have a right to know what is in our food tins packets and fresh food should be labelled by food companies as free range* or factory farmed or whether pesticides were used so that we know exactly what we are eating i realise my ideas might lead to higher food prices but i have no doubt at all it would be worth it

yours faithfully **shahar rishani**

Free range eggs come from hens which live in natural conditions.

52 Checking the text flow

When you have punctuated the letter correctly, read it through, as always, to get a sense of the way the text flows. Are the beginning and ending clear and decisive?

53 Further thoughts

How far do you agree with Shahar's view that it's worth paying more for food that is produced ethically?

In what ways do you think intensive methods of food production could be unfair to farm workers? Try to give some specific examples.

Caring for animals

54 Discussion

Do people who keep animals as pets have more responsibilities, in your view, than people who keep animals as a source of business?

Does everyone have the right to keep a pet? When would having a pet not be a good idea?

Make a note of the points that come up in your discussion. Keep them safely, as they will be needed later.

55 Rhetorical questions

Rhetorical questions are a special kind of question. If you use a rhetorical question, you do not expect an answer. It's a device to get more attention for your opinions when presenting an argument.

Study the following rhetorical questions. What is the opinion of each speaker?

1 'Don't you think it's about time people showed more sympathy to farmers?'
2 'Who can honestly say they would enjoy eating a battery hen?'
3 'Which is worse: to pay a tiny bit more for food or to make innocent animals suffer horrors under intensive systems?'
4 'Wouldn't we all be happier knowing our food was ethically produced?'
5 'Do we really need all these new products and convenience foods?'
6 'Who can worry about animals when little children are starving?'
7 'The theory is that pets are safe and happy with their owners, but is it the whole truth?'
8 'How can you put a price on a child's life?'

56 Restructuring statements into rhetorical questions

Try to rewrite these statements in the form of rhetorical questions.

1 A vegetarian meal is not always healthy.
   Is...

2 No one can say the farmers are wrong.
   Who...

3 We can save an animal or save someone's life.
   Which is ....

4 No one knows the extent of the problem.
   Who...

5 We buy fur coats and leather handbags. I am not sure we really need them.
   Do we...

6 I think we would all be happier knowing that our food was free of chemicals.
   Wouldn't..

7 I think it's about time we remembered endangered species at home.
   Isn't ....

8 I think we should consider farm workers before worrying about animals.
   Shouldn't..

Look back at the letters in exercises 46 and 51 and underline the examples of rhetorical questions.

You may like to use the rhetorical question device in your own arguments. One or two are usually enough.

57 Vocabulary: Young animals

Humans have children; sheep have lambs. Choose a word from the box to match with each animal/bird. You will need to use some words more than once.

> calf kitten cub foal kid chick/chicken
> pup/puppy cygnet duckling

1 bear	**7** goat
2 duck	**8** horse
3 hen	**9** elephant
4 cow	**10** whale
5 cat	**11** swan
6 dog	**12** lion

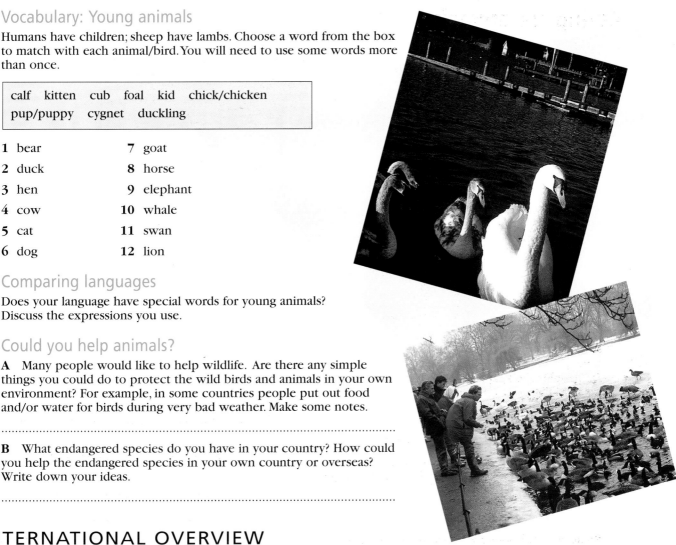

58 Comparing languages

Does your language have special words for young animals? Discuss the expressions you use.

59 Could you help animals?

A Many people would like to help wildlife. Are there any simple things you could do to protect the wild birds and animals in your own environment? For example, in some countries people put out food and/or water for birds during very bad weather. Make some notes.

....

B What endangered species do you have in your country? How could you help the endangered species in your own country or overseas? Write down your ideas.

....

INTERNATIONAL OVERVIEW

Wildlife all over the world is hunted for food and for the trade in animal parts and skins. The habitat of many animals is destroyed when people plant crops, cut down forests or create pollution.

Study the chart which shows the effects of whaling on the world's whales. Which species has been most affected (as far as it is known) by whaling?

THE IMPACT OF WHALING	*Pre-whaling*	*Current*
Blue whale	160,000-240,000	9,000
Fin whale	300,000-650,000	50,000-100,000
Sperm whale	Perhaps 3 million	Possibly 2 million
Grey whale	16,000-30,000	Around 22,000
Bowhead whale	52,000-60,000	Fewer than 8,500
Humpback whale	150,000	Around 20,000

60 Reading for gist

Skim read the following leaflet which gives information about two
ways of supporting King's Park Zoo. A lot of the vocabulary should be
familiar from previous exercises. Try to work out the meaning of
unfamiliar words from the context.

WILD ACTION APPEAL

THE ADOPTION SCHEME

King's Park Zoo, as well as being a great place to
visit, plays an important part in protecting
endangered species. The Zoo is often the last
sanctuary and breeding ground for these animals.
We have 160 different species of animals, birds and
reptiles, many of which are endangered in the wild.
We need your support to help these animals win
their battle against possible extinction with breeding
programmes, funded by the adoption scheme.

Most animals in the Zoo are available for adoption.
Many individuals and families, as well as groups, take
great pleasure in adopting their favourite animal.
Companies, too, can benefit from the scheme and
find it a worthwhile and cost-effective form of
advertising.

WHAT ADOPTERS RECEIVE

All adopters will receive an adoption certificate and
regular copies of 'Zoo Update', the Zoo's exciting
newsletter. For a donation of £35 you will receive 4
free entry tickets; for a donation of £60 or more you
will receive 8 free entry tickets and a personalised
plaque on the animal's enclosure.

Our **Wild Action** appeal was launched in 1997 to
support work with endangered species in their
threatened natural habitats. Donations to the
appeal will go directly towards the following
projects:

RAINFOREST ACTION, COSTA RICA

Costa Rica's tropical forests contain a wealth of
wildlife — 200 species of mammals, 850 species of
birds, 220 species of reptiles and 160 species of
amphibians. All these are at risk, including the
jaguar, ocelot, margay and jaguarundi. **Rainforest
Action Costa Rica** is securing a biological corridor
of rainforest that is intended to stretch throughout
Central America, providing a safe haven for
indigenous wildlife. £18 will save half an acre of
Costa Rican rainforest.

THE TIGER TRUST

The Tiger Trust is creating two natural habitat
sanctuaries in Thailand for the Indo-Chinese tiger,
which is facing the threat of extinction. Tiger
Mountains I and II provide a near-natural existence
for tigers orphaned by poaching.

Only 5,000 tigers remain in the wild and hundreds
are being trapped and shot by poachers for an
appalling trade in tiger bones and body parts. £20
will go towards looking after Sheba, a two-year-old
Indo-Chinese tiger, who was found next to the body
of her mother. She now lives with other rescued
tigers on Tiger Mountain II in Thailand. You will
receive a colour photo of Sheba and a tiger T-shirt.

61 Reading comprehension

Now answer these questions.

1   Which animals are available for adoption?
2   How does the zoo use the adoption money it raises?
3   What does a £35 donation to the adoption scheme give you?
4   What is the aim of Rainforest Action Costa Rica?
5   Where are Tiger Mountain I and II, and what is special about them?

62 Building a newsletter article from a first draft

Ramon wanted his school to support the zoo's conservation work. He decided to write an article for the school newsletter, explaining why it was a good idea and how the school could benefit.

Try to rewrite his rough draft of main points in the form of a finished article. The final paragraph is missing: try to think of a strong way to close the article.

STRUCTURE

Structure the article into paragraphs. Use a strong opening and definite final paragraph. Use defining clauses to make sentences more complex. Would you like to use some emphatic structures or rhetorical questions as a way of adding emphasis?

Link ideas with linking words and expressions, and use opinion language to introduce your views.

CONTENT

Ramon makes several very interesting points. Could you provide any extra examples or explanations of your own?

Can you show any further audience awareness in the letter? Think, perhaps, about your own school. How might the schemes be of particular interest to pupils? Try to show some audience awareness in your final paragraph.

Proof-read your work for punctuation and spelling errors.

FEEDBACK

When you feel you have produced a reasonable draft, why not show your work to a friend? Listen carefully to his/her comments. Would you like to add anything or change anything?

HOW WE CAN HELP ENDANGERED SPECIES

We could adopt a zoo animal. We could visit it on school trips. The zoo would send us a regular newsletter which would give us information about breeding programmes for endangered species. We could even get a plaque at the zoo with the school's name on it. The adoption scheme is a way of raising the zoo's income. The money helps the zoo with its breeding programmes. The breeding programmes encourage the animals to reproduce. The zoo is also running an appeal called Wild Action. Money from the appeal will help to preserve the Costa Rican rainforest. The money will also support two groups working to protect tigers. Only 5000 tigers still survive in the wild. Poachers kill the tigers and sell the skins, body parts and even the bones to make cosmetics and manufactured goods. The groups set up reasonably natural sanctuaries for tigers orphaned by poaching. These natural sanctuaries protect the tiger cubs.

Exam-format questions

Writing

1. Walking around your neighbourhood, you have observed some disturbing examples of cruelty to animals. You are also concerned about cases of cruelty you have heard about on TV and radio. Write a letter to your local newspaper explaining your views and making some positive suggestions on ways to reduce the problem.

   In your letter you should:

   - describe the problem
   - say why you think animals deserve fair treatment
   - suggest ways to control the problem.

   You should write about 150–200 words.

2. Your school has decided to make the first week of next term 'Animal Week'. Write a letter to your school newsletter putting forward some ideas and suggestions for ways pupils in your school could help animals. The following comments may give you some ideas, but you are free to make up ideas of your own.

   "Let's buy products not tested on animals."

   "We could create a wildlife habitat, such as a pond or meadow, in the school grounds."

   "Many wild creatures are killed or injured by litter. Let's start a litter patrol."

   "Eat organic!"

   "We need more information about wildlife in our area. Let's carry out a nature survey to see where animals are living and whether there is anything we can do to help them."

   You should write about 150–200 words.

3 Many people say wildlife sanctuaries, breeding programmes and projects to help endangered species are a waste of time. Write a letter to your local newspaper putting forward your own views and arguments.

In your letter you should:

- outline the reasons why such projects have been set up
- explain their purpose in helping animals and educating people about animals
- put forward your own views about the value of such projects.

You should write about 150-200 words.

Oral assessment

Pets

Pets are very important in some people's lives, whereas for others, pets are of no interest at all. Discuss your ideas about animals as pets with your partner or the examiner.

In your discussion you could talk about the following:

- the reasons why people enjoy having a pet
- animals which make good pets
- the responsibilities people have towards their pets
- whether everyone has the right to keep a pet
- why a pet may not be suitable for every home.

You are free to consider any other ideas of your own. You are not allowed to make any written notes.

1 Plan your **opinion essay** first. Think about content. Try to have enough interesting ideas to expand fully: don't run out of ideas halfway through. Engage with the subject and try to make the argument sound serious and important. Come across as convincing and you will convince other people.

2 Structure your essay so that it is clear and logical. Try not to 'backtrack' halfway through to ideas you mentioned earlier. Use paragraphs and linking words.

3 Use an appropriate tone. Opinion arguments are often quite measured, and you may want to give consideration to what other people say.

4 Devices such as rhetorical questions or restructuring sentences for greater emphasis will make your writing stronger and more persuasive.

5 Try to use a mature and varied vocabulary which is appropriate to the topic.

6 Punctuate carefully, using commas, full stops, question marks and so on. Proof-read your work for punctuation errors.

7 Check your spelling carefully, especially words you know you usually misspell, or words which present special problems such as plural forms, silent letters and suffixes.

8 Try to give attention to your **handwriting**. If your composition is interesting and well structured, and your handwriting is attractive, your work will be a pleasure to read. If you feel you have particular difficulty forming certain letters or keeping handwriting on the line, try practising using special handwriting worksheets.

Try experimenting with different kinds of pens in order to find one which helps you write better. A good quality pen is a good investment if you can find one that is not too expensive.

EXAM STRATEGY

9 In the exam, many candidates stop while writing a composition to count the number of words they have produced so far. This is a waste of time. Get used to seeing what 150 words, for example, look like in your handwriting. You will then be able to see whether you are writing to the right length. The lines on the exam writing paper are also there to help you.

The word limit given is a guide to the required length – a few words either side won't make any difference to your marks.

Unit focus

In this unit you have learned to write letters and articles putting forward formal **arguments and opinions**. This is practice for Paper 2, Part 3.

You have listened to a radio talk and answered true/false questions. This is practice for Paper 3, Part 3, and Paper 4, Part 2.

You have produced a set of notes on a detailed reading text. This is practice for Paper 2, Part 2.

You have produced short answers to questions on an advertising text. This is practice for Papers 1/2, Part 1.

The rewards of work

1 Discussion

Why do people work? Earning money is one reason. What other reasons are there? With a partner, try to add four or five more ideas to the list.

Reasons why people work
They get a sense of achievement.
They feel good about themselves.

2 Skills and qualities for work

Match the following skills and qualities to the occupations you think they are essential for.

1	patience	**A**	novelist
2	good communication skills	**B**	dentist
3	artistic flair	**C**	nursery teacher
4	an ear for languages	**D**	firefighter
5	business acumen	**E**	interior designer
6	physical stamina	**F**	cellist
7	courage	**G**	labourer
8	musical talent	**H**	tycoon
9	dexterity	**I**	linguist
10	imagination	**J**	journalist

3 Pre-reading tasks

A Think of any new products you have tried in the last year. Why did you try them? If you saw them advertised, did they live up to the advertiser's promise? What was the 'image' of the product conveyed in the media? How were the new products you tried different from similar products already available?

B You are going to read about how a totally new chocolate bar is produced. What challenges do you think are involved in this process? Examples:
You have to make it taste delicious.
You have to have the right equipment to make it.

4 Predicting

Look carefully, without reading, at the pictures in the text 'A bar is born' on pages 174 and 175. What do you think the pictures show?

Now read the text for general meaning. Try to work out the meanings of any unfamiliar words from the context.

A bar is born

Despite trends towards healthy eating, the chocolate confectionery market has grown by 20 per cent since 1990. In 1994 the UK spent over £3.1 billion on chocolate – a figure that works out at approximately £50 per person per year. Of other European countries, only the Belgians and the Swiss consume more chocolate per person.

Almost all mass-produced chocolates in Britain are variations of the basic ingredients of chocolate, caramel, nuts, raisins and biscuit. With popular new ingredients so hard to find, manufacturers are forced to look for new ways of combining the old favourites into new products.

❶

Opportunity

All chocolate manufacturers have marketing departments to think up ideas for new products. These departments analyse consumer fashions and lifestyles and try to identify opportunities for new products. Mars introduced mini-bars when they discovered that many parents cut up a full-size bar into smaller portions for their children.

Some new products come about through new technology rather than marketing. In these cases scientists or engineers will have invented a machine that can do something new to chocolate which is noticeably different from anything that has been produced before.

It might take anything from six months to a number of years to conduct all the necessary research to assess whether the proposed new product is likely to succeed.

Each research exercise may cost up to £100,000. For every 10 ideas for new products, only one will get beyond research assessment, so the real cost of getting a new product to the development stage is approximately £1 million.

❷

Product development

One of the key criteria for producing a new chocolate bar is that it should be difficult for rival companies to replicate. No manufacturer wants to spend a great deal of money developing a brand that will quickly attract stiff competition.

Creating a new bar may involve making minor adjustments to existing machinery, or it can mean investment in a whole new factory costing millions of pounds. So it is vital that the new bar can be produced economically.

Chocolate is a price-sensitive market. Even though a manufacturer might come up with a delicious formula for a new bar, it would not go ahead with production unless it could be made for the right price.

Sometimes new products cannot be made at all. One manufacturer found that, in one bar it was developing, it was unable to stop the wafer becoming soggy, and another found that the raisins always sank to the bottom of the bar. Both these projects were abandoned.

The chocolate must also always be consistent; even the smallest change in the balance of ingredients can affect the taste significantly. Manufacturers want consumers to buy the same brand over and over again, and if a bar cannot meet this requirement it will not go into mass-production.

The process of development is one of constant refinement. Manufacturers rarely make their ideal product first time round, and it is not unusual for them to have up to 30 attempts at getting it right.

❸ Packaging

Care is taken to ensure that the packaging is consistent with the type of bar produced. A bar ¹¹⁵aimed at teenagers may well be packaged in a red and yellow packet to appear cheap and cheerful. Blue is considered to be a sophisticated colour and is ¹²⁰often used to package top-of-the-range brands. Whatever the design, manufacturers will make sure that it stands out enough to be noticed on the sweet counter ¹²⁵where it will have to compete with 50 other brands.

The name of the bar must also reflect the right image.

❹ Advertising

¹³⁰Most new chocolate bars are launched with a press and TV advertising campaign. Advertising companies begin planning their campaigns by ¹³⁵deciding what message they want to convey about the product. For example, is it a luxury or is it a snack? They then work on a number of ¹⁴⁰advertisements before deciding which one is likely to work best.

This process may take between three and 18 months. Filming the advert may cost up to ¹⁴⁵£250,000, and buying the television air-time to screen it may cost up to £3 million.

❺ Testing

Manufacturers and advertisers ¹⁵⁰conduct extensive testing at all stages in the development and launch of a new product. Groups from different parts of the country are asked to give their ¹⁵⁵opinions on either the taste of the chocolate or the impact that an advert has had on them. These comments then form the basis for future refinements.

❻ The launch

¹⁶⁰Many new brands do quite well initially, as it is comparatively easy to get people to try a new chocolate bar once. However, ¹⁶⁵for a launch to be successful, sales must be sustained over a long period of time. Achieving this is extremely difficult. Nine out of every ten new products ¹⁷⁰launched fail.

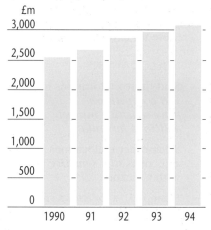

Chocolate confectionery
Market value, UK figures

£m

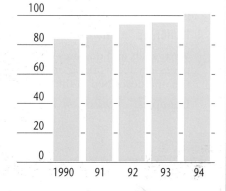

Spending
Weekly UK spending per head on chocolate products (pence)

homework

6 Reading comprehension

1　Explain why marketing departments study people's behaviour, habits and way of life.

2　Why is it important that a new chocolate bar should be difficult for other companies to copy?

3　What kinds of information does a company want to find at the Testing stage? Name two things.

4　In the UK, which year had the smallest increase in weekly spending on chocolate per head of population?

5　Write a paragraph of about 75 words explaining why many new chocolate bars made in the factory never reach the stage of being packaged, advertised or sold.

7 Post-reading discussion

Has the article surprised you in any way? Why/Why not?

Do you think the way new chocolate is launched could apply to other products?

8 Vocabulary

Look back at Section 2, Product development. Make a list of all the words in this section which are connected with making and selling a product.

Examples: *companies, manufacturer*

Put a **?** against words you don't understand. Look these up in a dictionary.

COLLOCATIONS

Find these collocations in Section 2 of the text:
stiff competition
price-sensitive market
delicious formula

What other collocations could be made with the adjectives *stiff, sensitive* and *delicious*? Make a list with a partner.

Examples: a *delicious cake, a sensitive child, a stiff breeze*

9 A rewarding job?   10/7/02.

Work in pairs or groups of three.

How do you think the people involved in developing the new chocolate bar might feel about their work? Write down your ideas.

Examples: *excited, frustrated*

What skills and qualities do you feel would be necessary for working on a new product, such as the one described in the article? Make a list.

Examples: *enthusiasm, determination*

10 Sharing ideas

Look back at the notes you made in exercises 1 and 2 about reasons for working, and skills and qualities needed for specific occupations. Do any of them apply here? Add them to your lists above.

Share your ideas with the other groups. Listen carefully and add any other interesting ideas.

11 Understanding visual data

Visual data, graphs, charts etc. are often included in newspaper and magazine articles, especially those of a factual type.

It is important that you understand the information being conveyed visually. The information either mirrors information in the text in a different format or adds extra information.

Re-read the opening paragraph of 'A bar is born'. Then study the two bar charts headed **Chocolate confectionery** and **Spending**. How do the charts

a　reflect information in the first paragraph?
b　give extra information?

12 Role play: Product development meeting

It is 10 a.m. You are a member of the Product Development and Marketing team, which is meeting to discuss the production of a new bar of chocolate. At the end of the meeting you need to decide:

* who the chocolate will be aimed at
* the name and packaging
* your advertising strategies.

In groups of four, choose from the roles. Study your role carefully. Make sure you understand the information so that you can express it during the meeting.

DESIGNER

You think there is a need for a new bar of chocolate. It should be aimed at young children as this is where the market is strongest.

You specialise in the design of the wrappers. You prefer a bright red, green or yellow wrapper, something which will stand out and catch children's attention – definitely not anything which looks grown up or is too subtle. You would also like images of animals and their young put on the wrappers. This will encourage parents to buy the chocolate for toddlers.

You want the name '*Choccie*' or '*Chic-Choc*'. You think this will encourage parents to buy it for their children's lunchboxes or as a treat after school. You think the taste should be very sweet and milky, which will not appeal to more sophisticated palates.

You are rather forceful in meetings. Give your opinions firmly and clearly. (You may want to look back at the opinion language on page 156.) You also hate to be interrupted.

SALES EXECUTIVE

You are convinced there is a need for a new bar of chocolate aimed at families, to include adults and children of various ages. You have some ideas for names for the product: '*Golden Bar*', '*Delight*' and '*Soft-Centred*'. You dislike childish-sounding names which suggest the chocolate is for young children.

The advertising should suggest the chocolate is an all-round family choice, not something too sophisticated or very child-orientated. The advert could show people eating it at work, on trains, or just enjoying it on family outings, etc.

You are going to suggest the product is advertised in magazines and on radio rather than on television. TV advertising costs too much and will not necessarily increase sales.

You are a good listener. You do your best to get on with everyone and calm 'ruffled feathers'.

MARKETING EXECUTIVE

You expect that the market research you are carrying out will show there is a need for chocolate that will appeal to older teenagers and adults. In your opinion, people are bored with the taste of the chocolate bars you already produce and want something which tastes more of chocolate and less of sugar and milk.

You think the name and image should be as sophisticated as possible. The colour of the wrapper should be black, blue or gold. The advertising should suggest the chocolate is a luxury. Eating it is a pleasure and makes an occasion special. It is not a quick snack or an item for children's lunchboxes.

You are not happy with any of the names suggested for the chocolate. You think that consumers will confuse these names with other brands.

The chocolate market is very competitive and the advertising budget needs to be high. You want to advertise the product on TV.

HEAD ENGINEER

You are very unhappy with the plans to produce a new bar of chocolate. You have been working on many different kinds of formula and each time the product is unsatisfactory. It goes soft easily, it's too sweet or isn't sweet enough, it's too dry, or it crumbles very easily.

The most satisfactory result so far was a bar of chocolate that tasted very similar to one you already make. You think that if the factory invested in a new machine that could produce the chocolate in a different shape and size from the original, then the new product would seem different enough to be successful. One possibility would be to cut the chocolate into small circles and sell it in large, family-size bags.

Facts and figures

13 Approximations

Study the following exact amounts. Say them aloud carefully, checking the pronunciation with a partner. Where does the stress fall in *per cent?*

1	4.9%	**5**	98.8%
2	10.4%	**6**	19.2%
3	52.3%	**7**	23.8%
4	74.7%	**8**	32.9%

Now match the exact amounts to these approximations.

A getting on for three-quarters
B a good half
C over one in ten
D under one in five
E almost a quarter
F practically all
G nearly a third
H about one in twenty

When facts and figures are presented, both exact amounts and approximations might be used. For example, you may hear '*19.8% of the town's population, that's getting on for one in five men and women of working age, are unemployed.*'

What are the advantages of using approximations to present information? Are there any disadvantages?

14 Questioning statistics

A Statistical information looks authoritative but you need to treat it with caution. Pressure groups, for example, may use statistics to influence public opinion.

What has the following survey found out? How does it compare with your own experience?

A recent survey found that children who come from homes where the mother works have half as many absences from school as the children of non-working mothers. Working mothers seem quite prepared to send their children to school when they are unwell.

B Before deciding whether the above conclusion is valid, you need to ask more questions. For example:

- Who asked for the survey to be carried out?
- Why was it carried out?
- Who took part in the survey?
- What was the size of the sample?
- Exactly what kind of questions were asked?
- Were the groups of children closely matched in terms of age, background, social class, etc.?

Why are these questions important? What kind of answers do you think you might get?

C With your partner, make notes on the questions you would want to ask before accepting the validity of the following 'facts and figures'.

The majority of the population thought that young people under the age of 18 should not be allowed out after 9 p.m.

....

....

A survey found that Merrymead was much better than the other schools. It had by far the best exam results.

....

....

15 Criticising statistics

Study the statement below and then read the reactions to it. Make sure you understand the expressions in **bold** type.

A survey of young people found the majority were not going to bother to get a decent job when they left school or college.

It's **a total distortion of the truth**. The teenagers I know would do anything to get on a good training scheme.

They're **fudging the facts**. We all want a good job.

I can't stand surveys which **bend the truth**. I'd like to know exactly who they asked and the questions they used.

They're **twisting the results** so they don't have to give us careers guidance.

Who dreamed that up? It's rubbish!

Look back at the statistical information given in exercise 14. Practise criticising the statements with your partner. Do you both sound indignant enough?

16 Young lives: Good or bad?

A survey of young people produced the following results. Read each statement carefully and decide with a partner whether it gives a good or bad impression of teenagers. Mark each statement **P** if a positive impression is being given, and **N** if the impression given is negative. Underline the words which help you decide.

1   23% valued spare-time jobs more highly than their school studies.
2   Over three-quarters were worried about the effect of their spare-time jobs on their school studies.
3   Over a fifth said that working at casual, part-time jobs was the only way they could pay for ordinary everyday things they needed, or buy treats such as sweets or magazines.
4   18% objected to the amount of pocket money they received but were not prepared to work to earn extra spending money.
5   Over a quarter of teenagers were dissatisfied with the amount of freedom their parents allowed.
6   74% were happy with the amount of freedom they were allowed.
7   Reading was a popular activity for two out of three of those interviewed.
8   A third never pick up a book outside school.
9   The majority do nothing to help their community.
10   One in three teenagers do voluntary work for their community.

Decide which statistics you would choose to present if you were:
a   an employer who feels teenagers are a bad employment risk
b   a youth leader encouraging firms to develop training schemes for young people.

17 Rewriting in a more formal style

The following letter was written to a newspaper by a teenager who disagreed with a report it had published. Discuss the letter with your partner and try to decide whether it is written in an appropriate tone and register for its target audience.

Consider the use of:
•   slang
•   colloquialisms
•   contractions
•   rhetorical questions, question forms, and question tags.

Underline those aspects of the letter you and your partner are both unhappy with.

Dear Editor,

Hi! It's me again! Paul Stanton from your go-ahead comprehensive just outside town. Your report 'Young Lives Shock!' just got me hopping mad! You, too, I bet! I mean, the report says 'We are unconcerned about employment'. Talk about fudging the facts, eh? All my mates are dead worried about getting a decent job. I also read 'teenagers value their spare-time jobs more than their studies'. Who dreamed that up? My dad's a single parent and there's no way he can afford to buy me the trainers and CDs I want. No way! So I work for them, right? I work in a café twice a week after school and, yeah, I do find it hard to concentrate the next day, but I do extra homework to catch up. Nothing wrong with that, eh? That stuff about teenage entertainment was kind of distorted too, wasn't it? 'The youth of today show a strong preference for the company of their peer group over that which their parents can offer.' I mean, who wouldn't rather be down at the youth club than stuck at home watching the old man snore? But it didn't say we dislike our parents, did it? I reckon you were pretty upset about that report in your paper, too, mate. Anyway, write me back. It's gonna be great hearing your views!

Love,

Paul

When you are ready, try to rewrite the letter in a more formal style, and divide it into suitable paragraphs. Remember: a letter to a newspaper can include some aspects of informal style, such as the occasional idiom or colloquialism. However, the general impression should be formal.

Show your finished letter to your partner. Does he/she agree that the 'balance' of your style (neither too formal nor too informal) is about right?

INTERNATIONAL OVERVIEW

Education after leaving school

Highest tertiary enrolment
Number enrolled as % of relevant age group, 1993

Country	%	Country	%
Canada	100	Russia	45
United States	81	Belarus	44
Finland	63	Austria	43
New Zealand	58	Australia	42
Norway	54	Kazakhstan	42
France	50	Argentina	41
Armenia	49	Denmark	41
South Korea	48	Spain	41
Ukraine	46	Peru	40
Netherlands	45	Latvia	39

The table shows the 20 countries which have the highest take-up of tertiary education as a percentage of the relevant age group. (Tertiary education is any kind of education undertaken after the school-leaving age.)

Which countries have over half of the relevant age group in tertiary education?

If your own country is not in the 'top 20', have you any idea how it compares? How could you find out?

Job stereotypes

18 Pre-listening discussion

What kinds of shops do you usually like visiting?
Which shops do you enjoy the least?
How would you rate the service in most shops?
If you could improve shops in one way, what would you do?

19 Predicting content

You are going to listen to Zoe, a personnel officer who works for a chain of electrical stores, talking in an informal way about her job. She aims to help the stores run more efficiently and profitably.

What aspects of her job do you think Zoe might be going to mention? Tick off the points on this list.

- [ ] Making suggestions about new products the stores could sell
- [ ] Helping managers decide whether they need full-time or part-time members of staff
- [ ] Suggesting that shop staff have extra training to improve their skills
- [ ] Encouraging managers to go for promotion
- [ ] Disciplining staff who are performing badly
- [ ] Advising sales managers if their sales are falling

20 Vocabulary check

Before you listen, make sure you understand the meaning of these words and phrases.

- personal sales targets
- influential
- wide spectrum

21 Listening for gist

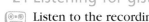 Listen to the recording. Which of the points that you ticked are mentioned?

22 Detailed listening

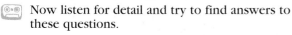 Now listen for detail and try to find answers to these questions.

1   What kinds of training does Zoe suggest for sales assistants? Give two examples.
2   How do managers often approach the problem of staff who are not meeting sales targets?
3   How does Zoe help managers avoid recruiting only people they personally identify with?
4   When does she suggest that the store's sales figures from the previous year should not be used in projecting future sales?
5   Describe her relationship to the store managers.

23 Post-listening discussion

A   Zoe says she finds managers want to recruit people who are '*just like themselves*'. What kind of people do you think she has in mind? How do you

think they would look and behave, and what way of life would they have?

B   Stereotypes often form around particular occupations. What would you expect a 'typical' person doing each of the following jobs to be like?

- labourer
- pop star
- prison governor
- scientist

C   Do you think the stereotype of an occupation helps you when you are choosing which career to follow? Why/Why not?

D   Can you think of someone who doesn't fit the norm for their job? Try to explain your views.

24 Common work-related expressions

Zoe describes store managers as being '*on a treadmill*'. What do you think she means?

Can you work out the meaning of the following expressions from the context?

1   I meet friends from work socially but we never *talk shop*.
2   The new assistant is hard-working and enthusiastic – *a real go-getter*.
3   He got a *golden handshake* worth £20,000 when he retired.
4   Although the policeman was *off-duty*, he arrested the thief.
5   I'm called an 'office assistant' but really I'm just a general *dogsbody*.
6   Not liking the structure of big companies, I got work where I could *be my own boss*.
7   He's not *a high-flyer*; he doesn't have any brilliant ideas, but you can depend on him.
8   Because of their working conditions, *blue-collar workers* are more likely to have accidents at work than *white-collar workers*.

25 Pronunciation: Linking sounds

Practise reading this advert aloud, checking your pronunciation with a partner. Does he/she feel you are reading smoothly and naturally? Notice that if a word ends with a consonant and the next word begins with a vowel, the sounds are linked.

> ### BRIGHTEN UP YOUR SUMMER – GET A JOB WITH US!
>
> If you need extra cash and are 16+
>
> #### WE NEED YOU!
>
> Lots of vacancies in our seafront restaurant.
> It's fun, it's easy, hours to suit!
>
> **Ring Ian on 01774-456156.**

Now mark the linked sounds in this advert and practise reading it aloud to your partner.

HEADLIGHTS HAIRDRESSING

CAREER OPPORTUNITIES FOR SCHOOL-LEAVERS

Trainees needed. Learn in a leading salon. If you've got energy and enthusiasm, we can take you to the top.

Contact Isabel.
Telephone 01223 569432.

26 Writing a job advert

You work in a laboratory. One morning you find this note on your desk from your boss.

Tim
The lab is getting so messy that I've decided to advertise for someone to come in on Saturdays to wash the glassware, sweep up and keep the area tidy. We can pay £4 per hour and travel expenses as well. It might interest a student. Can you draft an advert for the Evening News? Call it a general assistant or something. Use the lab telephone number. Amy Jones will take the calls.
Thanks.
Joanna

Write a suitable advert based on the note. Then mark the linking sounds and show it to a partner. Does s/he agree with the word linking?

Ask your partner to read it aloud. Correct the pronunciation if necessary (tactfully, of course!).

Recruitment with a difference

27 Pre-reading task

A Do you enjoy 'fast-food'? When (if ever) do you visit fast-food restaurants?

What do you think are the strong points of these restaurants?

B You are going to read an article about a fast food restaurant which is run by deaf and mute staff. Write down four questions you would like to see answered in the article.

Example: *How do customers communicate with the disabled staff?*

....

....

....

....

28 Vocabulary check

Make sure you understand the meaning of these words and phrases, which you will meet in the text.

- hearing impairment
- recruiting
- criteria
- agile
- mentor

29 Reading for gist

Now read the article. Are any of the questions you wrote down in exercise 27 answered?

When Aly Sarhan, 28, was asked to head a new branch of the Kentucky Fried Chicken restaurant in Dokki, Egypt, run by the deaf and mute, he didn't know what to expect.

5 "Working in the midst of 30 deaf and mute youths is like working in a foreign land," says Sarhan, who took a crash course in Arabic sign language.

For Sarhan, however, the experience has been an eye-opening one, and has changed his attitudes
10 towards the handicapped. "My staff's hearing impairment does not stop them from doing anything a hearing person can do. They certainly have a whole load of determination in them," he says.

The idea for a deaf and dumb-run KFC — the first
15 in the Middle East — was born when KFC's top management decided to "pay their dues towards society," according to Sarhan. "We found that deaf and mute people existed in large numbers in Egypt, so we decided to do something for them," he says.
20 The obvious place to start recruiting from was the Deaf and Mute Society in Heliopolis. The KFC board used the same criteria they apply when choosing hearing applicants. Successful candidates had to be tactful, presentable, agile, and no older than 25 years
25 of age. "It was so difficult turning people down, so we decided to pick the most eligible applicants, in addition to a long waiting list," Sarhan says. For KFC, this was groundbreaking work. The board was uncertain what to expect and leaned towards caution
30 by drawing up a large waiting list.

Sarhan, one of the youngest store managers working at KFC worldwide, says his biggest concern in the beginning was how to communicate with his employees. "I did not know a single sign, so I had to
35 use an interpreter. Whether the kids got to like me or despise me depended on the interpreter. I was determined, however, to learn the language and remove any barriers between us," he says.

That was easier said than done, he remembers.
40 "Arabic sign language is one of the most difficult languages you can learn, because it is mainly composed of movements rather than distinct signs,"

Sarhan says. Working with his staff for only 11 months, Sarhan is still a weak signer, but he knows
45 enough to help him get by and gain the trust and acceptance of his employees.

So far, the restaurant has been a big success and helped create a supportive environment for the employees. "What made the kids so enthusiastic
50 about our new endeavour was the fact that they get to be in a place where being deaf is the norm. Most of them have been through bad work experiences in which they were the only people with hearing impairment in the place, which made them feel lonely
55 and left out," he says.

This supportive environment, Sarhan says, has made many of the deaf employees depend on themselves more. "Many of the employees had been spoilt and pampered all their lives by their parents,
60 out of pity, which made them rather bad-tempered and lazy. Once they began to like us, it was like we had tapped a well of undiscovered energy," he says.

At the Finy Square KFC branch, pictures on the menu and light signals compensate for the lack of
65 verbal communication. Clients simply have to point toward the picture of the food item they want on the picture-menu. "Despite that, lots of people come in with the feeling of being at a loss drawn all over their faces. They start making signs, and are relieved to
70 find out I can talk. I start carrying out the client's role without signing, to show them how easy it all is," he says.

The newly-married Sarhan says that he considers his staff part of his family now. He has become
75 something of a mentor for them and has helped to create a friendly environment. "This place has helped the deaf and dumb employees psychologically, not just financially. I hope more companies think of embarking on similar adventures. It truly is
80 exhilarating to help make a difference in people's lives," he says.

by Manal el-Jesri

30 Comprehension check

1 Why did the restaurant choose to employ deaf and dumb staff?
2 How did the management decide what would be the right criteria for selecting applicants?
3 Contrast the way employees felt about work before they began their jobs at the restaurant with their feelings about work now.
4 Describe the personality changes the employees undergo.
5 What does Aly feel he has gained from this work? Name two things.

31 Post-reading discussion

A Aly hopes other companies will follow the example of his restaurant and employ disabled staff. Do you think he is being too idealistic? What are your own views?

B Aly says '*It truly is exhilarating to help make a difference in people's lives.*'

Jobs which are 'people-orientated', such as nursing, teaching, personnel, or the hotel trade, bring different rewards and stresses from 'product-orientated jobs' such as those in engineering, carpentry or design.

Which kind of work would you find rewarding, and why?

C Aly is described as being a 'mentor'. He supports and inspires his employees.

Many schools nowadays have 'mentoring schemes' whereby pupils are matched with highly successful adults of a similar background. The mentors give hope, encouragement and practical advice to their students. Sometimes students spend time at the mentor's workplace, 'shadowing' him or her. Do you think this is a good idea? Why/Why not?

Who would you choose for your mentor and why?

32 Vocabulary study

A Try to put these adjectives into order, from most active to least active. Use a dictionary to check unfamiliar words.

> manic   lazy   energetic   bone idle
> hyperactive   indolent

B Now put these adjectives into order, from most positive to most negative.

> friendly   loving   cold   affectionate
> supportive   indifferent   critical

C Which word is the odd one out?

> bad-tempered   moody   grumpy   cross
> fraught   equable   irritable   irate

33 Similes

Remember that using similes enriches your writing and makes it more sophisticated. Study these similes from the text.

> '... (it) is like working in a foreign land.'
> '...it was like we had tapped a well of undiscovered energy.'

Complete the following sentences with suitable similes.

1 The room was so hot. It felt like .....
2 The wind was as cold as .....
3 The house was so dirty. It was as if .....
4 Samira was thrilled with the news. She reacted as though .....
5 We're not allowed any freedom. It's like .....
6 I was so depressed when I couldn't get a job. It was as if .....
7 It's so frustrating when you won't see my point of view. It's like .....

34 Spelling: ...able or ...ible?

A In the text you met the adjectives *presentable* (line 24) and *eligible* (line 26).
The adjective endings -*able* and -*ible* are often confused. From the word *depend* we get *dependable*, but *convert* gives us *convertible*.

Complete the adjectives in these sentences, using a dictionary if necessary. Then learn by heart the spellings you find most difficult.

1 I'm afraid I won't be avail..... until after the 13th.
2 The house was almost invis..... in the fog.
3 Fortunately, the disease was cur..... .
4 I'm sure she'll make a respons..... parent.
5 I found his story absolutely incred..... .
6 This is a sens..... idea.
7 Let's take your car — it's more reli..... than mine.
8 Cheating in exams is not advis..... .
9 Heavy snow made the house inaccess..... .
10 Tiredness tends to make him irrit..... .

B Now complete these adjectives with the endings -*able* or -*ible* and then use each one in a sentence of your own.

1 wash.....
2 ined.....
3 digest.....
4 desir.....
5 approach.....
6 excit.....
7 bear.....
8 incomprehens.....

35 Phrasal verbs

Notice how these phrasal verbs are used in the article. Then use them in a suitable form in the following sentences.

turn down (line 25)   *leave out* (line 55)
draw up (line 30)   *carry out* (line 70)
get by (line 45)

1 Gavin earns so little money, I don't know how they _____.

2 She was careful to _____ all the instructions exactly.

3 We're going on holiday next week, so I'm afraid I shall have to _____ your invitation.

4 All the children in my son's class were invited to the party as we did not want to _____ anyone _____.

5 The management have _____ new guidelines for staff interviews.

36 'Eye' idioms

Aly says the experience of working with disabled people has been '*an eye-opening one*' (line 9). What do you think he means by this?

Match the first parts of these sentences (1–8) with their endings (a–h).

1 Jim wanted to paint the room green, and Vicki wanted blue,

2 As she had to do the ironing,

3 The bride looked wonderful in her wedding dress. She really

4 When I first saw the Pyramids, I thought they were so amazing that

5 Although it was very late, we walked home,

6 The children weren't supposed to be eating sweets

7 Visiting a foreign country for the first time

8 The new manager was so much more astute than the old one that it was impossible

a I couldn't keep my eyes off them.
b is quite an eye-opener.
c keeping an eye out for a taxi all the way.
d to pull the wool over his eyes.
e but I decided to turn a blind eye to it.
f was a sight for sore eyes.
g I kept an eye on the baby.
h so I'm afraid they didn't see eye to eye.

Preparing for work

37 How well does school prepare you for work?

A What kind of career would you like to have when you leave school or college? What general things do you feel you have learned at school which will help you?

Write down any ideas which seem relevant, even if you don't have a clear picture in your mind of the exact career you want to follow.

Examples:
I've learned how to use my initiative when I do projects.
I've learned foreign languages which will give me international opportunities.
I've learned to be more punctual, which is essential in most jobs.

....

....

....

B Have you held any positions of responsibility at school (e.g. helped run a club or society) which might be useful when you apply for college or work? What have you learned from 'working' at school? Note down your ideas.

Examples:
I've learned how to get on with different kinds of people.
I've become more mature.

....

....

....

Keep your notes, as you'll need them later.

38 Before you read

Many schools have a prefect system. Pupils who are prefects help the school run smoothly by keeping a check on other pupils' behaviour, doing litter patrols, helping in the dining room, etc.

Do you think this is a good idea? Could there possibly be any drawbacks?

Pupils who show special abilities are chosen as Head Prefect or Head Boy or Girl. In many schools, one of their main tasks is to represent the opinions of the pupils to the teachers.

Do you have a Head Prefect in your school? What are their duties? How is he/she chosen?

39 Reading, analysing and writing

Read this article from a school newsletter. What is its purpose?

HEAD PREFECT ELECTIONS by Luke Adams

I know you all have your own ideas about the best candidate for Head Prefect, but if you can spare a minute to read this I'll explain why Matthew Baron is by far the strongest candidate.

Matthew, who has been a senior prefect for a year, has shown the most fantastic negotiating skills. Do you remember when we were banned from the swimming pool at lunchtime? Matthew was the one who persuaded the teachers to let us use it by offering to supervise it himself. The fact that we can go on school trips is due to Matthew's hard work, too. He worked round the clock to raise funds for a reliable mini bus to take us on outings. He might not be as keen as some of us on playing team sports, but he is a regular supporter at all our matches.

Outside school, Matthew helps at a home for disabled teenagers. His experience has made him much more understanding of people's problems, which makes all the difference in a large, mixed comprehensive like ours.

Read the article again and underline examples of:

*   complex sentence constructions, including defining and non-defining relative clauses (revised in Unit 8, exercises 36 and 37)
*   comparisons, including comparative/superlative constructions
*   collocations describing qualities and skills
*   idioms
*   audience awareness.

Now write the closing paragraph to Luke's article, trying to use the same style.

Matthew is ....

....

40 Comparing two styles

Now read this second newsletter article. What are the main differences between this article and Luke's? Make a list.

Example: *There are no paragraphs.*

HEAD PREFECT ELECTIONS by Kirsty Mackenzie

You've got to vote for Nicola Wilson. It's not fair if she isn't made Head Prefect. She set up a social club. She worked after school every day. She worked on Saturdays as well. Before that we didn't have a club. Now we have a club. Everyone goes to the club. It is good. She has stopped the bullying. The bullying was happening a lot. She spoke to the bullies. She made them stop. Now everyone is nice to each other. She started a 'Welcome Day' for new students. Now new students are happy. They are not lonely. We had to wear skirts in winter. It was horrible. We were cold. Nicola explained we wanted to wear trousers. Now we can. That was because of Nicola. The other prefects talk about themselves. They say how good they are. But Nicola doesn't. She works in a hospital on Saturday. She visits patients. They are patients who have no visitors. She knows more about people now. You must vote for Nicola.

41 Rewriting in a more mature style

Try to rewrite Kirsty's article so that the style is more fluent and mature. Look back at Luke's article for an example of a more sophisticated style.

When you've finished, show your letter to a partner. Listen carefully to his/her comments. How far do you agree with them? Will you change anything?

42 Brainstorming

Work in small groups. Make notes about unemployment under the headings below, using the prompts to give you ideas.
Remember: brainstorming allows you to write down anything you think of at the time. Don't worry about relevance at this stage.

Try to think about your own country. Note examples of problems and remedies which are relevant to your own situation.

Unemployment – a global issue

WHY ARE PEOPLE UNEMPLOYED?

*   *Industries such as ..... have closed down because ..... and so ..... .*

*   *We import goods such as ..... and people prefer to buy these rather than the similar products we make at home, because ..... . This results in ..... in our own industries.*

*   *Modern technology has ..... .*

*   *The level of education and training is ..... .*

*   *Industries have moved out of city centres because ..... and now city centres are ..... .*

*   *People are leaving their farms in the countryside which means ..... and going to the towns which results in ..... .*

WHAT WOULD HELP PEOPLE GET JOBS?

*   *Government money could be given to ..... .*

*   *Industries such as ..... could be encouraged to set up in our area.*

*   *Training schemes such as ..... could be organised.*

*   *Industries which use old, out-of-date equipment could ..... .*

OTHER IDEAS

*   *The school leaving age is now ..... and it could be changed to ..... which might help ..... .*

*   *Colleges should offer more courses in ..... because ..... .*

*   *Unemployed people could visit advice centres to find out ..... .*

*   *We could have a mentoring scheme for students to help them ..... .*

*   *Careers guidance at school could ..... .*

When you have finished, compare your notes with those of other groups and add any useful ideas. Keep your notes carefully, as you will use them later.

43 Reading a model letter

Study this letter which was written to a local newspaper. The writer makes four separate points. What are they?

1 ....

2 ....

3 ....

4 ....

Unhappy to be on the dole

Dear Editor,

I do not usually write to newspapers but when I read your report which suggested that young people were happy to be on the dole, I felt I had to respond.

I am a school leaver, and in my opinion school leavers need much more detailed careers guidance. Moreover, I think schools should start a 'mentoring scheme' which would match pupils with successful career people. Spending one day a week with a mentor would be a real eye-opener and provide us with the work experience companies say they want but which students find so hard to get!

Furthermore, the majority of the firms in our area are 'hi-tech' whereas most school leavers around here are not computer literate. Firms should form a partnership with schools to develop training schemes which would enable us to learn the skills needed for the job.

I would also like to add that the statistic in your report '85% of pupils had no idea what life without a job is like' is a complete distortion of the truth. Many of us have parents who are out of work and we definitely do not want to be in the same boat.

When you are at school, getting a good job is like a high wall you have to climb over. Young people need all the help they can get, not criticism.

Yours faithfully,

Jennifer Goodman

---

44 Analysing the letter

The highest marks in the exam go to compositions which show examples of 'verbal sophistication' and where the quality of writing is 'sustained'.

The following checklist shows some aspects of verbal sophistication. Re-read Jennifer's letter and find examples of verbal sophistication for each item on the list. How is the quality sustained?

Defining clauses ....

Comparative structures ....

Idioms ....

Similes ....

Linking devices ....

Opening sentence ....

Conclusion ....

Style and register ....

45 Writing a letter of reply

Write a letter to Jennifer describing the employment situation in your country and explaining what you think would help people in your country get jobs.

Remember:

- Try to use an appropriate, mature style.
- Keep to the topic.
- Start a new paragraph for each new topic.
- Open and round off the letter sensibly.

46 Choosing appropriate vocabulary

When you read an exam question, you need to identify the topic as clearly as you can and think of language connected to it. As always, try to choose language which is lively and varied and really conveys a sense of occasion.

This also helps you avoid 'rubric error'. This means answering the question in a way which is not relevant to the topic. For example, a question about medical experiments on animals should not produce a composition about taking your pet on holiday!

Read the exam questions below and the vocabulary which follows. Working in small groups and using dictionaries, decide what vocabulary is unlikely to be connected to the topic. Make sure you all agree.

Question 1

You had an important exam and left home in very good time. However, something extremely unexpected happened on your journey. You arrived at the exam room only just before the exam was due to begin. Write an account of what happened for your school newsletter.

What language is unlikely to be connected to this topic? Cross it off from the following list.

decide my future	emergency services
with seconds to spare	dawdled
panicked	invigilator
hasty	not a moment to lose
yelled	indifferent
shoved	alarmed
budget deficit	stampede
anxious	strolled
grabbed	broke out in a sweat
absolutely desperate	loudspeaker
snatched	announcements
sales figures	share prices
darted	sheer despair

Question 2

Despite your expectations, you have been selected for a special training scheme which will help you get the job of your dreams. Explain the way you felt when you heard the news and how this training scheme will help bring you closer to your chosen career.

Cross off the inappropriate language.

sarcastic	aggrieved
bitterly disappointed	over the moon
relieved	ecstatic
thrilled	challenge
walking on air	develop new skills
repelled	isolated
practical experience	cast down
delighted	disenchanted
amazed	subdued
many benefits	swelled with pride
breathed	worthwhile
a sigh of relief	forsaken
huge burden off	irritated
my shoulders	colleagues
golden opportunity	

Question 3

You have to move house because your parents have been promoted in their jobs. Although you will not be living very far away, you are sad to leave your old home. Write a letter of welcome to the new occupants of the house explaining what you particularly liked about the house and why.

Instructions as before.

hostile	memorable
treasured memories	sense of history
poison pen letter	contentment
sick and tired	unjust
nostalgic	macabre
favourite hideaway	know the place by heart
light, airy and spacious	charming
deeply depressed	outraged
rambling garden	quality of life
security	terrified
sentimental value	not of this world
small, cosy, comfortable	contemptuous
ill-at-ease	delightful
disgusted	ideal spot

47 Timed writing

Choose one of the topics which you find appealing from the exercise above. Write about 150-200 words.

Allow yourself 15-20 minutes maximum to write the composition.

READING ALOUD

Read your composition aloud to your group and pay close attention to the feedback. How far do you agree with the comments, and what would you change?

Exam-format questions

Writing

1 *'It was hard work but worth it.'*

Describe work you have done which was for the benefit of your school or community. In your article you should describe:

- the sort of work you did
- how your school or community benefited
- what you feel you have gained from the work.

The following may give you some ideas, but you are free to make up ideas of your own.

"We raised money for a local charity."
"I knew my school needed a club so I started this one."
"I helped supervise the younger children during the trip."
"We transformed the waste ground into a vegetable garden."

You should write about 200 words.

2

> ## Spend the summer in America!
>
> Responsible students needed to help in children's holiday camp.
>
> **Must have good organisational skills, be keen on sport and able to supervise children aged 8-11 years.**
>
> Fares and accommodation provided.

Reply to the above advertisement, describing the experience, qualities and skills you have which make you suitable for this position.

You should write about 150 words.

3 A recent survey discovered the reasons why school leavers were still unemployed six months after leaving full-time education.

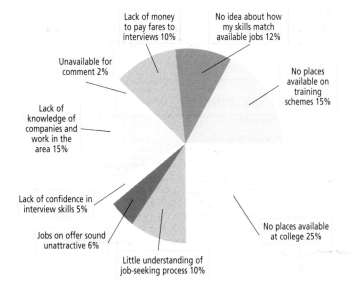

Write a letter to your local newspaper commenting on the information and suggesting ways **some** of these problems could be overcome.

Write about 150-200 words.

Listening

For questions 1–6 you will hear a series of short sentences. Answer each question as briefly as possible: full sentences are not required. You will hear each question twice.

1 Maria is ringing up to change the time and date of a job interview. What alternative is she offered?

2 You are listening to the radio when you hear the following advertisement. What training course is available?

3 Your class is listening to a careers talk for school leavers. What two personal qualities are needed to enter training schemes for the police force?

4 A friend tells you she wants to do voluntary work. What advice has she received?

5 You are visiting your grandmother. What does she want you to do and why?

6 A cousin phones to say he will be unable to come to a family celebration. Where will he go instead?

Oral assessment

1 Worthwhile work

What do you think is the most important and worthwhile work in the world today? Choose one or two jobs you think are particularly important. Say why you think these jobs are important and how society benefits from them.

In your discussion you could also consider such things as:

- the particular qualities and skills needed for such jobs

- how more people could be encouraged to do this kind of important and worthwhile work

- whether the pay received by people who do these jobs reflects the value of the work

- whether you, yourself, would like to do this work

- the sort of job you would ideally like for yourself in the future.

2 Choose a topic

Choose one of the topics below and talk about it for five minutes. You will be asked a few questions about it when you have finished. You may take a minute or two to write some brief notes before you begin.

1 'Unemployed people simply do not want to work!'
2 My dream job
3 Community service
4 The best way to help young people understand what work is all about is .....

You can't, strictly speaking, 'revise' for the exam. However, you can refresh your memory by studying your vocabulary records, reading through good examples of your own work and the model examples in this book. Take regular, short breaks and do something relaxing. You probably can't concentrate effectively for more than 20 or 30 minutes at a time.

Ask your teacher for exam practice papers. Time yourself answering the questions. Why not practise with a good friend? It's less lonely and more encouraging than working alone.

Concentrate on staying relaxed and calm. Have a light meal, fresh air, exercise and a good sleep the night before. Visualise yourself completing the paper well and in good time, and imagine the good results you will receive. Avoid the company of people who enjoy agonising over exams. Laughter is good therapy so you may like to do something light-hearted the night before, like watching a humorous video.

The order in which you tackle the Reading and Writing paper is a matter of personal preference, but it's generally a good idea to answer those questions you feel most confident with first. Part 2, which includes notes and summaries, can be left

until last if you feel this is your weak area. Aim to complete the paper; just a few extra marks on a question makes a difference to the overall score.

Make sure you don't run out of time because you have spent too long on answering one section of the paper. The number of marks for each individual question are shown at the end of the question.

Always read the questions very carefully. Don't be tempted to answer comprehension questions without reading the passage first. You will probably miss important links in the text. For summaries and compositions, make sure you understand the 'angle' of the question.

Never try to twist a pre-prepared essay to fit the topic of the composition if it really is not relevant. This is a transparent device which examiners will recognise, and you will not be given marks for a composition which is not relevant to the topic. It's far better to tackle the question confidently and write something fresh which answers the question set.

Try to stay calm and relaxed during the exam. Flex your fingers so they do not become stiff, and stretch from time to time. Make sure you are sitting comfortably and in the correct posture.

Be prepared for a question testing your understanding of a graph, chart or table of figures. This is often tested in Part 2 of Paper 2.

Unit focus

In this unit you have answered questions on a detailed reading text which included a question on information in a chart. This is practice for Papers 1/2, Part 2.

You have produced short answers to questions on a detailed reading text. This is practice for Papers 1/2, Part 1.

You have listened to a detailed talk and answered short-answer comprehension questions. This is practice for Paper 4, Part 3.

You have practised writing letters and articles giving your **opinions**. This is practice for Papers 1/2, Part 3.

Scores for quiz, page 5
Are you living the life you want?

Scores

Mostly A's
To be happy there has to be some momentum in your life, but you've hardly got off the launch pad! You're seeking first and foremost to protect and preserve your security. This involves a defensive approach and few risks. It's almost as if you're waiting for life to come and dish out the happiness. Try indulging a whim or two and see what happens.

Mostly B's
Congratulations! You're probably as happy as a person can be. You've a strong sense of what your wishes, wants and priorities are, and you're prepared to live in a way that suits you, even though it may be unfashionable or present the wrong image. You try to strike a fair balance between your needs and those of others. You're at home with yourself, know your strengths and limitations and don't allow your failures or the failures of others to get you down.

Mostly C's
You are trying hard to achieve happiness. What you don't realise is that happiness isn't an achievement, but an attitude. You're striving for all the things we are told will make us happy, but may be disappointed because you're taking your values from outside. You often feel guilty about your supposed failures. Try being more tolerant of yourself and of others.

Teacher: Sam and Carol, you've each chosen to talk about quite different films. Sam, you've chosen 'Crocodile Dundee' and Carol, you've selected 'The Hand that Rocks the Cradle'. May I ask why you chose these particular films?

Carol: I wanted to talk about a thriller because it's my favourite genre.

Sam: I wanted to say why I enjoyed a comedy adventure.

Teacher: They sound very interesting! Could you both tell me a bit about the plots?

Sam: 'Crocodile Dundee' is about an Australian outback hero, called Crocodile Dundee. An American journalist interviews him because she's heard about his reputation for defeating crocodiles. The film is set in two great places, New York and Australia, and it's basically about the hilarious adventures they have.

Carol: In 'The Hand that Rocks the Cradle', a normal, middle-class American family employ a nanny to look after their children. The nanny thinks, wrongly, that they are responsible for her husband's death. While she's working at their house, she's actually planning to murder them.

Teacher: Characters are extremely important in films. Carol, would mind telling me about the nanny?

Carol: Well, she seems sweet-natured but underneath she's very bitter and revengeful.

Teacher: So her appearance is very deceptive! What's the hero of 'Crocodile Dundee' like?

Sam: He's a tough guy but I felt I could identify with him because he's honourable and he's got a great sense of humour. The character is played by Paul Hogan. He's ideal for the part, because he has a sort of rugged, outdoor appearance.

Teacher: Can you give me an example of how his personal qualities were shown in the film?

Sam: In one scene, he's visiting New York when he's almost mugged by a young man with a flick knife. Dundee says 'Call that a knife?' and pulls out a really huge knife he uses in the bush. You know he's not going to use it but the mugger is terrified. I couldn't stop laughing.

Teacher: I know 'The Hand that Rocks the Cradle' is set in America. Could you explain in more detail why you think the setting is effective, Carol?

Carol: Well, the setting is very suburban. This makes the atmosphere more sinister because it shows how evil and danger can come into the lives of ordinary people.

Teacher: You've said that 'Crocodile Dundee' has two fascinating locations, Sam – New York and the Australian bush. Something else I'd like to know is whether there are any special effects?

Sam: Yes. A really good special effect is when Dundee confronts an angry bull in the bush and is able to soothe it with his bare hands.

Teacher: Carol, thrillers should be full of tension. Were you personally in suspense?

Carol: It was so scary that I was on the edge of my seat! There's a really frightening scene where the nanny picks up a pillow to put it behind the baby's head and I really thought she was going to harm the baby.

Teacher: Do you think it's right that the film shows how evil people can be?

Carol: Yes, because the underlying message is that evil is overcome by the forces of good. The real suspense is waiting to find out how that happens.

Teacher: Sam, did 'Crocodile Dundee' have a message?

Sam: I think the message is that courage and caring for others is more important than the background you come from.

Teacher: Carol, why would you recommend the film?

Carol: It's an exciting thriller and it's interesting for anyone who wants to work in a position where trust is important – caring for children, for instance.

Teacher: Sorry, I don't quite understand why you say that.

Carol: In the film, you see how much nannies are trusted and what could happen if a nanny abuses that trust.

Teacher: Finally, why do you think other people would enjoy 'Crocodile Dundee', Sam?

Sam: It's so relaxing and lighthearted. I've been working hard for my exams, and it's such an escapist film that I forgot about everything. It's fun for children as well as adults.